Donatella Della Ratta is Postdoctoral Fellow at Copenhagen University. She is the author of *Media Oriente: modelli, strategie, tecnologie nelle nuove televisioni arabe Al Jazeera. Media e società arabe nel nuovo millennio* (with Augusto Valeriani) *Un Hussein alla Casa Bianca: cosa pensa il mondo arabo di Barack Obama* and of several book chapters on Syrian media and politics.

Naomi Sakr is Professor of Media Policy at the Communication and Media Research Institute (CAMRI), University of Westminster, and Director of the CAMRI Arab Media Centre. Her publications include *Arab Television Today; Satellite Realms: Transnational Television, Globalization and the Middle East; Transformations in Egyptian Journalism* and *Women and Media in the Middle East* (all published by I.B.Tauris).

Jakob Skovgaard-Petersen is Professor of Arabic and Islamic Studies at the University of Copenhagen. He is the author of *Defining Islam for the Egyptian State: Muftis and Fatwas of the Dar al-Ifta* and (with Bettina Graf) *The Global Mufti: The Phenomenon of Yusuf Al-Qaradawi*.

University of Edinburgh

30150   027543625

'*Arab Media Moguls* is a landmark contribution that fills a gaping vacuum in the literature on the nebulous and opaque political economic structures of media ownership in the region. At once both investigative and analytical, this volume lays out the topography of media control across the Arab world, showcasing how the overlay of political interest/ alliances, the construction of audiences-as-markets, and megalomaniacal personalities informs much of today's media content. Commendations to the editors and authors for a truly indispensable work.'

Adel Iskandar,
Assistant Professor of Global Communication,
Simon Fraser University

ARAB MEDIA MOGULS

EDITED BY
**Donatella Della Ratta, Naomi Sakr
and Jakob Skovgaard-Petersen**

I.B. TAURIS
LONDON · NEW YORK

Published in 2015 by
I.B.Tauris & Co Ltd
London • New York
www.ibtauris.com

References to websites were correct at the time of writing.

Library of Modern Middle East Studies 148

ISBN: 978 1 78453 277 2 (HB)
ISBN: 978 1 78076 732 1 (PB)
eISBN: 978 0 85773 501 0

A full CIP record for this book is available from the British Library
A full CIP record is available from the Library of Congress

Library of Congress Catalog Card Number: available

Printed and bound in Great Britain by
TJ International Ltd, Padstow, Cornwall

Notes on Contributors

Donatella Della Ratta is Postdoctoral Fellow at Copenhagen University, where she obtained her PhD for research on the politics of Syrian TV drama. She is a former Postdoctoral Fellow at the Annenberg School for Communication at the University of Pennsylvania, and a former affiliate of the Berkman Center for Internet and Society at Harvard University. She is the author of *Media Oriente: modelli, strategie, tecnologie nelle nuove televisioni arabe* (Rome, 2000) and *Al Jazeera. Media e società arabe nel nuovo millennio* (Milan, 2005), co-editor of *Un Hussein alla Casa Bianca: cosa pensa il mondo arabo di Barack Obama* (Bologna, 2009) and author of several book chapters on Syrian media and politics. She has managed the Arabic-speaking community of the international NGO Creative Commons since 2008, and maintains a blog on Arab media at http://mediaoriente.com and tweets at @donatelladr.

Ehab Galal is Assistant Professor of Media and Society in the Middle East at the Department of Cross-Cultural and Regional Studies, University of Copenhagen. He holds a PhD from the University of Copenhagen that reflects his research interest in the treatment of identity, lifestyle and the positioning of Muslims on Islamic satellite television. His work has appeared in English and Danish in journals and books, including *Religious Broadcasting in the Middle East* (Hroub ed., 2012) and *Mediatization and Religion: Nordic Perspectives* (Hjarvard and Lövheim eds, 2011). He is currently examining audience responses to Islamic programming on Arab television, which includes fieldwork among Arabic-speaking audiences in four countries.

Tourya Guaaybess is Assistant Professor in Media Studies at the University of Clermont-Ferrand and Associate Researcher at the French national scientific research centre, CNRS, Paris. She has been a Marie Curie Fellow at the European University Institute (2001–3) and served as Assistant Professor at the University of Kyoto in 2010. She has worked on Arab media since 1997, particularly on broadcast media and with a historical and political economy approach. She is author of *Télévisions arabes sur orbite* (Paris, 2005) and *Les médias arabes, confluences média-tiques et dynamique sociale* (Paris, 2012), co-editor of *Les Arabes parlent aux Arabes* (Paris, 2009) and editor of *National Broadcasting and State Policy in Arab Countries* (Basingstoke, 2013).

Zahera Harb is Senior Lecturer in International Journalism in the Journalism Department, City University, London, and a former broadcast journalist who worked for over a decade in Lebanon for Lebanese and international media organisations. She is the author of *Channels of Resistance: Liberation Propaganda, Hezbollah and the Media* (I.B.Tauris, 2011), co-editor of *Narrating Conflict in the Middle East: Images, Discourses and Communication Practices in Lebanon and Palestine* (I.B.Tauris, 2013) and review editor for the *Journal of Media Practice*.

Joe F. Khalil is Associate Professor in residence at Northwestern University, Doha, and visiting Research Fellow at the London School of Economics. He holds a PhD from Southern Illinois University Carbondale and has more than 15 years of professional television experience as director, executive producer and consultant with major Arab satellite channels. He is co-author of *Arab Television Industries* (with Marwan Kraidy, 2009) and is currently working on a book entitled *Youth Generated Media*. His work has appeared in journals such as *Television and New Media* and anthologies including *Encyclopedia of Social Movement Media*, *International Handbook of Children, Media and Culture*, and *Meanings of Audiences*.

Marwan M. Kraidy is Professor of Communication and Director of the Project for Advanced Research in Global Communication (PARGC) at the Annenberg School for Communication, University of Pennsylvania. A recipient of fellowships from the John Simon Guggenheim Memorial Foundation and Woodrow Wilson International Center for Scholars, Kraidy has published more than 100 essays and six books, including *Reality Television and Arab Politics* (Cambridge University Press, 2010), which won three prizes. Kraidy has been the Edward Said Chair of American Studies at the American University of Beirut, Visiting Professor at the Sorbonne in Paris, Assistant Professor of International Relations at the American University in Washington, DC, and Assistant Professor of Critical-Cultural Studies at the University of North Dakota. He is currently writing *Creative Insurgency*, focusing on the human body as a locus of power and resistance in revolutionary times. He tweets at @Mkraidy.

Katharina Nötzold is a political scientist and Associate Research Fellow at the Arab Media Centre at the University of Westminster's Communication and Media Research Institute, where she was previously RCUK-Research Fellow. She was Managing Director of the Berlin Graduate School for Muslim Cultures and Societies and worked for the Center for International Peace Operations in Berlin. She holds a PhD in Media and Communications from the University of Erfurt, Germany. Her published work includes *Defining the Nation? Lebanese Television and Political Elites, 1990–2005* (Berlin, 2009) and articles on Arab media and media representation of migrants and Islam. She is a former editor of *Westminster Papers in Communication and Culture*.

Sarah El-Richani is a doctoral candidate at the University of Erfurt, researching the Lebanese media system from a comparative perspective courtesy of a German DAAD scholarship. She won a Quintin Hogg Scholarship to obtain her MA in Journalism from the University of Westminster, having graduated from the American University of Beirut with a BA in English Literature and Philosophy. She worked for two years as MENA Programme Officer for the London-based ARTICLE 19, and continues to carry out consultancies for NGOs working on media issues. She is on Twitter (@srichani) where she writes on Middle-Eastern politics, media and other topics.

Najat AlSaied holds a PhD from the University of Westminster for research on the production and reception of Arab satellite television content dealing with development issues affecting disadvantaged women. She holds Masters degrees from the American University in Washington in Heath Promotion and Disease Prevention and in Computer Information Systems. She previously worked at the Islamic Development Bank in Jeddah, the Pan American Health Organization in Washington, DC, and the US Department of Housing and Urban Development, and has served as editor-in-chief of a women's e-magazine covering topics such as women's rights, education, art and health, published by the Saudi Research and Publishing Company in Dubai Media City.

Naomi Sakr is Professor of Media Policy at the Communication and Media Research Institute (CAMRI), University of Westminster, and Director of the CAMRI Arab Media Centre. She is the author of three books, *Transformations in Egyptian Journalism* (2013), *Arab Television Today* (2007) and *Satellite Realms: Transnational Television, Globalization and the Middle East* (2001), and has edited two collections, *Women and Media in the Middle East: Power through Self-Expression* (2004) and *Arab Media and Political Renewal: Community, Legitimacy and Public Life* (2007). Her research focuses on the political economy of Arab-owned media, with particular reference to satellite television, corporate cultural production, development of journalism and human rights.

Jakob Skovgaard-Petersen is Professor at the New Islamic Public Sphere Programme, Department of Cross-Cultural and Regional

Studies, University of Copenhagen. His field of research is modern Islam, with a focus on the establishment of a modern Muslim public sphere and the role of the Muslim *ulama* in modern Arab states. Lately, his research has primarily focused on Islam's position in the pan-Arab television networks, and on renewal of the classical Islamic literary genre. His key publications include *Defining Islam for the Egyptian State* (Leiden, 1997), *Middle Eastern Cities 1900–1950: Public Spheres and Public Places in Transformation* (co-edited with H. C. Nielsen, 2001), and *Global Mufti: The Phenomenon of Yusuf al-Qaradawi* (co-edited with Bettina Gräf, 2009).

Note on Names and Classification of Sources

The names of individuals and organisations mentioned in this book have been transliterated from Arabic into English according to the style they themselves choose or the style most current in media coverage. The editors accepted the resulting inconsistencies in transliteration to make the text more accessible to readers unfamiliar with Arabic. For the same reason, diacritics and apostrophes have been minimised in the rendering of Arabic words, and the Arabic letter *qaf* has generally been represented with the English letter 'k'.

Two methods have been adopted for citing sources, depending on their type. Primary sources, such as interviews, internal reports, newspaper or magazine articles, press releases, speeches and conference presentations are cited in full in the endnotes, but not in the bibliography. Secondary sources, such as books, book chapters, monographs, journal articles, academic theses and published reports are cited in both the endnotes and the bibliography.

1

Arab Media Moguls: An Introduction

Jakob Skovgaard-Petersen

Does the phenomenon of the media mogul have a future in the Arab world? Doubts about the global future of the archetypal mogul have been driven by the spread of small digital media, competition law and the rise of new generations with different outlooks in family-run media firms. *The Economist*, prompted by Rupert Murdoch's fumbling performance before a parliamentary committee in the UK in 2011, described the mogul as a 'dying breed'. Yet the pronouncement proved highly controversial, provoking questions as to whether or not the controls over content distribution that allegedly helped moguls to build their empires had really been fatally undermined by the many-to-many digital distribution channels of the internet. With media moguls seen by some as distorting what media professor James Curran has called the 'national conversation',[1] an understanding of media moguls' efforts for or against free media appears all the more pressing in Arab countries facing political polarisation and uncertainty.

Who are the Arab media moguls? We know about the moguls of the USA and Europe, and a few from other parts of the world. However, although some of the Arab moguls are known, at least to the publics of the region, their modes of operating are shrouded in secrecy. This is curious, because Arab media matter. Within a span of just two decades, major Arab news outlets such as Al-Jazeera and Al-Arabiya have become global brands, and all major world powers have invested in their own Arabic-language television stations. In 2011, revolutions in the Arab region were partly instigated, and certainly spread, by means of new Arab media, small and big. There are Arab migrants on every continent, and they tend to be avid consumers of Arab media. Indeed, Arabic is one of a handful of truly global media languages.

If Arab media matter, Arab media moguls matter too. Media systems are conditioned on factors such as law and regulatory policies, general economic indicators and market size. Media ownership concentration is a significant variable. This is particularly the case if the field of media is insufficiently monitored and regulated, and if media power can be used to project political influence. The Middle East provides fertile grounds for media moguldom. The Arab media moguls have emerged with the opportunities afforded by steps towards liberalisation and privatisation in the media sector, and with the rise of an expanded Arab media market that has transcended national borders. They rose under the watchful eyes of political authoritarianism, but they made sure not to challenge the rulers directly. The autocrat rulers, on their part, envisaged tight media regulation and censorship, not to prevent media concentration but to curb political opposition and foster a submissive public. The authoritarian power-holders could live with the rise of moguls, and the moguls could live with them. Over the last two decades, at least in some states, an Arab media geography has emerged where the major companies of production, finance and broadcasting are concentrated in just a handful of Arab cities. This geographical concentration is a theme that Joe Khalil addresses in his chapter of this book.

Redolent with fascination and exaggeration, the term 'media mogul' is in itself an expression disseminated by the media. The late nineteenth century's concentration of US and European businesses into major

Acknowledgements

This volume grew out of two gatherings held in 2011. The first was a conference in April, organised and hosted by the Arab Media Centre under the title 'Investment and Entrepreneurship in Arab Media', as one of its annual international conferences. The Arab Media Centre is a research subgroup of the Communication and Media Research Institute (CAMRI) at the University of Westminster in London. Its 2011 conference was a collaborative effort with the New Islamic Public Sphere Programme at the University of Copenhagen and with CAMRI colleagues leading University of Westminster degrees in media management. The second gathering was a workshop hosted by the Danish–Egyptian Dialogue Institute (DEDI) in Cairo in November with help from the New Islamic Public Sphere Programme, at which a number of contributors to the present volume shared their preliminary research on the issues and personalities covered in the book. As editors, we wish to record our gratitude to the institutions named here for their support and to thank the authors for making the book project an enriching experience.

Contents

degeneration, as the second and the third generation will gradually lose the vigour and vision of the founder of the empire. Perhaps because it is Orientalist in itself, the term media mogul thus seems to lend itself rather too easily to an Arab context. It is necessary to set aside lazy assumptions about autocratic power systems and ask whether, in fact, the media mogul archetype takes on its own form in the Arab world. We believe that it does. We contend that within the last 20 years a group of Arab media moguls has emerged who have successfully challenged the state-owned media of individual Arab states and built companies for the pan-Arab market. However, we also contend that the specific political, social and economic circumstances of the Arab world have created its own specimen of the media mogul. How have political authoritarianism, oil economies, religious revivalism and political turmoil influenced the rise of the media moguls? How have changes in regulation and privatisation processes in the region (including the rise of media cities) changed or re-shaped their businesses, or impacted their growth strategies? Can it be demonstrated that moguls played a role in pushing through market liberalisation or privatisation? Are they really entrepreneurial risk takers, or what talents do they have? Who are their key barons, and how do they spot and develop media talent? Do they have a personalised or eccentric style of management? Are they rivals, or do they collaborate? How close are they to political power, and what does that entail? Do they try to influence politics to enhance their business opportunities? Or did they set up their businesses in order to further their political ambitions?

To answer these questions, we have opted for an analysis of the careers and positions of the major Arab media moguls. Information about these figures is surprisingly hard to come by, as their business dealings are rarely in the open, and the available biographies verge on uncritical praise. Each chapter of this book investigates a set of features and dimensions of the mogul, ranging from the private and personal to the national and transnational. We set out to probe family roots, the role of family in business and the issue of succession. We explore the kinds of risk taken, hiring and firing strategies, access to finance and approaches to debt. We investigate each mogul's relationship to the inner circles of political power, the opportunities provided by steps towards relaxation of media monopolies, the place of media in the mogul's business empire and the nature of the medium on which the empire was built. We look closely at styles of management and whether each mogul is engaged in politics or not.

The Mogul Moment

The analyses demonstrate certain family resemblances among the media moguls, although there is also significant variety. As mentioned, pan-Arab media are not evenly spread throughout the Arab world. The traditional production centres in Cairo and Beirut have been supplemented by important new centres in Dubai, Doha and Riyadh, reflecting not only the economic power of the Gulf, but also its capacity to attract business and talent. Almost all the moguls are based in these cities. The Arab moguls are essentially television moguls who have expanded into other media. This is a result of the dominance of the television medium in Arab media consumption, but also to the specific moment in the 1990s when satellite technology enabled the establishment of television channels that could broadcast across borders to the entire Arab world, and even to relatively affluent sections of the Arabic-speaking population in Europe. As a consequence of restrictions in the Arab world itself, entrepreneurs were initially forced to set up these stations in Europe, but, in the early 2000s, these were relocated to the newly established media cities in the Arab world itself. Setting up a television channel, or a network of channels, thus demanded both risk taking and access to major financial resources. The Arab moguls did not work their way up from newsboys; they had money to begin with. However, given the inhospitable environment for free media, they undeniably took risks.

As in Europe during the 1980s, the combination of economic liberalism and the relaxation of certain media controls provided impetus to the sudden rise of media conglomerates, and thus to the emergence of media moguls. However, whereas Western Europe generally provided a stable legal and regulatory framework for business, this was hardly the case in most Arab countries. Political connections were vital. If these were in place, the regulatory system was more amenable, and the commercial competition less fierce, than in Western countries. As Toby Dodge has pointed out, the 'paucity of political representation' in authoritarian political systems across the Middle East during the global drive for economic liberalisation acted to limit societal threats to regime survival.[3] In this context, economic liberalisation – in the sense of notional restrictions on monopolies and promotion of business competition – was no more than a top-down means of cementing political control, because entrepreneurs enriched by the so-called liberalisation process were tied to the regime and did not seek to push liberalisation any further than the regime itself wanted it to go.[4] Certainly, the need for personal connections with the top ruling circles was also a risk, and it could backfire. Yet, there was always the possibility, and sometimes threat, of moving the company to another country, or overseas, as many television station owners did in the 1990s.

As Arab rulers came to realise that the days of state-controlled media were numbered, some began to consider ways of luring in the private companies. As we have seen, the moguls accepted the basic premise that their companies generally stayed within certain editorial lines and essentially accepted the legal and political circumstances set by the regimes. In return, they were given sufficient editorial freedom to be able to deliver more interesting debates, more daring news and better entertainment than the state channel system that preceded them.

Media moguls' motives are not always transparent. Often it seems that politics and economics are intertwined. In the case of Arab moguls, however, it is apparent that profit cannot be an overriding expectation, because distortions in the advertising market and restrictions on editorial content combine to undermine the commercial potential of media operations in the region. Where economic motives are involved, these are often related to the moguls' other non-media businesses, which can benefit from belonging to an empire that controls one or more significant television stations. As for political motives, controlling a network of media is a good way to demonstrate loyalty and thus curry favour with a country's rulers. It may also be the case that the mogul wishes to make a cultural investment in a long-term effort to influence public opinion or taste. The stated purpose of 'combatting extremism' may have been popular with the regimes *and* been a sincere motive for several moguls in the 2000s.

Whatever the motives for investment, television stations do not survive without cash. The few stations that have known periods of profit, most notably the Lebanese Broadcasting Corporation (LBC), have also required periodic restructuring and heavy investment, while the remaining stations need investors to keep them afloat. Even if the costs of market entry have fallen, the dearth of viable business models has led to a search for investors with deep pockets, and hence an increasing role for Gulf money. To move from a small national market to the broad pan-Arab market, some local Lebanese advertising and television moguls succeeded in wooing leading Gulf businessmen to invest in the expansion of their companies. This was true of Pierre Daher and the late Antoine Choueiri and Rafik Hariri, as shown in the chapters by Sarah El-Richani, Zahera Harb and Katharina Nötzold, respectively.

Significant though Gulf money is, it does not amount to a 'Saudisation' of Arab media content. Indeed, nudging the Saudi audience in a more liberal and tolerant direction appears to be the stated motive of several of the Saudi entrepreneurs. As demonstrated in the chapters by Najat AlSaied and Marwan Kraidy, Saudi moguls such as Walid al-Ibrahim and Alwaleed bin Talal declare themselves to be committed to a 'reformist' or 'modernising' agenda, providing Saudi viewers with entertainment and discussions that would not be available on Saudi state television. Nevertheless, however liberal these moguls consider themselves, they are first and foremost members of the topmost elite in undemocratic and illiberal countries, and the reformist tenets of their channels are not intended to change the power relations in them. A telling illustration of this overall priority was Alwaleed bin Talal's summary sacking of Tarek al-Suwaidan, who as his 'baron' had established the Al-Risala Islamic television channel to promote a reformist and participatory version of Islamism. In August 2013 the channel protested against the military's armed takeover in Egypt, which removed the Muslim Brotherhood's choice of president, Muhammad Morsi. Tarek al-Suwaidan is closely connected to the Muslim Brotherhood movement, whereas the Saudi government was an active and vocal supporter of what many in Egypt and outside regarded as a coup d'état. Writing on his Twitter account, Prince Alwaleed described the Muslim Brotherhood as a 'terrorist movement' and announced that he had dismissed al-Suwaidan for admitting he belonged to it.[5] Such acts seem not to dent the self-proclaimed reformists' credibility with mainstream media outside the Arab world. As pointed out by Sakr in her chapter on the Egyptian mogul Naguib Sawiris, the applause of Western capitalist media to the expansionist behaviour of Arab media moguls seems to conform to a pattern of lionising the mogul as the embodiment of healthy, liberal capitalism as a global trend, conveniently ignoring any concerns about political cronyism by focusing on his personality and cultural outlook.

The Transition Moment

If political authoritarianism has proven conducive to the rise of the Arab moguls, what will happen if the political system is replaced by another with a higher degree of transparency and public accountability, as could yet be the case after the revolutions of 2011? So far there is little evidence that the media moguls are destined to go the way of their erstwhile political patrons.

If anything, the recent popular protests have forced the moguls to take new political risks. Lebanon is a good example of this. Many Lebanese consider the Arab Spring to have begun with the March 2005 demonstrations in Beirut, which mobilised a much higher percentage of the population than in any other country. The massive demonstrations on 8 and 14 March came in the wake of the assassination on 14 February of Rafik Hariri, prime minister, billionaire and owner of a media empire, with the television channel Al-Mustaqbal at its centre. The crown prince of the media empire, Saad Hariri, also took over the political mantle, and was later elected prime minister, like his father, but in very different political circumstances. The Mustaqbal television station, which had mainly served entertainment, then began a year-long campaign in search of justice and retribution for the murder of Rafik Hariri. As Katharina Nötzold describes, this campaign was relatively unsuccessful, but Saad Hariri's status as a top politician was not dependent upon his media business.

The Tunisian and Egyptian media moguls treated in this book have largely been successful in abandoning the old regime and embracing some aspects of the revolution. Tarek Ben Ammar and Najib Sawiris were both on good terms with former presidents Ben Ali and Mubarak in their respective countries, as demonstrated by the fact that they were allowed to set up independent media. In the Tunisian media scene, which is much smaller and more controlled than that of Egypt, the private Nessma TV was a novelty, even if it was mainly an entertainment channel. Donatella Della Ratta tells the story of Ben Ali's late December appeal to Tarek Ben Ammar, who duly arranged a televised roundtable about the protests. The show was seen by Tunisians as encouragement to talk freely about corruption and only made more people take to the streets. This enabled Ben Ammar and Nessma to project themselves as revolutionaries.

Similarly, Naguib Sawiris' ONTV had on at least one occasion cancelled a show for being too critical of the Mubarak regime. During the revolution, Sawiris was one of a panel calling itself the Committee of Wise Men, whose members sought to mediate between the government and the youth in the street, and his mobile phone company Mobinil complied with the collapsing regime's wish to close down the mobile network on 28 January 2011. Nevertheless, only a few months after

President Mubarak was forced to step down, Sawiris founded the Free Egyptians Party. More importantly perhaps, as pointed out in the chapter by Tourya Guaaybess, Sawiris' channel ONTV, and his partly owned newspaper *Al-Masry al-Youm*, had for years introduced debates and criticism of Egyptian politics, raising the level of expectations of the population 'little by little, and gradually lowering public tolerance thresholds *vis-à-vis* the regime' (see page 177 of this volume). Sawiris and another Egyptian media mogul, Sayyid El-Badawi, are best viewed as pragmatists who knew how to get on with a regime they did not really approve of, and this practice of constant negotiation and adaptation is likely to continue as the holders of power in Egypt change.

In this respect, the fortunes of the Egyptian and Tunisian moguls are perhaps not so different from those of the moguls in the Gulf, even if the revolutions of 2011 were potentially a threat to the Gulf regimes. As well as the news channels, the general entertainment-led channels of the major television stations also gave full coverage to the revolution in Egypt and the domino effect it unleashed. The phenomenon was simply too big to ignore. On the other hand, the Gulf-based channels initially disregarded the uprising in Bahrain, or sought to interpret it in a sectarian light. By the end of 2011 they had generally returned to their customary focus on entertainment, with some concessions to the public appetite for political talk. That is to say, the gap between popular aspirations and Gulf rule had widened, in the Gulf itself too, challenging mogul media to adapt.

Gradually, however, a new mediascape was taking shape. New television channels such as Tahrir, 25tv and Al-Miyadeen emerged to challenge the news coverage of Al-Jazeera and Al-Arabiya. New small media with small financial needs appeared, and new young faces gained popularity. In several instances, the moguls' channels and companies were able to engage some of the new actors, or buy some of the new channels, and they were generally much less compromised than the old state media. More worrisome perhaps to the moguls was the coming to power of Islamists in Egypt and Tunisia, and the rise of Salafi media. In the polarised political climate of 2012–13, many of the moguls and their media were squarely in the camp of the anti-Islamists.

More than in other parts of the world, Arab media moguls have had a head start by being in a position to take advantage of and play a part in the dramatic expansion of the pan-Arab television market and its value since the 1990s, and the ensuing inter-Arab political competition. It is noteworthy that media owners are benefitting from the lack of effective mechanisms for pan-Arab regulation of pan-Arab media. At the same time, it is striking that most of the region's media moguls are of mixed parentage and heritage, which gives them a foothold across national (Saudi–Lebanese) and even regional (Euro–Arab) borders. However, it is also notable that the Arab uprisings of 2010–11 were accompanied by a growing availability of national television coverage for publics in Tunisia, Egypt and elsewhere, as well as a growing reliance on alternatives to mainstream linear television for sources of entertainment and news. National markets are less predictable and less profitable for investors, and the fragmentation of pan-Arab television enhances the mobility and autonomy of content producers, while social media gives those producers alternative outlets. Moguls stand to benefit from a continuation of the authoritarian power structures with which they have been allied over previous decades, and from the very slow progress likely to be made anywhere in the region toward tough and effective competition laws. At the same time, however, the generation that rose up against authoritarianism is also tired of the autocrats' allies and the old guard. The personal profiles and trajectories examined in this book reflect a particular, historically specific configuration of inter-Arab relations, pan-Arab media and regional development. As explored in each chapter, the concept of media mogul is not applicable in every case. In a future context, characterised by prolonged political instability and a digitally converging media scene, what does seem likely is that media business survival rates will still depend on the taking of mogul-scale entrepreneurial risks.

2

Modalities of Media Governance in the Arab World

Joe F. Khalil

This chapter advances the argument that private media owners, including those who emerge as media moguls, operate within particular structures and that these structures help moguls to advance their goals of combining entertainment with politics, providing specific visions to the public and exerting power on politicians.[1] Framed against accelerated political and economic liberalisation, deregulation, media entrepreneurship and transnational Arab and international investments in regional media industries, the chapter investigates the modalities of Arab media governance. Broadly defined, 'governance' refers to complex and dispersed processes of interactions among a number of policy-making stakeholders, and of control often extending beyond the traditional governmental activities.[2] The growth of private ownership of Arab media outlets over the last 20 years is closely related to specific modalities of media governance manifested in symbiotic relationships that develop between a number of stakeholders, including governments, politicians and owners.

The questions raised by this chapter relate to the kinds of development that strengthen or challenge the power of the mogul, and the modalities by which he (they are rarely women, for reasons beyond the scope of this chapter) defuses threats, creates opportunities and operates in collaboration or competition with other stakeholders. To address these questions appropriately, the focus here is on the loci of production and distribution. During the past two decades, the significance of location has grown exponentially as leading private media owners have enhanced their control over production and distribution, and consequently have transformed the modalities of media governance. To an unprecedented extent, media activities previously under the purview of the nation state are now financed and controlled by moguls. Until recently, governments reluctant to allow private media ownership could impede moguldom, for a while, by the application of draconian laws, economic dirigisme and backroom dealings. Today, governments, political elites and moguls have developed modalities of media governance that allow for negotiation and accommodation.

To deal with these multilayered modalities, this chapter is divided into two broad sections. The first analyses modalities of media governance, summarising interpretations of how the contemporary Arab media landscape evolved as it did. The second section provides four examples of such interpretations. Both sections aim to address the multi-directional trajectories of creative and capital flows between the various media centres and the roles of the biggest media owners.[3] On one level, the chapter follows potential moguls' activities from their intraregional operations and their European experience to their relocation to the Arab world. On another, it provides an analysis of the relationships among Arab satellite investments, investors and the place of investment from a historical and political–economic perspective.

Modalities of Governance

In recent years the term 'media governance' has become part of the standard vocabulary used to explain changes in media. Although it appears to be a catch-all term, media governance is increasingly at the centre of much debate among media institutions, regulators, governments and civil society organisations operating locally, regionally and internationally. The debate around media governance could be summarised from either a power-centred or a relationship-focused perspective. The power-centred perspective views media governance as located with various stakeholders. Giddens suggests that the term is appropriate to cover the various power centres and their relations, as well as regulations that affect media performance.[4] In the same vein, Hamelink and Nordenstreng suggest that media governance is a 'framework of practices, rules, and institutions that set[s] limits and give[s] incentives for the performance of the media.'[5] Extending beyond statutory regulations, Freedman argues that media governance 'refers to the sum total of mechanisms, both formal and informal, national and supranational, centralized and dispersed, that aim to organize media systems.'[6] In this view, the modalities of governance are power-centred, allowing various stakeholders, moguls included, to shape media performance.

Another perspective draws our attention away from the power struggle to suggest a structured, more balanced relationship among the various stakeholders. For example, McQuail suggests that media governance includes the various institutionalised practices of organisation and responsibility within media institutions, and between those institutions and society.[7] In order to generate more dynamic growth, others see the governance infrastructure as responding to the needs and changes in the market as well as the restructuring of industrial organisations.[8] In this view, the modalities of governance are relationship-focused tools that are both receptive and adaptive to the various interests, technologies, politics, economies and communities that make up media systems.

Emerging information and communications technologies have periodically contributed to reshaping the dynamics of governance in the Arab world. Composed of 22 states that share a common cultural and historical heritage, the Arab world has an estimated combined population of over 300 million. One mistake is to look at the region as a monolithic entity in the traditions of the *Four Theories of the Press*.[9] Instead, Rugh advances alternative models to describe press models in the Arab world.[10] He divides them into three categories: mobilisation (e.g. Egypt), loyalist (e.g. Tunisia) and diverse (e.g. Lebanon). Similarly, Ayish distinguishes three different media models: traditional government-controlled, reformist government-controlled and liberal-commercial.[11] It is beyond the scope of this chapter to detail these models, but, by and large, national Arab media policies fall into one of three or four models. To gain a better understanding of how media governance operates in the Arab world, it will be helpful to compare the 'old order' characterised by state-centred modalities and an 'evolving order' that, since the 1990s, has included media moguls as central players.

The impasses of twentieth-century national media policies can be characterised by an attachment to development programmes, propaganda objectives, national unity and the promotion of citizenship defined through national identity and ruler/party politics. From the 1940s until the 1990s, Arab governments, with few exceptions, were able to continue their dominance over print and the airwaves, preventing or limiting private ownership of media and policing access to satellite receivers, audio and video tapes. Newspapers, radio and then television were used by most Arab regimes to foster national unity, achieve social development and maintain control over information flow. In brief, this 'old order' often replicated colonial press laws (Ottoman, French, British) and was characterised by a strong state, governmental or political control of radio and television broadcasting (clearly establishing a monopoly over the latter), and greatly influencing print media. Although operating with relative freedom, the press was entangled in political and ideological battles as proxies of local or regional governments, political parties or power centres.

To seek out moguls in this context is to consider charismatic publishers (e.g. Kuwait's Ahmad al-Jarrallah of *Al-Seyassah*) or powerful families (e.g. Lebanon's Tueini family of *Al-Nahar*) whose role often involved struggles over editorial independence as much as profits.

Apart from outdated, outmoded and sometimes absent regulatory arrangements, varied and variable instruments of political pressure or informal social control could always be found in different Arab countries. In many instances, constitutionally guaranteed private properties were ignored or, if respected, the operating environment was generally restrictive and limited the growth and expansion of media investors. At the same time, social and religious establishments exerted more influence than direct power, establishing taboos and supporting particular political discourses.

The evolving order of modalities of media governance described here is the outcome of several forces – moguls included – working together and often with quite closely intertwined interests. Since the 1990s, the power of social and political actors has been increasingly dependent on their access to satellite television channels, as the Arab television industry transitioned from government-owned national terrestrial services to privately owned regional satellite channels. In order to escape government monopoly, and following the Arab private press, these channels established themselves in London and Rome. From these cities they addressed a broad cross-section of the Arab population. Instead of focusing on one particular country, they identified common denominators among their audiences in news and entertainment. In fact, they provided a counter-narrative to the stale didactic programming and reporting of state media. However, the ascendance of moguls as private owners of 'offshore' media has never implied a depoliticisation of media.[12] There has been, and largely still exists, a considerable range and intensity of political influence, as captured by a number of Arab media researchers.[13]

Interpreting the Modalities of Arab Media Governance

The fundamental course and scope of Arab media moguldom can be interpreted in a number of ways. In the first, technological change is credited as the main driving force, with three interconnected developments at its heart. From early discussion in the late 1960s to the launch of the first Arab-owned satellite, Arabsat, in the mid-1980s, the first of these developments was the recognition and application of satellite communications technologies. For instance, the advent of the fax and satellite allowed for unprecedented two-way connectivity between the Arab offshore press and the Arab world. The second development was the accelerated integration and digitisation of all communications vehicles for satellite distribution (video signal compression being particularly significant). As a result, better quality was achieved with less bandwidth. The third change was the steep decline in the costs of telecommunications transmission, including telephone and satellite. Egypt's NileSat, launched in 1998, competed directly with the Arab-owned, Saudi-dominated Arabsat. This regional competition took place at the same time as similar European competition between a number of newly privatised national telecommunications providers. From this viewpoint, the ability to use and lower the costs of this technology can be seen to be instrumental in the development of these enterprising media ventures.

In a second interpretation of the rise of Arab media moguldom, the 'CNN effect' is credited with awakening interest in unmitigated, uncensored news. This accelerated the adoption of new technologies as a way to influence public policy makers. Most Arab audiences never imagined that the Iraqi government closely monitored Peter Arnett's reporting of the first Gulf War. Perhaps because of the Gulf War, and despite the government's attempts to ban consumer access to satellites, consumers created a number of ways to acquire such access, for example, by owning one or via a neighbourhood cable hook-up. What started with the CNN effect was completed with the 'Al-Jazeera effect', the belief that Al-Jazeera had a liberating effect on the region's media.[14] The Qatar-based Al-Jazeera and Lebanese Broadcasting Corporation International (LBCI) were capable of raising the level of permissible discourse in news and entertainment, respectively.[15] Both became role models for the channels that followed.

A third interpretation of Arab media development attributes the pace and scale of change in the Arab media landscape to the unleashing of market forces, which provided opportunities and incentives to venture into private media ownership. This was closely related to the shift in politico-economic policies linked to the triumph of liberalism and consumerism in the latter part of the twentieth century. The transition was not only the result of politico-economic liberal policies like Sadat's *Infitah* ('open door'), but was also accelerated by the increased ability of oil-rich countries to control and manage their petro-dollars.

A fourth narrative stresses the general globalisation of social and cultural life as well as economic trends. For media moguls, globalisation has produced a number of opportunities to increase control over their investments, maximise profits and reduce the threats inherent to interconnected networked markets. Globalisation has undermined both the legitimacy and the feasibility of nation states claiming outward sovereignty and exerting pressure on the movement of labour and capital. For mass media organisations, globalisation has produced a high level of convergence of all kinds, as well as integration in an increasingly global media industry. A column can be written in one country, compiled in another, and printed and distributed in further different countries.

A fifth narrative stresses the impact of conflict on the movement of media moguls and their strategic investment choices. Although the Arab–Israeli conflict has been central to regional politics, other conflicts of varying scope and intensity have perhaps had the largest impact on media. Such conflicts range from swift local coups such as those in Egypt (1952) and Qatar (1995), which established large state-sponsored media empires, to more protracted wars such as those in Lebanon (1975–90) and against Iraq (2003), which resulted in the mushrooming of media outlets. Some conflicts, such as the so-called 'War on Terror', had transformative and enduring effects, such as an increase in the number of stakeholders and the choice of media investments, including the re-introduction of international propaganda broadcasts to the region. Regardless of their nature or scope, media moguls approached these events as opportunities for developing business and increasing their affluence.[16]

For the purposes of this chapter, it is unnecessary to single out any one of these alternative explanations of the emerging preconditions of moguldom. We need to note that change in the modalities of media governance is a reflection of all the trends mentioned, to varying degrees. This evolving order, although it may have reached a settled stage, is clearly differentiated by the marked increase in centralised operations, transnational interconnectedness and integration in global media industries, the commercialisation and marketisation of all forms of media products, and by the decline of the state-owned media systems of the 'old' older.

These various modalities of media governance are increasingly integrated into a regional and global media market that includes organisations, copyrights, finance, development, production and distribution. As noted earlier, they represent a complex four-tiered matrix that applies to various degrees across the Arab world, with Lebanon at one extreme, where the state is a marginalised player, and Saudi Arabia at the other extreme, where the state is the strongest player. The following is an illustrative discussion of these four layers that together make up the modalities of governance in Arab media. Each layer operates in some media sectors more than others, with varying degrees of intensity and impact depending on the country's geopolitical, economic, social and cultural conditions. The key point here is to reveal how media moguls have benefitted from, modified and greatly influenced the various conditions related to the development of Arab media. A second and equally important element is that politics – whether local, regional or international, state, party or feudal – remains a powerful shaper in media development. Because space precludes a consideration of all modalities related to all media platforms, each section will focus on television as the most widespread medium, taking due regard to historical specificity.

Local Modalities: National Media

Most Arab states are characterised by non-existent, late or incomplete democratisation, often little modernisation, and a business sector associated with a dirigiste state. It is too early to predict what, if any, changes will be brought about by the Arab uprisings, but Arab countries still display features of 'state paternalism' or 'political clientelism', as well as 'panpoliticismo', whereby politics dominates much of economics and society.[17] Arab nation states, taken as a group, provide examples of situations in which politics permeate and influence many social, economic and judiciary institutions and, indeed, media and cultural activities. The development of private institutions has been delayed due to a political culture favouring a strong state role and control of the media by political elites. Of course, within this macro picture, a closer analysis will reveal certain differences across the various Arab states. Such differences, when they exist, are the outcome of different historical paths, cultural sensibilities, economic opportunities and political structures.

Against this background, the term 'local modality' refers to the conditions in which the state remains a central and strong player as media financier, regulator and censor. Over recent decades these modalities have provided a balance between the state's interest in maintaining a monopoly over communication while simultaneously encouraging the emergence or expansion of local media owners from within its ranks. In fact, local modalities help sustain a system in which the state and its political elites control the flow of information and entertainment. Even in states such as Lebanon, where television was established as a commercial venture, political and business elites owned the licences while the government oversaw the newscasts.

Across the Arab world, it is possible to outline certain characteristics that facilitate moguldom. There is a pervasiveness of politics in broadcasting that seeps into the appointment of board members, allocation of budgets, licensing and business deals. While gradually moving away from state monopoly over media, governments have introduced liberalisation and privatisation measures that could best be described as cosmetic. One measure, for example, includes the control of media through proxies – usually a group of friendly oligarchs. Another involves the promotion of politically friendly media by limiting licences to entertainment rather than political programming. Meanwhile, political elites maintain their control over media infrastructures, particularly access to satellite broadcasting. At the same time, the state media apparatus is strengthened through training, rebranding and the launching of new channels. To meet this target, politically friendly production companies are often specifically established to supply programmes and services that do not challenge the status quo.

With effect from the late 1980s, the media scene in Syria saw the rise of local media patrons benefitting from such local modalities. Although more than 100 production companies emerged in Syria, the main owners of these companies came from a close circle of political elites. Al Sham International for Production stands as an example of what happens when an oligarch falls out of political favour. Owned by the sons of the former vice-president, Abdel-Halim Khaddam, Al Sham International was responsible for revamping Syrian drama and re-introducing it to the Arab world. Benefitting from their political associations, the company's managers could set the price, schedule the programme and define the terms of contracts on behalf of the national broadcaster. Not long after Abdel-Halim Khaddam announced his separation from the regime, Al Sham International found itself unable to operate and was shut down amid legal and commercial controversies stirred by the regime itself, as well as companies competing with Khaddam. These local modalities allowed other members of the political elite to have a financial interest in media. They included relatives of Hikmat al-Shahabi, the former chief of staff of the army (Aleppo for International Art Production); Mahmoud al-Zoubi, a former prime minister (Bosra International); and the son of former general Bahjat Sleiman (Al Wasseet Media Group).

The 2000s saw the Syrian regime appearing to flirt with liberalising its media sector. This included discussions about a new media law, the introduction of a media 'free zone' to attract foreign investments, and the licensing of new broadcast and print outlets. Each flirtation was accompanied by tighter government control over the means of production. For instance, Rami Makhlouf, the maternal cousin of President Bashar al-Assad, intended to launch the television channel Ninar, and published *Al-Watan*, the first private newspaper since the 1960s.[18]

To sum up, the central feature of the local modality in a contemporary Arab setting has been a political drive on the part of authoritarian elites to substitute state ownership, or at least strict state control, with looser private media ownership in the hands of a few loyal and trusted individuals.

Network Modalities: Arab Media Clusters

One important characteristic of media moguls, as is the case with most business owners, is their appetite for expansion beyond nation-state boundaries. Operating from urban media clusters, successful media moguls combine high-quantity production with high-quality regional networking. Although exact definitions of networks and networking are hard to find,[19] network modalities are those that allow for partnerships and cooperation in finance, technology or creative labour among local, regional and/or international players. Through these modalities, local partners emerge through control over production and creative resources of value to regional or international trade in media products.

Most media clusters are 'not directly comparable because of different purposes, histories, structures and sectors emphasized.'[20] Undoubtedly, most clusters are the outcome of unique historical processes of cumulative policies, conditions and accidents. Therefore, these network modalities can only be discussed in broad strokes. As clusters, there seems to be a shared use of a common pool of financial, human, technological or other resources. The ability to exchange information and knowledge among members of the cluster enables the creation of network extensions. In turn, these extensions often lead to greater interest in developing new business partnerships. Clusters also allow for close contact with consumers and a greater ability to address audience requirements given their strategic geocultural positioning. Furthermore, clusters seem to generate a greater degree of organisation and better division of labour. Media moguls associated with clusters stand to reap the benefits of the network modalities while undergoing expansion regionally and globally. At the same time, they are able to mitigate risks by relocating their activities across the network.

With the beginning of Arab television broadcasting in the 1950s, Beirut and Cairo became the dominant media clusters of the Arab world. The historical involvement of Beirut and Cairo in various media platforms is well documented. Although each city independently developed its own media cluster, they have a long history of networking successfully with one another. Under the Ottoman Empire, Cairo became a key refuge for many of Beirut's journalists and newspaper publishers. In return, Beirut was a haven for exiled or self-exiled Egyptian film makers in the 1950s and 1960s.

The conditions for the success of each cluster depended on specific conditions. Since the 1950s, the regime that ruled in Egypt has considered media to be a national priority, for both political and economic reasons. Internally, it aimed to consolidate state power and promote development programmes. Externally, it aimed to foster Egypt's image through propaganda and soft power. As economic conditions reflected the shift from Nasser's dirigiste to Mubarak's neo-liberalist policies, public–private partnerships grew. Increasingly, business and political elites promoted intraregional networking that built on and extended the popularity of Egyptian cultural products. Similarly, Lebanon's success as a media cluster promoted and benefitted from a broader interest in the arts, education, apprenticeships and the development of a creative class. Given its geopolitical position, Lebanon played the role of refuge for political dissidents. It also acted as an incubator for many of the intellectual and artistic currents during the 1960s and 1970s. Coupled with a laissez-faire market economy and free movement of capital, Beirut nurtured bustling media scenes in which private national and foreign entrepreneurs were able to develop their intraregional networks.

The ability of media moguls to benefit from network modalities in times of risk has been tested, at least once, in both Beirut and Cairo. During the Lebanese war (1975–90), a number of media owners relocated to neighbouring countries (e.g. Jordan and Egypt) and European cities (e.g. Paris, London and Athens). Similarly, many Egyptian players relocated to Dubai and Athens after the 1978 Camp David peace accords with Israel led to Egypt being suspended from the Arab League for the next decade. Generally, the choice of where to relocate was determined by the degree of similarity of the modalities available in the host city and those in the home city. Indeed, the more these modalities resembled each other, the easier it was for transplanted entrepreneurs to reconstruct their teams in the new city and quickly get back to business. More importantly, they were able to maintain, sustain and sometimes expand their networks in the process, and then relocate them back to Beirut and Cairo. In fact, Beirut and Cairo re-emerged in the 1990s as central nodes in the creative industries supply chain. Examples include the film and television productions of Saddek al-Sabbah's Sabbah Media Group and the advertising sales achievements of the late Antoine Choueiri's Choueiri Group.[21]

The network modalities available in media clusters such as those in Beirut and Cairo are not unique to the region. The current Arab media ecosystem boasts numerous clusters, each providing specific advantages and cultural products conceived and promoted by media owners. For example, Amman has been home to historical drama producers such as Adnan Awamleh's Arab Telemedia Productions.

Transnational Modalities: Arab Offshore Media

A second layer of media organisations, in which ownership and agendas compete with nation-state politics, complicates notions of national governance. The term 'offshore media' refers to privately owned institutions that escaped the control and censorship of state regimes. Established outside the Arab world in European cities, these media can also be called migrant, émigré, transnational or international. The fact they are privately owned is not a guarantee against government influence, however, as transnational modalities allow powerful state and non-state players to select content unevenly, target audiences and achieve revenues. With transnational modalities, the leading players are able to develop media empires that cut across nation states and mitigate financial, political and other risks and constraints.

What started as an exodus of dissident print media during Lebanon's war was followed by a second wave of political dissidents and activists, as well as regime proxies from all over the Arab world. It was not until the 1990s that a third wave – one of politically savvy businessmen – established satellite channels broadcasting to the Arab diaspora as well as the Arab world. While Athens and Paris had their share of offshore Arab media productions, London and Rome had the largest and most significant activities throughout the 1990s. In London, Walid al-Ibrahim and Saleh Kamel founded the Middle East Broadcasting Center (MBC) in 1991, and in 1996 Kuwait Projects Company (KIPCO) partnered with Viacom to offer the pay-TV service Showtime. In and around Rome, Saleh Kamel established his Arab Radio and Television Network (ART), and shortly thereafter Mawarid Group's Orbit pay-TV channels established their headquarters in the Italian capital.

As media clusters, London and Rome offered transnational modalities allowing investors to produce and distribute entertainment and content; acquire, prepare, compile and distribute news; and, perhaps most importantly, develop a transnational advertising market. These transnational modalities can be summarised in three broad themes. The first relates to the history of Arab media presence in Europe, which afforded access to human resources, infrastructure and a creative milieu. Coupled with this enabling environment for the development of entertainment and independent news coverage, a second transnational modality was characterised by minimal state control and censorship. While many networks (for example, Orbit and MBC) chose to adopt self-censorship measures, others, such as Arab News Network (ANN), operated as dissident media. The third modality is closely related to the benefits of economic globalisation, namely a rapid increase in cross-border movement of labour, goods, services, technology and capital, particularly at the time of Europe's reunification in the period after 1989.

In practice, media owners were able to relocate Arabs and others to European cities, seek advertising accounts and other services, and transfer funds to and from the Arab world. Taking advantage of the technological advances available in Europe, they were able to embark on a modernisation project that selectively applied technology, management and production strategies. In practice, they were able to integrate Arab media in a global industry as they solicited technologies from Europe and the USA, headhunted an international management team and adopted international production standards. Combined, these transnational modalities allowed offshore media to be positioned strategically *vis-à-vis* the audience/market and prepare for an eventual relocation back to the Arab world. In fact, the very few remaining offshore media are those that, for political reasons, are unable to relocate to Arab countries. In addition to oppositional media, this includes a number of Saudi-owned establishments that are not necessarily opposed to the regime, but that have nuanced perspectives that at times challenge aspects of the status quo.

Supranational Modalities: Arab Media Cities

Towards the end of the 1990s, the economic policies of certain Arab governments sought to benefit from the expanding media sector by creating media 'economic free zones'. These designated areas, usually associated with a number of incentives, aim to act as information, communications and technology hubs, and as incubators for economic, sociocultural and creative activities. These so-called media cities were established in Egypt in 1997 and in Jordan and Dubai in 2001. In 2012, there were more than ten existing or planned media cities around the Arab world. The emergence of supranational modalities provides a media ecosystem for a recentralisation of media operations in specific clusters or zones. These supranational modalities consist of specific incentives that lower the barriers to entry for aspiring media entrepreneurs, encourage the development of commercially oriented media and arguably mitigate concerns about freedom of expression.

In media free zones, governments develop high-end infrastructure, provide incentives (co-production, access, talent, locations and facilities) and create legal structures (taxation, immigration and ownership arrangements). Meanwhile, media owners, including those operating off-shore, have relocated to these media cities and are allowed to operate outside the immediate constraints applied to national media. In what could be perceived as a symbiotic relationship, governments and media organisations have vested interests in developing supranational modalities for these media cities to succeed. By existing in frameworks that bypass, transcend or extend beyond nation states, Arab moguls and states have been relatively successful in accommodating mutual priorities. As a result, an 'anywhere but here' media phenomenon has emerged that eschews direct censorship and questions political ideologies, social values and religious taboos, while refraining from meddling in local and national politics. Apart from occasional threats to cut signals and a failed attempt to regulate satellite broadcasts by the Arab League, these transnational channels have weathered political and social pressures.

In addition to providing a home for repatriated offshore television channels, media cities and their associated supranational modalities have contributed to transforming media in the region. Quantitatively, privately owned satellite channels grew tenfold in ten years and have been located predominantly in these media cities. More importantly, these channels are owned by an emerging breed of media owners with wide-ranging backgrounds, interests and goals. For example, Saudi Arabia's Fahad al-Shmaimri extended his family's religious publishing business into an Islamic pay-TV group of channels, Al-Majd Company, operating from Dubai and Amman. Others have capitalised on niche interests; for example, Gamal Ashraf Marwan (Melody Group)[22], Suhail al-Adboul (Nojoum TV & Music) and Muhsen Jaber (Mazzika and Alam el-Phan) have all created value chains in the music industry. In brief, these supranational modalities have been a contributing factor in the emergence of new players, increasing business practices, identifying niche markets and integrating Arab media both horizontally and vertically.

Towards Re-localised Modalities of Media Governance

Examining the various modalities of media governance reveals multi-layered and competing factors, stakeholders and structures. This chapter aimed to describe and analyse these modalities by focusing on media history, localities and media entrepreneurs.

With the benefit of hindsight, the changing economic conditions in Europe, the increased interest in democratisation and the events of 9/11 precipitated the repatriation of offshore channels from their European bases to the Arab world. Also, during the period leading up to 2001, a number of channels based in the Arab world succeeded in attracting a regional audience in entertainment (LBC), news (Al-Jazeera) and music video (Melody Group). Balancing economic imperatives and editorial challenges, these now transnational channels continuously negotiate direct state control.

At the same time, radical Islamic groups, human rights activists and youth groups rely on alternative communications platforms to expose and circumvent repressive government policies. For example, these groups have communicated their messages via ideologically competing television channels (for instance, Saudi dissidents appeared on the Qatar-based Al-Jazeera). Another tool they use is the internet, with online forums, chat rooms, blogs and, most recently, Web 2.0 all presenting opportunities to promote counter-hegemonic messages. After years of activism, young people were able to mobilise mass movements in Tunisia, Egypt, Libya, Yemen and elsewhere in what was briefly known by some as the 'Arab Spring'.

The ensuing expansion of participation in Arab public discourse has led to a remapping of the media landscape, as local audiences, empowered and emboldened by their reclaimed liberties, advocate for media that mirrors their aspirations. New publications, broadcast channels and social media platforms illustrate the complexity of the new media environment. This new environment's reliance on media freedom activates strong local impulses including investments, coverage and audience interest, among others. The advent of a strong 'local pull' challenges modalities of governance, from the state and regional or global actors to myriad local political, social, economic and professional actors. Drawing on the history of Arab media, together with this chapter's discussion of the layered modalities of media governance, the fate of Arab media entrepreneurs, and most of all the Arab media moguls, depends on their ability to adapt to and perhaps transform the emerging economic and political challenges. The extent to which they are able to develop commercially viable and politically flexible business models remains to be seen.

3

Antoine Choueiri: 'President' of Arab Advertising

Zahera Harb

When Antoine Choueiri died in 2010, obituaries readily dubbed him a 'media mogul'.[1] However, the title he was mostly known by during his lifetime was 'Le President', reflecting a widespread belief that he had single-handedly controlled the Arab world's advertising market for more than 35 years. From its launch in 1971, the Choueiri Group grew over the next four decades to market and manage the advertising space of 26 satellite television stations, 15 print titles, nine radio stations in the Arab world and the largest billboard network in the Gulf region. Choueiri's activities were not limited to advertising, however. For example, he led the Lebanese basketball club, La Sagesse (*Hikmeh*), to win the Asia Cup and qualify for the World Cup. This chapter explores the political and economic factors that made 'Le President' such a recognisable figure in business, media and sport in the Arab world. It examines Choueiri's tactics, alliances and business decisions and how they led to him becoming one of the most influential people on the Arab media scene.

Taking the definition put forward by Tunstall and Palmer, that a media mogul is someone who 'owns and operates major media companies, who takes entrepreneurial risks, and who conducts these media businesses in a personal or eccentric style',[2] this chapter explores how far Choueiri – a 'self-made' billionaire who started working at the age of 16 to pay for his studies and rose to head a media empire – measures up to the definition of a media mogul. In the process it considers what these traits of moguldom reveal about the nature of Arab politics, about norms of conduct in the region's media businesses, and about the nature of 'risk' and 'eccentricity' in the context of Arab media.

Magazines as a Launchpad

Antoine Choueiri's first bright idea, according to those closest to him, was to see the potential for advertising in magazines. According to his own account, published in *ArabAd* in 1998 when he was named '*ArabAd* man of the year', he 'came to advertising by coincidence'.[3] He started out as an employee of the Beirut-based luxury goods enterprise, Abu Adal Group, becoming accountant and then chief accountant.[4] Later, as managing director of Les Editions Orientales, publishers of the first pan-Arab magazine, *Al-Ousbou al-Arabi* (*The Arab Week*), Choueiri became aware of the symbiosis between advertising and magazines, whereby magazines benefit from advertising revenue while providing valued space for advertisements. His wife, Rose Salameh Choueiri, and daughter, Lena Nahas, regard this realisation as 'visionary'.[5] Yet Rose also implicitly claims some credit for those early achievements by referring to them using the pronoun 'we'. 'We took *The Arab Week*', she says, 'which was very popular, but did not carry much advertising. When we became their representative things changed.'[6]

Not having the means to develop his ideas as an employee, Choueiri founded Lebanon's first media representation company, Régie Generale de Presse, in 1971. Rose remembers that period vividly because of the risk involved in leaving paid employment to start a company from nothing. With hindsight she sees it as a positive move, which, she says, promoted magazine advertising and established its importance for media prosperity and independence.[7] Choueiri became media representative of the Lebanese political magazine *Al-Diyar*, the popular showbiz magazine *Al-Moued* and the mouthpiece of Lebanon's Phalange Party, *Al-Amal*.

After 1975, when civil war broke out in Lebanon and Lebanese journalists and advertising agencies migrated to Paris, Choueiri did likewise. Within three years he had taken on representation of three Paris-based, pan-Arab political magazines, each of which was presumed to rely on Arab government subsidies as well as advertising revenues in order to survive. Various Arab governments and the Palestine Liberation Organization (PLO) had their own stakes in the war in Lebanon and regional politics and pursued these by backing certain publications. One of the magazines represented by Choueiri, *Al-Watan al-Arabi* (*The Arab Nation*), was launched in 1976–7 by Walid Abu Zahr, a Lebanese businessman with Iraqi connections. It received revenues from the Baathist regime in Baghdad in return for the 60,000 copies sent to Iraq every week.[8] *Al-Mustaqbal* (*The Future*), founded in 1977 by Faisal Abu Khadra, a Palestinian businessman living in Saudi Arabia, was later taken over by Nabil Khoury, a journalist and writer of Palestinian origin who had previously edited *Al-Hawadeth*, the third magazine represented by Choueiri. Of the three, *Al-Mustaqbal* was the most profitable. According to one-time deputy editor Assad Haidar, it sold 1,500 pages of advertising a year at US$1,500 per page, and reached a circulation of 120,000 copies at its peak, many purchased by Arab governments at full price.[9] This proved unsustainable when petrodollars slumped in the mid-1980s, resulting in the title's eventual sale to Lebanon's Rafik Hariri.[10] *Al-Hawadeth* was hit by the assassination of its owner, Salim al-Lawzi, in 1980. Al-Lawzi, a prominent Lebanese journalist, was a harsh critic of the Syrian regime and its role in Lebanon. His brutal murder was attributed to Syrian intelligence forces and was later compared by a Lebanese lawyer to the dropping of an atomic bomb on Lebanese journalism.[11]

Innovation in Untapped Markets

With the civil war continuing, the Choueiris kept their business split between two capitals, with Antoine based in Paris and Rose responsible for running the company's office in Beirut. Lena describes the move to Paris as a joint decision by her parents.[12] However, selling advertising space for magazines subsidised by oil-exporting Gulf states made Choueiri aware of these states' low investment in advertising at a time when they were enjoying a boom in export revenues in the wake of the oil price explosion of the mid-1970s. Industry veteran Ramzi Barakat told the Abu Dhabi-based newspaper *The National* that Choueiri hated losing. Barakat said he possessed 'a legendary drive' to explore new venues and markets.[13] By 1978, Choueiri's company was operating not only out of Beirut and Paris but also heading to Saudi Arabia. There, because advertising was not allowed on television, he needed first to create new media platforms.[14] Lena Nahas recalls that living in Europe had shown Choueiri the importance of television as a medium for advertising, and so he turned to video as a popular medium in Saudi Arabia. After establishing a new company, Video Force,

> he made deals with Egyptian movie producers to provide him with the movies' master copies and he started selling spaces and inserting ads at different intervals of the movie. He established a video cassette printing house in Saudi Arabia. He would get the film from the producer, take it to Saudi Arabia and insert ads inside it and distribute it across the Saudi market.[15]

Video Force, the first company of its kind in Saudi Arabia, was Choueiri's first step to building his business in the Gulf region. Rose Choueiri recalls that her late husband believed that media organisations, advertising agencies and media representatives form a triangle in which each component is equally dependent on the other two. Antoine's son Pierre, Chief Executive Officer of the Choueiri group, and his daughter Lena, Chief Financial Officer, say they both believe the same thing. Buoyed by the success of video advertising, Choueiri investigated other available advertising spaces. Because it was difficult for him as a non-Saudi to represent Saudi news-papers, he looked to billboards instead. With a friend, Abd-al-Ilah al-Qureishi, he created Arabian Outdoor, erecting billboards in collaboration with local municipalities. They started in Riyadh and Jeddah and spread the business to other parts of the kingdom. According to his surviving family members, Choueiri was always more interested in strategic long-term investment, 'ten-year outcomes', than in immediate profit or even short-term loss.[16] The value of taking long-term risks was demonstrated when Video Force was eventually obliged to close. The closure came when Saudi television started broadcasting advertisements and these were no longer allowed on video. However, Choueiri had established a presence in the Saudi market, which would serve him in later years.

Accusations of Monopoly

In the early 1980s, the Lebanese Forces, a Maronite Christian militia formed during the civil war, approached Rose Choueiri in Beirut to ask if Antoine would be interested in becoming media representative for the new television station they were establishing, the Lebanese Broad-casting Corporation (LBC). Antoine flew to Beirut to meet the founders and sign the contract. This was his first new venture in Lebanon since his departure for Paris in the 1970s and, according to Rose, it seemed like a big risk. In a politically and religiously divided country still at war there were questions about the physical safety of the LBC premises, as well as the size of the television advertising market on which it could rely given Lebanon's sectarian and geographic divisions, and therefore doubts about the station's financial viability. In Rose's words,

> Everyone was telling him not to take the risk with LBC, but he insisted. He knew it had the potential to be a major player in the TV industry in Lebanon and the Arab region. He didn't hesitate. He used to say he had faith in this country and its people. He had faith in the people who were running the TV and their potential.[17]

Choueiri himself explained in 1998 that he had been persuaded to work with LBC in the 1980s because he could see that its manager, Pierre Daher, had a 'vision for the future' and because his wife Rose had stayed with Daher and his wife when things were bad in Lebanon during the civil war.[18] Working with LBC renewed Choueiri's Lebanon operations at a time when the Lebanese media market was growing rapidly. He approached Ghassan Tueini of *Al-Nahar* newspaper and became the advertising sales representative for both *Al-Nahar* and its French sister publication *L'Orient-Le Jour* by buying Tamam, the company that used to represent *Al-Nahar*, renaming it Press Media Tamam. His next move was to create what Lena calls a 'Lebanese infrastructure', founding separate companies to represent separate media outlets. He formed Audio Visual Media to represent LBC, Inter Radio to represent Radio Free Lebanon, which also belongs to the Lebanese Forces, and Press Media to represent the print sector. Rose remembers that Choueiri believed the Lebanese advertising market could be doubled in value. 'He used to compare the media market to a pie', she recalls. 'He used to say the bigger the pie the bigger are the slices. The bigger the market, the bigger the profit. Everyone would have a fair share.'[19]

By owning companies that were supposed to be competing with each other for advertising in the same market, Choueiri made friends and enemies. Some accused him of monopolistic behaviour. Others appreciated that he protected the price of advertisements in different platforms. Advertisers resented it, but Choueiri is remembered for saving media organisations from having to reduce the price of their advertising space in order to compete for revenue.[20] He claimed there was competition but that it was all about quality, not price. He believed in statistics, says Lena. He used to read all readership and viewership statistics and encouraged his employees to work with media organisations to get the top ratings. Rejecting accusations levelled at Choueiri for trying to monopolise the Lebanese market, his daughter says his strategy was to represent the most successful media players, offer advertisers access to a popular medium, and inspire loyalty among those working with him. She recalls her father asking how it could be a monopoly to represent just two out of more than ten television stations in Lebanon.[21] Challenged on the issue by *ArabAd*'s interviewer in 1998, Choueiri relied on a technical definition of monopoly in an answer that begged as many questions as it answered. 'Monopoly', he said, 'is when advertisers have no real choice in terms of which media they want to advertise in, and this is not the case in Lebanon.' Sidestepping the meaning of 'real choice', he continued, 'there are six TV stations here, 20 radio stations and numerous publications. If I represent the most important of these, this does not mean that I am practising monopoly.'[22]

Indeed, accusations of monopoly resonate with the fact that there was really only one sole source of media statistics in Lebanon, namely Stat Ipsos. Some media owners have questioned the credibility of Stat Ipsos surveys, seeing them more as a weapon used to deprive them of their rightful share of the advertising market. Talal Salman, publisher and owner of Lebanese daily *Al-Safir*, says he remembers suspecting Choueiri of monopolising the market. He even called him the 'giant' or 'ogre' who was aiming to take over everything that came his way.[23] Yet, one day Choueiri approached Salman, proposing to represent *Al-Safir*. 'He came to see me', Salman recounts,

> and I remember saying to him how would this work? You represent my competitor. His answer was simply: you and *Al-Nahar* are the best-selling newspapers in the country. If I represent you both I would be selling ad spaces in both newspapers hence offering clients better exposure for their products. He organised a meeting between Ghassan Tueini [of *Al-Nahar*], himself and me. Tueini was convinced. Sharing the same broker would be good for both of us. Choueiri's motto was: I bring you ads, I make profit and you make profit. He always acted as the middleman.[24]

That was how Choueiri became 'king' of the advertising market, Salman explains, by setting his own rules for the buying and selling of advertisements and advertising spaces, but also adhering to local norms for what was considered fair and honourable behaviour.

> Choueiri was a clever chess player. He understood the rules of the game. He understood the market. He investigated his competitors' weaknesses and acted upon them. He took risks. He was a good poker player (literally), but a fair player. He respected his deals and kept his word. He made verbal deals and stood by them. Many competing companies no longer exist. He took over 70 to 80 per cent of the market for brokering advertisements.[25]

By taking so much of the advertising pie, Choueiri left little for his competitors to claim. By gaining the accounts for both *Al-Safir* and *Al-Nahar* he became the representative of the most circulated newspapers in Lebanon. *Al-Nahar* stands on the centre right, with a predominantly Christian readership, while *Al-Safir* represents the centre left, with a predominantly Muslim pan-Arabist readership. Representing two competing media organisations at the same time and keeping both happy might look like an eccentric way of doing business were it not for the sectarian divisions in Lebanese media and their implications for undermining outright competition. It is a practice that Choueiri's son and daughter have continued.

Ahmad Salman, General Director of *Al-Safir*, asserts that Choueiri became the strongest and most active sales force in Lebanon. By acquiring the business of the country's two main newspapers he had better bargaining power with clients and *vis-à-vis* competitors in the media-buying business.[26] According to Salman, 'he brought us ads and strengthened our position in the market, and did the same with *Al-Nahar*'. 'But', he adds, 'we always had this feeling that children usually get: who does mummy love most, me or my brother?'[27] Choueiri might have founded a media cartel that dominated the advertising market, but both newspapers had already achieved their high circulation positions in the Lebanese market before their collaboration with Choueiri. In their view he had helped them to survive by guaranteeing a source of income. He considered both newspapers to be icons in the history of Lebanese journalism and believed he was helping them to protect that position.

According to his daughter, Choueiri was often driven by patriotic and nationalistic tendencies. Others believe his Christian identity also played a part. After the Lebanese civil war ended at the end of the 1980s,[28] Télé-Liban, the state-run television, underwent a major restructuring and relaunch. Choueiri, realising the importance of such a platform in postwar Lebanon, started negotiating with the company's board of directors to appoint him as Télé-Liban's media representative, which they did. However, his years with Télé-Liban were tainted by constant concerns from the station chairman at the time, Fouad Naim, that Choueiri was favouring LBC over Télé-Liban.[29] These concerns persisted until Choueiri was forced to quit the station after 1996, when the new media law in Lebanon prevented media brokers from representing more than one television station and one radio station locally. Choueiri chose to represent LBC's successor, Lebanese Broadcasting Corporation International (LBCI),[30] which Talal Salman says he had helped to establish, structure and develop without owning any of its shares.[31] It seems he was politically and spiritually connected to the station and was very close to Lebanese Forces head Samir Geagea. Ahmad Salman maintains that Choueiri cared so much about LBC that he acted as a peacemaker between Pierre Daher (LBCI chairman) and Geagea in a dispute over ownership of the station.[32] He was worried that the dispute would harm the company's image and credibility and damage its profits. In this way his preoccupations were political, nationalistic and financial, all at the same time.[33]

As already demonstrated, being politically affiliated with the Christian right in Lebanon did not stop Choueiri from doing business with people from other religions or political backgrounds. His wife Rose insists he read the Qur'an as well as the Bible and 'memorised large sections' of both.[34] Talal Salman speaks highly of Choueiri's political tolerance:

He approached *Al-Safir*, a newspaper that opposes completely his political views. He wanted to do business with us despite our political differences. He liked challenges. We used to have heated discussions on current and historical political grievances, but that never affected his business operations with us or anyone else for that matter.[35]

With Salman and *Al-Safir* it was a case of dealing with business partners not only from a different religious community but with political views that completely contradicted his own. As a newspaper, *Al-Safir* was highly critical and sometimes offensively critical of the Lebanese Forces and its leader Samir Geagea. By putting business ahead of politics, Choueiri came across to some of his Arab partners as a force against sectarianism. When he died, Walid al-Ibrahim, owner and chairman of the Saudi MBC Group, described him as a believer 'in one united Lebanon for all its citizens away from sectarianism'.[36] Abdul-Rahman al-Rashed, veteran Saudi journalist and general manager of MBC's news channel, Al-Arabiya, declared that Choueiri was the victim of a rumour mill. Even though he was 'truthful', 'honest' and had worked for the good of Arab media, Choueiri's image had been deliberately damaged, in Rashed's view, by those who did not share his interest in boosting overall advertising revenue across the Arab media sector.[37]

In 1996, under new Lebanese broadcasting legislation, LBCI started broadcasting via satellite and Choueiri also took over representation of the satellite channel.[38] LBCSat attracted big audiences in the Arab world and among the Arab diaspora across the globe. As a market leader it attracted a corresponding share of Saudi advertising. Choueiri knew the rules and regulations for advertising in Saudi Arabia and other Gulf states, which reflected cultural and religious taboos, and he saw to it that publicity agencies would abide by them when producing advertisements. He started MediaSat in Dubai for regional marketing of advertising space on LBCSat. It was at this point in the late 1990s that *ArabAd* magazine pronounced him 'man of the year'.[39]

'Completing the Circle', from Egypt to the Gulf

After establishing his parent company, Régie Générale de Presse, in 1971, the scope of Choueiri's ambition and transactions extended far beyond his home borders, but Beirut always remained a focal point. He realised early the importance of the Saudi market, then lost Video Force, but outdoor advertising was flourishing. It grew bigger with new designs and the introduction of platforms, including the MUPI, a double-sided backlit poster that can be illuminated at night, and the Megacom silkscreen printed poster. Arabian Outdoor extended its business to Kuwait and the United Arab Emirates (UAE). The local Gulf markets were growing bigger. In 1991 he signed a management agreement for the restructuring and management of Saudi Arabia's Tihama group of companies, engaged in advertising, retail bookstore chains, printing and publishing. He became media representative of the pan-Arab newspaper *Al-Hayat* and its offshoots, including *Laha* (*Hers*) magazine.[40] According to his widow, Rose, it was Choueiri who encouraged *Al-Hayat* to establish a specialised magazine for women, saying the region lacked such a thing.[41] In Dubai he expanded further by establishing Middle East Media Services (MEMS) to represent media based there, starting with Dubai TV and *Al-Bayan* newspaper and ending with all the media outlets owned by Dubai Media Incorporated in 2009.[42] In 2005, MBC Group was added.[43] Choueiri also expanded into Kuwait, where he represented the newly launched Al-Watan TV, linked to the daily newspaper *Al-Watan*, as well as *Samara* magazine and Cinescape cinema halls. His group also represented Qatar-based Al-Jazeera, the region's first relatively unfettered pan-Arab 24-hour news channel, for over six years.[44] However, the contract with Al-Jazeera was not renewed. Some in the business thought at the time that Al-Jazeera would be better off without Choueiri, but Choueiri's own family say that the separation took place in the wake of a political rift between Qatar and Saudi Arabia that led to a Saudi advertising boycott against Al-Jazeera, which had adverse implications for Choueiri's other businesses.[45]

Thus, they see it as a business decision, not one influenced directly by Saudi politics as such. Other media experts note his link, via MBC, to Al-Arabiya, which was created to compete with Al-Jazeera in 2003. Al-Jazeera at the time was seen as a problem by several Arab Gulf Countries, and its offices in both Saudi Arabia and Kuwait were closed. Importantly, however, Choueiri's contract with Al-Jazeera endured for the agreed time, with both parties respecting the contract's timeline.

The first decade of the new millennium saw Choueiri extend his business still further to Oman and Morocco, but Egypt was his dream market, as Rose reveals:

> He used to say we are missing an essential part in the circle, we are missing Egypt. If we get to Egypt then we could connect the circle well together. We used to tell him 'forget about Egypt' and he would reply that the future is for Egypt's markets. He took Melody group in Egypt. He felt that was not enough. He wanted Al-Hayat group. He didn't get it, his son did. We now have Al-Hayat Group in Egypt.[46]

In Egypt, as elsewhere, Choueiri was accused of monopolising the media industry and the advertising market.[47] However, Eli Khoury, Chairman of Quantum Holding, told *The National* newspaper that Choueiri acted more as a regulator than a monopolist:

> I think it's the absence of professional competitors that makes him the monopole of the industry. And being the monopole of the industry, he's done some really great stuff for the industry. At least he regulated competitiveness, i.e pricing. Otherwise, the industry would have suffered big time.[48]

In Khoury's view, a powerful middleman was needed to set prices and act as a kind of gatekeeper to prevent media organisations across the region engaging in a race to the bottom on ad rates.[49] Indeed, 'middleman' is how Choueiri used to refer to himself. Would a middleman have been able to control the advertising market and set prices if regulations on the concentration of media ownership had been stricter or more diverse and credible sources of audience data to reveal media entities' true market shares existed? Such questions highlight the nature of development in the pan-Arab media sector from the 1990s onwards. As pointed out in one of the many articles written about Choueiri after his death, his group's rise to such a dominant position in different parts of the market was due in large part simply to him being first to get there.[50] By 2010, Choueiri Group consisted of 12 companies representing different media platforms across the Middle East and North Africa, making it the largest business representing media in the region.

A Web of Personal Relationships

Those who worked with Choueiri say he did not believe in trying to diversify one line of business into many others. In some parts of the media industry, investors see economic advantage in diagonal expansion, involving cross-ownership activities in more than one sector.[51] For example, George Chehwan, owner of the real-estate company Plus Properties, also won advertising concessions, including at Lebanon's Rafik Hariri airport, through his media arm Group Plus. Choueiri, in contrast, reportedly insisted that a media representative should not open an advertising agency and an advertising agency should not open a media representative company.[52] Instead, his approach was to create new companies to deal with different media platforms across countries, each with its own general manager and team of media buyers and sellers. In Lena Nahas' view this avoids any conflict of interest and 'makes the client feel more confident' about the service being offered. She states that, 'to perform well', you 'shouldn't have interests here and there'. 'Our teams compete with each other to serve the media they represent and this is what my father wanted and encouraged.'[53]

Choueiri presented himself as someone with a wide circle of personal relationships and good political connections, giving him a vantage point from which to pursue a particular strategy for the whole market. He told *ArabAd* in 1998 that 'personal relationships are very important in business' in the Arab world and that he was 'proud to have the [Lebanese] president and his wife as friends', explaining that his role was to 'organise a strategy for the advertising markets as a whole, rather than concern myself with the everyday running of the individual companies'.[54] Yet, his personal relationships also seem to have involved the giving of advice about management structure, media content and how to develop audiences. Walid al-Ibrahim of MBC said that MBC used to consult with him about new programme ideas and programme grids.[55] He was also close to Pierre Daher of LBCI, Talal Salman of *Al-Safir*, Ghassan Tueini of *Al-Nahar*, Walid Abu Daher of *Al-Watan al-Arabi*, among others. His relationship with Daher was not helped when Prince Alwaleed bin Talal of Saudi Arabia increased his holding of LBCSat to 85 per cent and took responsibility for media buying away from Choueiri, handing it to Rotana Media Services, part of Alwaleed's Rotana Group, with effect from January 2009. The Rotana–LBCI partnership foundered, however, and Daher's relations with Choueiri are said to have got back on track. Two years after Choueiri's death, Rotana went public on its rift with LBCI.[56]

Admirers of Choueiri say he had an open-door policy with his employees, meaning that they could see him and talk to him at any time, but Rose Choueiri felt that he distinguished between work and family:

> Pierre and Lena worked with him, but he never treated them as son and daughter at work. If they did wrong he used to shout in their faces. Once he shouted in my face and I told him, 'You are shouting at me' and he said, 'Here you are not my wife, you are an employee who made a mistake'. Pierre started from the bottom of the ladder as an employee in reservations, Lena as well. He wanted them to learn the profession from [the] bottom up and appreciate every aspect of it.[57]

At work her husband had a sharp temper, says Rose, explaining 'If he wanted something, he would want it finished yesterday and not tomorrow.' Choueiri's daughter Lena believes that he was able to think strategically while also taking care of details. Of her father's employees, she says 'We grew up together', because staff who started working with the firm in their early twenties stayed on till they were in their thirties and forties 'with kids'.[58] This family ethos was reflected in the title of 'patriarch' given to Choueiri by other agencies, who came to him for help when they were in trouble. Eli Khoury told *The National* that the reputation for helping out was deserved:

> If you are a small company and you have just lost a client and you have some bills that could send you bankrupt, it's enough to walk into his office, tilt your head and say 'I'm dead if you don't help me' and he will tell you 'OK don't worry about it'.[59]

In his decades of forging alliances, Choueiri could also count 18 years of nurturing basketball in Lebanon and seeing it grow as a national sport through the televising of matches. It was in this sphere that the title of 'president' stuck. 'They used to call him the Emperor', Rose recalls, 'but he didn't like it. They used to call him the Godfather, which he was in a good way. They used to call him the Giant and the Patriarch, but the title he loved most was Le President.'[60] He was elected president of the Lebanese basketball club known as La Sagesse (*Hikmeh*) in 1992, and the club went on to win 19 championships in ten years, including three victories in both the Asian Club Championship and Arab Basketball Cup. Choueiri had always supported La Sagesse, donating money for the club and the school, which is overseen by the Maronite Archbishop of Beirut and run by an appointed member of the Maronite clergy. It was the archbishopric of Beirut who approached him to take over the club's presidency on the death of the previous incumbent. Rose remembers that he watched the club lose 8–0 to opponents in a game in Tripoli, in the north of the country, but was persuaded to work with them because the fans were still singing in support of their team even in the face of such a defeat.[61] He hired new players, bringing them in from the Lebanese diaspora, and pushed the team up the league. Rose sees this as a sign of his determination:

> He told me we want to become Lebanon champions and I said it is feasible. Then he came to me to say I want to achieve the Arab championship and I said you are hallucinating, but he achieved it. He told me I want to get the Asian Cup and I said you are being crazy, but he proved me wrong. Then the team qualified for the World Cup. His dream was to go to the Olympics, but he left the club before achieving it.[62]

Choueiri resigned, according to Rose, because he did not want to be a lifetime president of La Sagesse. The model for a new basketball stadium in Beirut remained in his office. The stadium was never built, but the sport's fan base increased, partly through LBCI's initiative in broadcasting live matches, where once football had dominated the sports scene.

Conclusion

This account suggests that the analytical category of 'media mogul', as employed by Tunstall and Palmer,[63] has both descriptive and explanatory value in the context of Arab media. Risk, eccentricity and a personalised style of management – the kind that accepts subordination to no-one – are all important factors in the rise of Antoine Choueiri and expansion of his Choueiri Group. Moreover, each factor also has the potential to reveal particularities of political culture in Lebanon and the Gulf. Leaving his home country to start a business in Europe was clearly risky, but it was necessitated by the long-running Lebanese civil war, and the level of risk involved in representing Paris-based publications was determined – and partly mitigated – by the source and political motivation of government subsidies provided in each case. Tapping new markets in Saudi Arabia involved risks as well as rewards, especially given the restrictions on Saudi media at the time. Backing LBC was perceived as risky in a country divided by sectarianism, but it was a calculated risk based on what Choueiri himself described as a 'very close friendship' with Pierre Daher and high expectations of the latter's role in LBC.[64]

Similarly, the features of Choueiri's style of management that seem eccentric and highly personalised shed light on the nature of the Arab advertising market and the Lebanese business scene. Talal Salman's comment, that he set his own rules for the buying and selling of advertising while also abiding by the local 'rules of the game', draws attention to the state of the media market in which he was operating, which had no laws to prevent monopoly and promote competition, depending instead on unwritten rules about trust and mutual support among a self-selected business elite. Choueiri's own admission about organising a strategy for the advertising market as a whole may not have been intended to refer to the fact that his companies controlled an estimated 80 per cent of the market, but the two phenomena were certainly in alignment. The dominant media voices represented by Choueiri were highly vocal in singing his praises when he passed away in March 2010.[65] Such are the rules of the game in a region where even those who criticised him when he was alive were ready to join the commemoration after his death.

4

Pierre Daher: Sheikh, Baron and Mogul of LBC[1]

Sarah El-Richani

The Lebanese Broadcasting Corporation (LBC) is one of the Arab world's oldest privately owned channels. Initially set up as a partisan media outlet in wartime Lebanon, the LBC can be seen as a precursor to the competing television stations in the capitalist and only loosely regulated pan-Arab market. LBC's dramatic development from a partisan media outlet to a successful local and regional commercial enterprise, despite a series of lingering legal, financial and political battles, is above all due to the vision and the wheeling and dealing of its chief executive, Sheikh[2] Pierre Daher. This chapter discusses the story of LBC,[3] Lebanon's leading station, and the parallel trajectory of its current owner Pierre Daher from a militia associate to a media baron in a larger conglomerate, and finally into a media mogul in his own right.

Lebanon's Media Landscape: A Special Case

The Lebanese media landscape has long been regarded as 'a special case among Arab systems'.[4] The political system, characterised by pluralism, weak state structures, deep-rooted confessionalism and patronage, has also made this 'democracy of sorts'[5] stand out. The Lebanese media provide a good illustration of the observation by Siebert, Peterson and Schramm that the 'press always takes on the form and coloration of the social and political structures within which it operates'.[6] The externally plural[7] Lebanese media system, with its weak public broadcaster and fiercely competitive private media, generally reflects the country's sectarian diversity and largely serves the political elite.

The Taif Accord, which ended the civil war in 1989, called for reorganisation of the media by limiting the large number of unlicensed radio and television stations. Audio-Visual Media Law 382, passed in 1994, granted licences[8] to political and/or sectarian groups, reinforcing the confessional system[9] and officially ending the state's monopoly over electronic broadcasting. Although the state broadcaster was promised a monopoly on the airwaves until 2012, this promise was already de facto broken during the civil war.[10] Owing to the size of the local media market and the polarisation of the country, the Lebanese audio-visual corporations became an integral part of the political game, with high levels of political parallelism[11] and a partisanship of audiences, particularly when it came to political broadcasting. However, despite the 'communal trenches' in which most of the Lebanese media remain,[12] some media, such as the leading LBC International (LBCI), have managed to pluralise internally and attract a wider audience from across the spectrum.

The Rise of LBCI and Daher

LBC was founded in 1985 by the nationalist Christian Phalange Party and managed by Pierre Daher, who was selected, thanks to his family connections, to head the operation. Daher, the son of a Phalange Party founder, and a friend and close aide to the men who led the party at that time, Bashir Gemayel and Samir Geagea, pledged at the channel's inauguration that 'just as there are fighters on the military front, here, we will be the fighters on the media front'.[13] Yet, despite this clear link between the station and the Lebanese Forces (LF) militia, the television station still managed to reach beyond its partisan audience, easily overtaking the state broadcaster Télé-Liban in both audience share and advertising revenues.[14]

With the end of the war and subsequent decrease in the influence of the LF, culminating in its dissolution and the 11-year incarceration of its leader, Geagea,[15] LBC severed its ties with the LF. Daher proved his ability to practise *realpolitik* by grasping the Pax Syriana phase and then seeking and securing the necessary political backing that would maintain LBC's survival. To this effect, in 1994 the newly formed company LBCI released a communiqué announcing its aspiration 'towards new horizons in its news programs, in harmony with the demands of the hour characterised by close collaboration with the Lebanese state, in the shadow of a law on the audio-visual media which will be quickly promulgated and which will clearly define [the LBCI's] rights and obligations in the framework of [national] understanding'.[16] The statement also acknowledged 'the support of brothers and friends, at the forefront of which is Syria under the leadership of President Hafez al-Assad, is alone in assisting the resistance of Lebanon and the consolidation of its edifice'.[17]

To secure the licence, Sheikh Daher again turned to Elias el-Hrawi, president in the post-Taif era, who gave him the green light. Daher secured 'political cover' by reportedly flinging 'himself on to the lap of the Syrians',[18] toning down the coverage, and bringing in Syria's close allies in Lebanon, former Deputy Prime Minister Issam Fares and Prime Minister Najib Mikati, among others, as shareholders. In addition to securing political cover, Daher teamed up with Antoine Choueiri,[19] an advertising mogul, to secure financial support for the station.[20] With a 20 per cent share of the Arab market, the Choueiri Group is seen by many observers as having long monopolised the market both in Lebanon and the region. Furthermore, Choueiri sympathised politically with the LF and therefore threw his weight behind the channel, giving LBCI an alleged monopoly on the advertising

market in Lebanon as well as securing substantial revenues from the Gulf[21] when LBC Group launched its satellite operation.

Still, had LBCI not been successful, the shrewd Choueiri 'wouldn't have chosen it as its *cheval de bataille* [war horse]', as Marcel Ghanem, the channel's lead talk-show host, put it.[22] Indeed, Daher, who allegedly 'only functions in line with figures and ratings and the income of the station',[23] is said to have succeeded in luring the pan-Arab audience by offering amusing entertainment shows 'with a lot of good looking girls in revealing clothes, which our Arab brothers appreciate'.[24] Locally, the political programming remains among the leading channels, with Al-Jadeed TV news surpassing it at times.[25] By maintaining a 'very tight culture and efficient equipment',[26] LBCI managed to toe the postwar line in a period where censorship and tight controls on freedom of expression were prevalent.

However, despite their announced intention to accept the status quo, LBCI faced pressure,[27] 'threats'[28] and censors attempting to influence content. Interviewed by the author, Daher said

> Politicians here think that if they own one per cent [...] this means they can impose [their] media policy which makes it not a medium but a tool. This is a business endeavour and as a shareholder you get your share of the wins or losses but you cannot interfere in the editorial. That's it.[29]

Suleiman Frangieh, a *za'im*[30] from the north of Lebanon and a shareholder brought in for political considerations after the end of the civil war, placed a political supervisor at the station in 1998 to ensure coverage of his news. Frangieh and Daher repeatedly and publicly fell out, with the former saying 'LBCI follows our political line and works under our supervision.'[31] 'I run the station', was Daher's retort. After losing an appeal to the Supreme Council to keep a political supervisor at the station, Frangieh sold his LBCI shares in 2001 to Issam Fares, a shareholder and affluent businessman who was elected to parliament and served as deputy prime minister from 2000 to 2005.[32] LBCI, however, managed to avoid the fate of the more outright oppositional channels such as MTV (which was shut down by the government in 2002) or New TV (which was refused a licence for four years and was subjected to intense pressure and harassment).[33]

Despite LBCI's controversial break with the LF, the array of shareholders brought in to increase capital, and the special programming during the Ramadan season (when advertising spending rises exponentially),[34] LBCI still managed to allay the concerns of 'the Christians' who felt they were effectively sidelined after the war. Extensive coverage was given to then-Maronite Patriarch Cardinal Mar Nasrallah Boutros Sfeir, a key political actor during this period. Perceptions of that coverage are reflected in Professor Nabil Dajani's assessment that LBCI is a 'forum for the Maronites and the Patriarch'. 'If he sneezes, they report it', Dajani said.[35] Although this is a cynical exaggeration, LBCI regularly covered Patriarch Sfeir's critical political and social sermons on prime-time news, as well as memorials and masses during Christmas and Easter. A study analysing the content of Lebanese television found that, of all Lebanese channels, LBCI identified most strongly with the sect it represented.[36] That, however, was no longer Daher's ambition. In spite of LBC's strong identification with its community, the cautious partitioning of the 'media cake' and the hypothetical partisanship of audiences, where audiences 'autistically'[37] consume the media that reinforces their views, Daher asserted that LBC 'doesn't aspire to represent the Maronite sect, it aims to represent all of Lebanon'. Over the years, LBCI successfully managed to appeal to a larger audience in what is already a small national media market, thereby meeting part of its declared 'mission'.[38] In recent years, and for political reasons having to do with the battle with the LF over the ownership of the station, LBCI attempted to move in the direction of the pro-Syrian March 8 coalition,[39] resulting in what some have deemed a 'confused identity'.[40] For Daher, however, this was a 'fantastic' and indeed a strategic choice. 'Sure. I'll give you both sides of the story', he insisted. 'Why should I be considered on the side of one or the other; I am with this side if what it's doing is in my view good and against this same side if what it's doing is wrong.'[41] Daher also rejected the particular Lebanese 'logic' whereby political backing is necessary to safeguard one's continuity. 'I want the state to protect me', he said, despite conceding that the state remains weak.[42]

Legal Battle with the LF

The withdrawal of Syrian forces from Lebanon in 2005 and Geagea's subsequent release from prison heralded a tussle over LBC. Pierre Daher claims[43] to have purchased LBC from Geagea in 1992 as the LF's power began to dwindle. According to Daher, Geagea said 'You like this, you are financially well-off, the son of Youssef Daher, you have connections to politicians, banks and investors, who better to take it?' Daher alleges to have paid US$5 million in addition to its liabilities, which he claims have been paid 'to the last cent and with "*habet misk*".[44]

Meanwhile, the LF contends that ownership of the television station should have returned to them following their leader's release from prison and the party's return to the political landscape. Indeed, they have strongly denied selling the institution, claiming Daher was 'occupying' the corporation[45] and that 'LBC is not a company to be sold and bought, it is a cause, it doesn't even belong to us, it's for the community, and was set up using our community's funds'.[46] In one Wikileaks cable documenting Geagea's meeting with a US diplomat, Geagea refers to Daher as 'a good friend and a political character, [who] was having some trouble adjusting to having a boss at LBC'. The wife of the LF leader Strida is reported to have smiled and 'sinisterly' said 'He'll get used to it'.[47] Rather than get used to it, however, Daher opted to fight. As negotiations broke down and the parties went to court,[48] LBCI called off an interview with Geagea and, in 2009, May Chidiac, the anchor and political talk show host who survived a 2005 assassination attempt on her life and is known to be a LF supporter, resigned on the air, referring to 'fierce battles'[49] waged against her within the station and expressing 'the wish' that Geagea and Daher reconcile.

Daher and Geagea did not reconcile and, in October 2010, the three-year legal and political court case came to its first climax with the release of an indictment in favour of the LF. It accused Daher of 'misuse of trust, fraud and embezzlement'[50] and requested his imprisonment and that of another board member. The indictment also held LBC and its eight affiliated companies – LBCI, XYZ Ltd, Lebanese Media Company Ltd, LMH Ltd, LBC Plus Ltd, LBC Sat Ltd, PAC Ltd and LBC Overseas Ltd – partly responsible. Typically, Daher announced that this was but 'a battle in a war'. Instead of an ownership dispute, he framed it as a struggle over media freedom and an attempt to subject the 'independent' corporation to 'partisanship or political restraints'. Media analyst Magda Abu Fadil said of the tussle:

> Pierre Daher isn't going to give it up and he is one hell of a smart businessman [...] he is going to appeal it to doomsday and he is making tons of money, he and his wife because he has diversified into all sorts of production companies. It's not just the old LBC, there are branches, it's a money-making venture [...] this guy is into big business and he ain't giving it up anytime soon.[51]

Indeed, Daher appealed the indictment, and subtly accused the judge of being influenced by the outgoing Minister of Justice, who happened to be politically affiliated to the LF.

Daher's subsequent political manoeuvring, coupled with the changing political landscape in early 2011 that brought a March 8 government led by Prime Minister Najib Mikati, an LBCI shareholder, may be seen to have helped this battle swing to his advantage. In March 2012 the court case was dismissed,[52] amidst claims by the LF that some March 8 forces and even March 14[53] forces were backing Daher in the battle and that the latest political positioning of the station was simply to secure this support.[54] In a subsequent turn of events, however, the Court of Cassation overturned the case's dismissal and ratified the earlier indictment against Daher, paving the way for the start of the trial.[55]

LBC Group and the Pan-Arab Broadcasting Scene

Regionally, Daher was able to tap into the large Arab market when he launched LBCSat in 1996, a company registered in the Cayman Islands. Due to the small size of the Lebanese market, LBC's satellite operation was set up to ensure an entry into the lucrative Arab advertising market, thereby allowing sustainability between what Daher terms the 'outside and inside'.[56] To this end, Daher secured the Saudi backing needed to ensure access to the Saudi market in order to take advantage of its demographic features, including a sizeable population with considerable disposable income as well as the possibility of accessing 'petro-dollars for TV production'.[57] In 1997, Daher and Sheikh Saleh Kamel, a Saudi businessman and owner of the television network ART,[58] founded Lebanese Media Holding, which owned LBCSat, LBC Europe, LBC America and the Production and Acquisitions Company (PAC). PAC would later employ the majority of LBC Group's staff. Daher's partnership with Choueiri later paved the way for the 2002 cooperation deal with pan-Arab newspaper *Al-Hayat*, owned by Saudi Prince Khalid Bin Sultan, son of Saudi Arabia's late Minister of Defence and Crown Prince Sultan bin Abdul Aziz. *Al-Hayat*'s media sales were already handled by Choueiri. The LBC–*Al-Hayat* partnership was presented as a news-gathering alliance aimed to strengthen LBC's political coverage, but it ended in 2010. In 2003 Kamel sold his shares in LBC to the Saudi Arabian global investor Prince Alwaleed bin Talal for US$98 million,[59] alleging that LBCSat management had 'resisted his meddling'.[60] Bin Talal is also the grandson of Lebanon's first prime minister, Riad al Solh, and may at some point have nurtured dreams of entering Lebanese politics.[61] The increased capital, in addition to Alwaleed's friendship with Lebanon's then president Emile Lahoud, provided LBCSat with resources to compete against the regional conglomerates.[62]

In 2007, LBCSat and bin Talal's Rotana merged. A year later, Alwaleed bin Talal increased his ownership of Lebanese Media Holding (LMH), the parent company of PAC, LBCSat and LBC Plus, to 85 per cent, and increased the capital to US$123 million. Daher, who argued that LBCI would benefit indirectly, even though it was kept outside the deal,[63] was then made general manager. In the terminology of Tunstall and Palmer, Daher had thus become a baron in the prince's media empire. 'Standalone channels are becoming a thing of the past', was how Daher explained the move. 'The free-to-air arena is becoming more crowded and more competitive. Consolidation is the best way to confront these challenges.'[64] At the time, Daher and Alwaleed seemed to be rivalling the Saudi-owned, Dubai-based MBC group, a leader in the Arab world's free-to-air market.

The merger between LBCSat and Rotana, however, was short-lived. On 11 April 2012, bin Talal liquidated PAC, leaving 397 staff members jobless, and replaced LBC satellite channels with Rotana programming. The LMH statement claimed that LBCI's

> failure to pay for programming produced by PAC and the ensuing dispute with the head of LBCI and former-head of PAC and Rotana TV, Mr. Pierre El Daher, have resulted in the inability of PAC to pay the salaries of its employees, and continue to sustain the ongoing costs of production and operations.

Other reports cited the Daher family's dispute with a Rotana baron, Turki Shabana, who was appointed by Alwaleed to run LBCSat, thereby bearding the lion in his disputed and partly owned den.[65] For its part, LBCI issued a statement rejecting the alleged 'falsehoods' of the LMH version of events. LBCI argued that LMH and PAC, owned by Rotana, were indebted to LBCI as the former had unlawfully terminated their contracts, in addition to setting out to weaken LBC Group. LBCI said:

> We would like to assure our audience, Lebanese and Arab, in Lebanon and abroad, that these attempts to undermine LBCI are doomed to failure. Building on our human, technical, financial, and other resources and on our resilience to overcome the difficulties that have faced us over the years, we assure you that, this too, shall pass.[66]

With this, the embattled Daher returned to the helm at LBCI. Randa El Daher, Daher's wife and deputy Chief Executive Officer (CEO), took to Twitter to announce 'LBC is Lebanese & will remain 4 the Lebanese [sic]'.[67] Nearly half of the jobless PAC staff were hired by LBCI, while others were secured jobs in various projects that LBCI had been contracted to undertake.[68] Soon after, in August 2012, in an attempt to increase advertising revenues, LBCI launched LBC Drama,[69] broadcasting non-stop series and soaps. When Rotana seized LBCSat and LBC's other satellite channels, LBC Group started new satellite transmissions under the name Lebanese Diaspora Channel (LDC).[70] LBCI also sealed deals with MBC, Rotana's rival, to broadcast their *Arabs Got Talent* programme. A tussle[71] over LBC's golden goose, the Endemol television format *Star Academy*,[72] seemed to end in Daher's favour when it was announced that *Star Academy 9* was set to begin in September 2013 on LBC, LDC and the Egyptian CBC channel.[73]

Discussion and Conclusion

In reviewing Daher's orchestration of LBC's transition, it can be seen that he progressed from LBC executive to baron in Alwaleed's Rotana empire and then to a mogul of sorts, presiding over his own smaller successful media companies. As noted in the introduction to this book, Tunstall and Palmer define a media mogul as someone who has built up their own media empire through launching, buying or taking over media outlets. They see a media baron, on the other hand, as someone who may take entrepreneurial risks but does not ultimately control a corporation. Other analysts also emphasise media proprietors'

> high levels of control over their properties. They hire [...] they fire [...] take a direct interest in content and approach [...] they are pragmatic and opportunist. Unlike many politicians they are controllers of ideology not its slaves. If supporting Party X is seen as good for business, Party X will receive support, yet just

occasionally Party Y may seem a better bet. Practical necessities temper the fervour of ideology.[74]

Tunstall and Palmer see media moguls as supporting political sides in return for political favours,[75] while the history of newspaper ownership in the UK has shown them exerting 'political influence in the battle to improve the opportunities for business' as well as for 'financing and refinancing [...] their assets'.[76]

These descriptions coincide closely with the actions of Pierre Daher. In the words of senior LBC reporter Tania Mehanna, Daher comprehends 'the dictates of the hour', as reflected in the shareholders brought in, as well as his station's editorial tilts, which 'fluctuate with the daily political stock market'.[77] These tilts resemble the often-cited example of Rupert Murdoch's switch from supporting the Tories to the Labour Party's Tony Blair in the UK's 1997 general election. Indeed, the political positioning and hue of the LBC emerges as a function of commercial interests, which for Daher reign supreme.

Daher, who was an executive when LBC was launched, eventually took the reins of power, becoming the effective owner of the station, his ownership battle notwithstanding. Although shareholders were brought in to protect and sustain the corporation, Daher maintained control over content and clashed with those who tried to interfere. In addition to taking the lion's share of the local market guaranteed by his relationship with advertising mogul Antoine Choueiri, Daher next sought to expand regionally to tap into the larger Arab market, partnering with Saudi Arabian heavyweights and accepting, formally at least, the role of a baron in Alwaleed's media empire. The temporary merger with Rotana and his earlier partnership with *Al-Hayat* created both synergies and profit. While it lasted, the partnership with Rotana also undoubtedly diversified and enlarged the advertising revenues. In an attempt to circumvent regulation, as well as potentially safeguard LBC's property should the ownership battle against him succeed, Daher set up a series of companies, including some registered offshore, overseeing productions, staff and equipment. In 2009, apparently with similar motives, Rola Saad, his sister-in-law, director and producer of *Star Academy* seasons 1 to 8, founded Vanilla Productions,[78] potentially in anticipation of a breakdown in relations with Alwaleed.

The role of family in LBC is in line with that envisaged by Tunstall and Palmer, who point to the manner in which an inheritor to the mogul, or 'crown prince', is often selected from among family members. While Daher remains very much in control, his family occupies high executive positions in the LBC media group. Some reports cited Daher's 'family management' of the channel as a reason behind the dispute. In addition to his sister-in-law (Rola Saad), Daher's wife, Randa, serves as deputy CEO,[79] her other sister, Yara Issa El Khoury, is in charge of set design, and Daher's daughter was head of the digital department.[80]

Moreover, even though the breakdown in relations with Rotana left LBC Group without regional financial and political backing, Daher sought to secure his relatively smaller empire with the launch of LBC Drama, deals on popular formats with Rotana's rival,[81] and possibly also through negotiations with pro-Syrian donors in the run-up to the June 2013 parliamentary elections that were eventually postponed to late 2014.[82] He shook up political programming after a 'crisis'[83] that saw Al-Jadeed's newscast gain a slight advantage,[84] and took the drastic step of replacing George Ghanem, a long-serving news anchor and veteran director of political programmes, with the left-leaning former *Al-Akhbar* editor Khaled Saghieh and replacing Ghanem's wife Dolly with a younger journalist, Dima Sadek, in an attempt to make the evening newscast more dynamic and attractive to a wider audience.[85] Daher also instituted a series of prime-time talkshow episodes and campaigns such as *Cheyef 7alak*,[86] tackling socio-economic, cultural and environmental problems. He candidly conceded that the social responsibility aspect of overcoming divisions in Lebanese society was accompanied by commercial considerations, explaining, 'To say public service alone – just doing it because it's useful – without at the same time having an impact on ratings, I won't do it, I cannot handle doing it, so I try to get both simultaneously.'[87]

Paradoxically, therefore, in spite of his legal and financial battles, Daher's business sense and calculated political manoeuvring has propelled LBC's evolution from a partisan outlet towards a more liberal commercial model in a deeply polarised nation. Daher, who spoke of introducing American-style commercial television to Lebanon even when LBC was still directly owned by the LF, managed to reach beyond the confines of the station's community and borders by focusing on entertainment with high production values, special Ramadan programming and relatively balanced reporting. He also pluralised the station internally by hiring a number of Muslim presenters, although the overwhelming majority of staff remained Christian.[88] With Daher, the Sheikh of LBC Group, always adapting to the changing political landscape and managing to gravitate from one centre of power to the next, his wife Randa resolutely tweeted that 'many tried to hurt LBCI image/shut it down they will not succeed'.[89] Daher himself nonchalantly shrugs off the constant need to make compromises, shift alliances and defend his media by observing, 'this is Lebanon'.[90]

5

The Hariris, Father and Son: The Making and Unmaking of Moguldom?

Katharina Nötzold

These days, any mention of a media-owning prime minister may bring to mind Italy's former premier Silvio Berlusconi. Yet, billionaire prime ministers who own media outlets are not all one of a kind, nor do the combined roles of media owner and politician automatically qualify the person in question as a media mogul. Lebanon's former prime minister, Rafik Hariri, who became known as 'Mr Lebanon', was certainly in command of a huge business empire before his assassination in 2005. He was friends with the French president of the day, Jacques Chirac, and the late crown prince of Saudi Arabia, Prince Sultan bin Abdel-Aziz. He was out for profit and ran the country as if it were a company, but even his detractors acknowledge that part of Hariri's ambition was a national one, namely for Lebanon to regain its place at the centre of Middle East business after the country's devastating 15-year civil war came to an end in 1990.

It was not a foregone conclusion that Rafik Hariri, born into a family of poor farmers in the southern Lebanese town of Sidon in 1944,[1] would become the 108th-richest man in the world, according to the *Forbes* annual rankings, the year before his death. This chapter charts Hariri's rise, and the relationship between his media investments and political and business manoeuvres. Rafik Hariri readily admitted that he created his media empire to further his political objectives for Lebanon.[2] But what were those objectives and was he a politician first and businessman second, or vice versa? What happened to his media empire after his death? Even if Hariri himself matched up to the entrepreneurial risk taking and 'personal or eccentric style' of the archetypal media mogul as defined by Tunstall and Palmer,[3] can the same be said of his son Saad? Or does Saad fit Tunstall and Palmer's theory of the 'crown prince', the 'second-generation media entrepreneur, who typically inherits major media properties from his pioneering father'?[4]

A Back Door into Lebanon's Political Elite

Rafik Hariri's original plan to qualify as an accountant was thwarted by financial difficulties. After winning a scholarship to attend the Makassed Islamic High School and enrolling to study accountancy at the Arab University in Beirut, he was forced to leave university without a degree in order to sustain his young family by working as a maths teacher and bookkeeper. He left Lebanon to find his fortune in the booming oil-rich countries of the Gulf. Starting out with little and after encountering several setbacks, Hariri built his construction empire in Saudi Arabia – first with his own company, then jointly with Nasser Rashid, a construction tycoon who had good connections to the Saudi ruling family, and then by purchasing the French company Oger.[5] Hariri transformed Oger into a leading construction company in the region. After he finished building a hotel in the Saudi Arabian city of Taif to a very tight deadline in 1976, and thus established personal relations with the Saudi ruling family, Saudi Oger became one of the main recipients of Saudi government contracts.[6] King Khaled had commissioned the hotel for an Islamic summit meeting and rewarded

Hariri for getting it built on time by granting him Saudi citizenship. Hariri's success with the hotel brought him the close friendship of Saudi Arabia's Crown Prince (later King) Fahd.

With his new-found wealth, Hariri turned to humanitarian projects in Lebanon, building educational facilities at Kfar-Falous and then founding the Islamic Institute for Culture and Higher Education in 1979. This institute, which became known as the Hariri Foundation, paid for thousands of Lebanese to live and study abroad.[7] Just as the Salam family had funded Sunni Lebanese, including Hariri himself, through the Makassed Islamic Foundation, so Hariri's philanthropy in supporting schools and healthcare facilities enabled him to replace members of the Salam family in the traditional role of *za'im*, or political head of the Sunni community in Beirut.[8] This was seen as a cornerstone of his success, as many of the Foundation's beneficiaries became potential political supporters.

In the early 1980s Hariri bought the French shares of Banque de la Méditerranée, later renamed BankMed.[9] Via Saudi Oger, the Hariri family also owned Lebanon's biggest insurer, MedGulf, the Mediterranean & Gulf Insurance and Reinsurance Company, stakeholder in MedGulf Bahrain and MedGulf Saudi Arabia. Other shareholders in MedGulf were the Lebanese firm LFZ (Lutfi El-Zein) Holding and Kingdom Holding Company, belonging to Saudi Arabia's Prince Alwaleed bin Talal.[10] Within a decade of buying into BankMed, Rafik Hariri had amassed a fortune estimated at US$2.5billion. In 1990–1, *Forbes* magazine ranked him among the world's top 20 billionaires.[11]

While Hariri was making his name in the construction industry in Saudi Arabia, his native Lebanon was descending deeper into civil war. During ceasefires, Hariri would send Oger trucks into Beirut's streets at his own expense to clear away the rubble. Investing his fortune in reconstruction at home was a route to political influence, underpinned by his close ties to the Saudi monarchy. As special envoy of King Fahd and 'sole conduit of Saudi funds in Lebanon',[12] he was a mediator who could bring valuable bargaining chips to negotiations between Lebanese militia groups in 1983–4 and between Lebanese President Amin Gemayel and Syria in 1985. It is an open secret that Hariri paid large sums of his own and Saudi money to various leaders of the Lebanese militias and forged close ties with members of the regime in Damascus with the aim of bringing an end to the civil war.[13] Having thus penetrated Lebanon's usually impenetrable system of sectarian power sharing,[14] Hariri was seen by many as someone with the wealth and connections needed to handle Lebanon's reconstruction, not least because of his major role in the national reconciliation conference that created the 1989 Taif Accord, which brought the civil war to an end in 1990.

After the civil war, Hariri emerged as a serious contender for the premiership, supported by those who trusted him to re-establish Beirut as the banking capital of the Arab world. The 1991 multilateral Middle East peace talks in Madrid contributed to hopes of a return to prosperity. At that point, Hariri had good relations with key Syrians, among them Abdel-Halim Khaddam, who was Syrian vice-president from 1984 to 2005.[15] Having reached the centre of power, Hariri was in a position to decide on the economic rules, not only of his own enterprises but those of the country at large. He espoused the neo-liberal market model, favouring private enterprise and seeking to run Lebanon like one of his companies. His first government was filled with trusted former employees.[16] Such an approach antagonised many politicians who had other business interests or those who preferred a bigger role for the state. When Hariri became prime minister in 1992 his government devised a reconstruction plan named Horizon 2000. A major component was Solidere, a Lebanese joint-stock company founded in May 1994 and largely owned by the Hariri family, which was put in charge of planning the development and reconstruction of Beirut's central district. Solidere was accused of expropriating property by giving owners shares in the company that were worth less than the value of their property.

Horizon 2000 aimed to privatise electricity generation, telecommunications, major roads and airports, with all the potential that this created for cosy deals with members of Lebanon's ruling classes. The awarding of licences for the mobile phone network to two companies whose owners were close to political elites in Lebanon and Syria was a case in point.[17] Horizon 2000 was also meant to provide Lebanon with economic stimulus from foreign investment. For this, Hariri used his political power to provide tax breaks for foreign investors. In 1992, the Council for Reconstruction and Development, established in 1977, was given more powers and instructed to report to the Council of Ministers and ultimately to Hariri himself.

Perhaps because of his overwhelming involvement in business, Hariri is said to have viewed state institutions as an obstacle to his reconstruction drive; he did not believe that Lebanese state institutions, constrained by the country's sectarian politics, would ever be truly reformed.[18] Instead, his solution was to establish and mobilise his own team with members of his companies.[19] He would set up private companies or link government agencies directly to the premiership, undermining mechanisms for oversight and accountability.[20] When he attracted funding pledges for Lebanon he did so through his own personal contacts with political leaders in the Gulf, Europe, the USA and the Far East.

Amin Gemayel, who was president of Lebanon between 1982 and 1988, has been quoted as saying that Hariri chose a body of advisers, including political scientists and economists, without regard for sectarian differences. This 'infrastructure', according to Gemayel, was essential to ensuring the means to 'talk to everyone, Christians, Muslims, the left and the right'.[21] Hariri's loyal ally, Fouad Siniora, served him for years as finance minister. Fadl Chalak directed the Hariri Foundation and the Council for Reconstruction and Development. The young economist Basil Fuleihan gave up a promising World Bank career and was later appointed economy minister.[22] Political journalist Nouhad Machnouk served Hariri as a political advisor. Hani Hammoud, Hariri's media advisor, also edited news and political programmes on Hariri's channel Future TV and his newspaper *Al-Mustaqbal*. This group of advisors included his lawyer Youssef Takla and Ghassan Tahir of Saudi Oger. He appointed them because he could rely on their loyalty, valued their advice, and believed they shared his economic and political visions.

The policy of appointing former employees to positions in government and the civil service exposed Hariri to allegations of corruption and favouritism, despite Hezbollah MP Muhammad Raad's declaration that 'We can honestly say that Hariri was not corrupt'.[23] Hariri's way of exploiting state funds and reconstruction contracts and establishing institutions that were directly subordinated to his office deflected any drive for transparency in post-war Lebanon. Despite some prestige projects such as the reconstruction of Beirut's Central District, ordinary Lebanese were left struggling to make ends meet and the public debt rose dramatically.

Concentration of Power through Media Acquisitions

Unregulated media outlets mushroomed during Lebanon's civil war, often linked to militias. By the end of the war, 40 private broadcasters had sprung up alongside the publicly owned Télé-Liban radio and television stations.[24] Hariri wanted a media network that would support his new political career and propagate his ideas and political programme. Embarking on a media-buying spree in 1992, he told the German Press Agency (DPA), 'I need a press that can complement my work in building a healthy country, not sabotage my job'.[25]

Hariri acquired two Paris-based media outlets. One was the radio station Radio Orient, bought from Raghid El-Chamma.[26] Having originally catered to the Arab-speaking community residing in France,[27] the station expanded its focus to an audience in the Levant and North Africa after being bought by Hariri. In 1996, Radio Orient's affiliate in Lebanon received an FM licence in the name of Future TV under the controversial Audio-visual Media Law.[28] Hariri's second purchase was the Paris-based weekly *Al-Mustaqbal* (*The Future*), which had launched in Paris in 1977 and, despite some successes, had gone bankrupt in 1989.[29] He started *Al-Mustaqbal* as a Lebanese daily newspaper in 1995.

Future Television began live broadcasting as a terrestrial Lebanese station on 15 February 1993, staffed by enthusiastic young journalists who saw in Hariri a symbol of hope for rebuilding Lebanon.[30] Its 24-hour family-oriented programming claimed to respect 'Oriental traditions and values'[31] but was varied enough to attract viewers quickly. After the station started trial satellite broadcasting to the Arab world in 1994, attaining 24-hour transmission in 1998, Future International became a successful pan-Arab satellite station with target audiences throughout the Levant, the Gulf and Egypt.[32] According to journalists at Future TV,[33] Hariri was so interested in the channel's content he sometimes asked editors to interview a particular minister for a news bulletin and his office would provide background material. In 2003 he also phoned daily to enquire about the welfare of Future TV journalists covering the Iraq war from Kurdistan, Baghdad and southern Iraq. When *Al-Mustaqbal* started in 1995 it supported Hariri and, after his death, the Future Movement and March 14 coalition.[34] In 2012, Radio Orient promoted a series of 20 episodes about Rafik Hariri's life, narrated by his wife Nazek, which could be listened to as a podcast.

Hariri's appetite for promoting his political and economic programme through media ownership extended beyond his Mustaqbal Group. In the early 1990s he bought 50 per cent of shares in Télé-Liban. Despite being government-run, Télé-Liban was half-owned by the private sector and the rest belonged to the government (according to Legislative Decree No. 100 issued in 1977).[35] In anticipation of the audio-visual legislation that would later regulate private broadcasting media, Hariri re-sold his Télé-Liban shares to the government. Once he was sure of acquiring a licence for Future TV he no longer needed Télé-Liban.

During the 1990s Hariri also started to buy up to 34.5 per cent of the shares in the influential Lebanese daily *Al-Nahar*.[36] *Al-Nahar's* General Manager Gebran Tueini later bought the shares back for an undisclosed sum,[37] but these shares are said to have returned to the Hariri family once again after Tueini's assassination in December 2005. According to a source that was brought to light through Wikileaks, Hariri's Mustaqbal Group owns 17 per cent of *Al-Nahar* shares.[38] When asked whether Rafik Hariri exerted editorial pressure on him, Gebran Tueini replied: '[...] yes and no. The relationship was comfortable, though. He endured much more from me than I endured from him, because he knew that he couldn't exert pressure.'[39] *Al-Nahar* regularly criticised Syria's policies in Lebanon, but without taking undue risks. The newspaper gave space to Hariri's views during his lifetime, but without always supporting his economic policies. After Hariri's assassination, Gebran Tueini was at the forefront of the so-called Cedar Revolution and the editorial policy of the newspaper consistently supported the March 14 movement over a long period.

Claims that Lebanese politicians own shares in companies cannot always be proved conclusively. Instead, evidence of share ownership has to be traced through politicians' families and business partners. This holds true for Hariri, whose control over shares was often achieved through ownership nominally assigned to his wife, children and close associates. In 2002, the majority of the shares in terrestrial Future TV were divided among his wife Nazek (10 per cent), brother Shafik (7.2 per cent), sister Bahia (10 per cent), his sons by his first marriage Baha'eddine (8 per cent) and Saadeddine (8 per cent), and associate Ghaleb Chamma (10 per cent).[40] Members of the Board of Directors of Future TV also own shares. At that time, the board included his lawyer Youssef Takla, Future TV's then CEO Nadim Munla, executive manager Ali Jaber and Hani Hammoud, then Director of News and Political Programmes of Future TV.[41] Such ownership patterns are legal under Lebanon's audio-visual media law, which states that all shareholders need to be Lebanese citizens, with no more than 10 per cent of the shares belonging to a single person or entity. A husband, wife and all direct relatives, especially 'under age' children, are counted as one person or entity.[42]

The 1994 Audio-visual Media Law was seen by political observers as a tool used by Hariri and the then pro-Syrian governing elite, including Parliamentary Speaker Nabih Berri, to limit the influence of any anti-Syrian forces still persistent in post-war Lebanon. After the law came into effect in 1996, only licensed radio and television stations were allowed to broadcast. Dima Dabbous describes how previously non-existent stations mysteriously met all the eligibility criteria almost overnight, whereas economically successful stations that were deemed too critical of Hariri's policies, such as New TV, were denied the necessary licence and had to stop broadcasting.[43] Likewise, the National Audiovisual Media Council (NAMC), set up to oversee the licensing process and to monitor and rein in stations that contravened the 1994 law, was also seen to be a direct tool in the hands of Rafik Hariri. Five of the ten NAMC members were to be appointed by parliament, while the other five were named by the Council of Ministers, then headed by Hariri. This meant that, at the council's formation, Hariri could impose most of his candidates because he commanded a parliamentary majority.

Rafik Hariri invested heavily in Future TV, especially its satellite operation aimed at the Gulf market. He had business reasons for wanting to promote Lebanon as a destination for tourism and a thriving service centre, so that Arab Gulf investors would inject the cash that was badly needed for reconstruction. Media coverage of Lebanon's relations with these investors was taken care of by the Audio-visual Media Law and its references to the Press Law of 1962, which outlawed any content deemed to 'weaken national unity', criticise heads of state, incite sectarian hatred, endanger national security or hurt relations with friendly Arab countries.[44] Although the NAMC was nominally involved in enforcing the law on Lebanese television stations, in fact it was the security apparatus that reacted swiftly in cases where the rules were said to have been broken. New TV, which obtained its licence in 1999 during a brief period when Hariri was not prime minister, faced temporary suspension on 2 January 2003,[45] after it advertised a documentary programme about Saudi Arabia. Rafik Hariri claimed in a live interview on Future TV that '[t]he promotional spot discussed the status of women, the state of the budget, and other issues' in Saudi Arabia. This, he said, made it 'obvious' that New TV acted against the laws that forbid 'impugning relations' with Arab countries.[46]

The Hariri family also expanded into telecommunications, creating Oger Telecom as an offshoot of the Oger Group. Oger Telecom operates through Cyberia in Saudi Arabia, Lebanon and Jordan, Cell C in South Africa and Turk Telekom and Avea in Turkey.[47] Cyberia, one of the two leading internet service providers (ISPs) in Lebanon, started operations there in 1996. It is 95 per cent owned by Oger Telecom and 5 per cent by Saudi Oger.[48] Its involvement in a range of communications, web design and marketing services in Saudi Arabia, Lebanon and Jordan[49] testified to the Hariris' regional ambitions.

Future TV was one of the first Arab broadcasters to use and benefit from technical convergence and cross-media platforms. Interactive tools such as SMS to Television, MMS (Multimedia Messaging System), the use of ringtones and special websites were used to enhance the television station's revenue.[50] The hugely successful entertainment programme *Super Star*, an Arab adaptation of the *Pop Idol* format owned by the international company FremantleMedia, premiered in 2003. It used voting for candidates by mobile phone and text messages for the first time on Arab television on a grand scale. After the first season finale, Future TV grossed over US$4 million in voting revenues alone,[51] in addition to revenues from advertisement packages[52] and through merchandising.

With the Arab satellite television boom in full swing, the Mustaqbal Group also tried other ways to attract younger viewers. The satellite channel Zen TV, established jointly with Dubai Media City in 1999, went on air in January 2001, broadcasting from Beirut. Its main attraction was the programme *DardaChat*, which tackled subjects then still considered taboo in the Arab world, such as the growing generation gap, sex, and emotional and relationship problems. These were subjects of concern to young adults, who were a neglected target audience in the early 2000s.[53] Critics argued that the station catered mainly to a westernised Arab urban middle and upper-middle class. A commentator at

Forbes at the time suggested that the station accorded with Hariri's 'political philosophy of melding Western innovation to Arab culture' as a way of avoiding the harshness of the inevitable influx of foreign products.[54] Hariri was aware that '[w]e are at a stage of being forced to open our doors to international products', and he embraced this vision coupled with the warning that 'If we do not open them to ours, our markets will be flooded [...] However, we can encourage local Arab products.'[55] Despite the enthusiasm of Zen TV's beginning and its pan-Arab transmission, it lasted barely three years, closing in 2004.[56]

Future TV's Emerging Split between Lebanese and Pan-Arab Objectives

Future TV is accused of being the Hariris' station, especially when it comes to political reporting. Although the network dutifully supported Hariri's reconstruction drive for Lebanon when he was prime minister from 1992 to 1998, it attacked the policies of the government led by Salim El-Hoss, prompting Hoss to complain in the very same terms previously used by Rafik Hariri himself, that 'a local satellite station was intentionally focusing on "unrealistic" news, which was having a negative impact on tourism, foreign investors and the diaspora'.[57] After increased criticism by the Hoss government, Hariri instructed his media outlets to refrain from broadcasting political programmes and news commentaries. He told them to restrict their local reporting to 'developments in the south and non-controversial issues'.[58] The former news director of Future TV claimed that '[w]hen we were in the opposition, Future news was much more combative and people liked to watch it'.[59]

Yet, the 2000 election campaign fought between Hoss and Hariri was increasingly marked by mud-slinging via the media. Hoss had no channel of his own, so he relied on coverage by the government-owned Télé-Liban while Future TV did the job for Rafik Hariri. Each station focused their news coverage on one or the other contender exclusively, completely ignoring the other candidate's election campaign. In the end, Télé-Liban's credibility was entirely undermined by the way the government of the day blatantly misused it. Future TV meanwhile became even more closely identified with Hariri, especially as attacks on the government petered out when he became prime minister again.[60] A large-scale content analysis of Lebanese news reports in 2002 and 2003 revealed that pro-Hariri reporting happened mostly on Future TV,[61] concentrating on his political activities, his meetings with world leaders and explaining his policies. However, the pro-Hariri bias was not so simplistic as to focus all coverage purely on Hariri personally. Instead, news reports carried interviews with MPs belonging to Hariri's parliamentary bloc, who indirectly represented him and his views.

The focus on Rafik Hariri became even more apparent after his assassination on 14 February 2005. The station abandoned any semblance of impartiality and openly sided with Hariri's politics. News readers were visibly shaken, the programme and website of the station aired films of Hariri's legacy, and the station was used as an instrument to demand the truth about Hariri's murderers and the installation of the Special Tribunal for Lebanon (STL). The television buildings were adorned with big banners demanding 'The Truth' behind the assassination, and newsreaders greeted their audience at the beginning of each newscast by counting how many days had passed since his death. During the election campaigns of 2005 and 2009, Saad Hariri and his Future Movement used Future TV as a means of support for Saad himself, his electoral list and the March 14 alliance. Future TV and the rival Al-Manar station, representing Hezbollah, were seen as the most sectarian channels as they rallied their supporters around their respective party flags in 2006/2007 when the March 8 movement attempted to overthrow the government of Fouad Siniora.[62]

During this period, Future TV contravened the 20 per cent time limit specified for news. Indeed, viewers were said to feel the station was 'shifting into news and current affairs, and away from entertainment'.[63] In what seems to have been perceived as a necessary sacrifice at the time, Future TV lost some of its audience in the Gulf and thus some of its revenues from entertainment programmes. On 9 December 2007 it launched the 24-hour news channel Future News as part of a plan to re-establish Future TV as a general entertainment channel or, as the then Chief Executive Officer (CEO) Nadim Munla declared, to identify the station as 'the channel of empowerment and optimism'.[64] Referring to the Israel–Hezbollah war in July 2006, Munla pointed out that the channel had been 'obliged to broadcast many news programs and talk-shows'. This, he said,

> created an inconvenience, since we had to reduce the time given to other programs. We had to come up with a news channel that deals basically with Lebanese issues. We are not going to compete with Al-Jazeera nor Al-Arabiya, since we are strictly dealing with Lebanese issues.[65]

In the summer of 2012, Future TV underwent further restructuring. Future News channel was phased out as a separate station and news broadcasts were again incorporated into Future TV, a network thus consisting of general terrestrial and satellite channels airing a mix of entertainment, news, talk shows and sports. With the revamp, which included a major facelift, a new logo, reshuffling of programmes and a new website, Future TV tried to regain its position among the top three Lebanese TV stations,[66] a position it lost during the period of heavy politicisation as a pro-Hariri tool. In the process it became clear that the station had suffered lay-offs, budgetary problems and internal fighting.[67] Meanwhile, despite well-intentioned efforts to introduce new programmes and attract more viewers, there was no disguising the network's political line under Saad Hariri. In the words of its marketing consultant, Claude Sabbagha, 'it is very clear what is the political position of the owner of the station, it cannot but reflect in the news, this is for sure'.[68] In other words, Saad Hariri could be seen to be following in the footsteps of his media mogul father in his deployment of media outlets under his control to promote certain political approaches and policies. However, meanwhile, the regional media landscape had changed.

Saad Hariri: New Head of an Empire Past its Peak

With the death of Rafik Hariri in 2005, Saad Hariri, born 35 years earlier, was thrust into the limelight much earlier than he probably expected. The succession to Rafik Hariri was settled quickly among the Hariri family and Saad, despite his political inexperience, was picked to 'assume the historic responsibility and leadership of all national and political affairs'.[69] Belgian scholar Ward Vloeberghs argues that Hariri's oldest son Bahaa, who seemed to be the natural heir, preferred to concentrate on his business activities.[70] Vloeberghs floats the argument that Saad was more inclined to see Syria as the main culprit behind Hariri's assassination, a view that was also supported by other March 14 politicians in Lebanon and by Hariri's main supporters in Saudi Arabia, as well as Jacques Chirac, who was French president in 2005.[71]

Rafik Hariri's assets passed to numerous inheritors. For example, shares in BankMed, owned by the Hariris' MedGroup, were divided between Saad and Rafik's two sons from his marriage to Nazek, Aiman and Fahd, with each of the three holding 24 per cent, and Nazek and her daughter Hind holding 15 per cent and 12 per cent, respectively.[72] In keeping with Arab family traditions, Saad incorporated the sons of his politically more experienced aunt, Bahia, into his political network. His cousin Nader was appointed chief of staff in Saad's office in 2005, while his younger cousin Ahmed was put in charge of leadership positions within the Future Movement.[73] Bahia Hariri won her parliamentary seat in subsequent elections and thus both she and Saad represented the Hariri family in Lebanon's parliament.

Unlike his father, who never had a university degree, Saad had earned a degree in Business Administration from Georgetown University in 1992, and started his career in his father's Saudi Oger company. Having been raised between Saudi Arabia and Lebanon, Saad had settled in Riyadh in 1996, with his family, to oversee the family businesses. His consequent strong links to Saudi Arabia attracted heavy criticism from his opponents in Lebanon's March 8 forces, who feared too much

Saudi Arabian meddling in Lebanese internal affairs. Nevertheless, Saad tried to mould himself into a respected politician in Lebanon and abroad. He relied on the loyalty of his father's close ally Fouad Siniora, who served as Lebanese prime minister from 2005 to 2009 before stepping down in favour of Saad. Like his father, Saad surrounded himself with advisors to cover important topics such as economics, politics, religious affairs, media and external relations.[74] Some had previously acted as advisors to Rafik.

He put another family member, Muhammad Ahmad Mokhtar Hariri, in charge of administration in several of the banking, construction and telecommunications companies, notably GroupMed, MedGulf, BankMed, Saudi Oger and Oger Telecom. He restructured some of his companies in Saudi Arabia and Lebanon, and it was under him that Mustaqbal Group saw the addition of Future News channel. He also positioned several of his lieutenants in strategic departments of public administration. Yet this did not go unchallenged in Lebanon, as it resembled the strategies of his father too closely and because the differences between the March 14 and March 8 coalitions were growing bigger by the day. There was particular concern about government support for the Special Tribunal for Lebanon investigating Rafik Hariri's assassination. The impression that Hezbollah members might be indicted for involvement pushed Hezbollah in early 2011 to bring down Saad Hariri's government in favour of Najib Mikati, another powerful Sunni businessman, with a power base in Tripoli.

For some time, rumours were rife about financial difficulties in the Hariri business and media empire, as employees of the various media and social organisations and Future Movement administration were heard to complain about unpaid salaries. While Saudi Arabia rescued Saudi Oger,[75] Saad Hariri was reportedly forced to sell 35 per cent of shares in Oger Telecom to Saudi Telecom in 2008,[76] with negotiations for further sales reported in 2011.[77] In April 2011, six years after Hariri's death, the Lebanese firm LFZ (Lutfi El-Zein) Holding signed a US$400 million takeover deal for the Hariri family's MedGulf.[78] As noted above, the Mustaqbal Group rationalised its operations. Hariri absented himself from Lebanon in 2011, citing security reasons for setting up residence abroad.[79]

It could be expected that a media mogul would respond to the increased usage of social media in the Arab world to stay at the helm of media-related developments. In the case of the Hariris, it can only be speculated that Rafik would have tried to get a foot in the door of new media businesses to further his political influence. Saad Hariri, among other Lebanese politicians, presents himself as an avid user of social media such as Facebook and Twitter, but this also has its pitfalls.[80] Future TV's redesigned website tried to incorporate new media such as a YouTube channel, advertised its App for iPhone and Android, referred to its presence on Facebook and Twitter, and invited its visitors to follow the station's presenters on Twitter. Yet, just as Lebanon's 'old' media landscape was perceived to be highly divided along sectarian and/or political lines,[81] these new communications outlets seemed to offer more of the same political–sectarian division, especially with the escalation of violence in Syria. Despite Lebanon's official stance of political neutrality in the Syrian conflict, Hezbollah acknowledged its active involvement alongside the Syrian army. Future media group meanwhile sided with the opposition to Syrian president Bashar al-Assad. Yet, several political bloggers in Lebanon have expressed their dismay at continued sectarianism. According to blogger *Beirut Spring*, several bloggers have stopped writing about politics as 'they are realizing that their sharp divisions are making it awkward to write their real point of view in polite social media company'.[82]

The future of social media in Lebanon is anyway such as to put it low down on the priorities of Saad Hariri or the Future Group. Overall, television remains the most important source for news and information,[83] while penetration of Facebook, Twitter and YouTube in Lebanon is often lower than in Gulf Cooperation Council (GCC) countries.[84] Lebanese social media users and businesses face persistently slow broadband capacities. They feel cut off from ever quickening developments in communications and fear losing jobs to businesses in GCC countries, blaming political unwillingness and incompetence for delays in expanding broadband facilities. Although Rafik Hariri might eventually have used his economic power to change this, his son Saad has other issues on his agenda.

Conclusion

Rumours about financial difficulties in business in Lebanon are always difficult to verify as they often emanate from sources close to a business's competitors. The origins of Saad Hariri's troubles are not openly discussed and it is hard to tell whether the fortunes of the Hariri empire in the wake of the Arab uprisings of 2010–11 were the result of a change in management style between Rafik Hariri (the media mogul) and his son (the 'crown prince'), a change in the media landscape, or a change in the region's political dynamics. Ultimately, however, a link can be seen between the fortunes of the Hariri empire and the family's political fortunes, based on the relationship between financial and political clout.

As noted in this chapter, the Hariri media empire shrank under Saad. Assets were diminished when they were split among Rafik Hariri's various inheritors, but there were other factors too, such as mismanagement, losses incurred during the global financial crisis, and excessive political generosity. When the Mikati-led government challenged Saad Hariri in key positions of influence, such as the Ministry of Communication and Solidere portfolio, the latter's decreasing financial means made it harder for him to bolster political support from the Sunni community. At the same time, even Saudi backing for Saad Hariri may have waned somewhat as a result of his personal disagreements with influential princes during the fraught political situation in Saudi Arabia and around the region in 2011.

Within Lebanon, deep splits emerged over which sides to support in the Arab uprisings. The Future Movement published a policy paper that presented the Cedar Revolution of 2005 and the subsequent Syrian withdrawal from Lebanon as having fathered the Arab Spring of 2011.[85] Saad Hariri openly voiced support for the Syrian opposition at a time when the fighting in Syria was encroaching ever further into Lebanon, exposing a rift between Sunni and Shia Lebanese. Yet the channels in Hariri's Mustaqbal Group, having never established a large network of correspondents in Arab capitals, were no match for the media power of pan-Arab satellite news channels or social media in covering the Arab uprisings. Today, the media tools with which Rafik Hariri pursued his political and business objectives are no longer the only means of communication by which to sustain a media empire and command economic and political influence. Social media have forced media moguls to contend with alternative voices on YouTube channels, Facebook and Twitter. Although Future TV has undergone some restructuring to incorporate social media, there were doubts as to whether it could regain its former success in a competitive media market, especially in light of Saad Hariri's absence from Lebanon. Despite Saad's official status as crown prince of the Hariri business and media empire, the first decade after Rafik's assassination left a question mark, not only over the empire's future, but also over Saad Hariri's future as a Sunni leader in Lebanon.

6

Saleh Kamel: Investing in Islam

Ehab Galal

'When I was six or seven years old, my mother used to make a special drink for us that in Egyptian is called *halabisa*.[1] I asked her to increase the quantity and then I sold cups of *halabisa* to my pals in the street where we played.'[2] This memory is part of Saleh Kamel's own story of how he became a businessman and multimillionaire. That this Saudi Arabian sheikh[3] invested heavily in media was a choice closely linked to his general business interests and his connections to other major players on the Saudi business scene. Since the launch of the Middle East Broadcasting Center (MBC) in 1991, Saudi businessmen have had a big influence on Arab satellite television. Saleh Kamel was involved in Saudi-owned satellite channels from the very beginning, first as a co-investor with Sheikh Walid al-Ibrahim in MBC and later, in 1993, as the founder of Arab Radio and Television (ART), the first Arab pay-TV network offering specialised channels. In 1998, ART introduced Iqraa as the Arab world's first 'Islamic' satellite channel. *Iqraa*, meaning 'read' or 'recite', was the instruction that Prophet Muhammad is said to have received from the angel Gabriel.

The launching of an Islamic channel reflected a religious theme underlying and linking Saleh Kamel's involvement in some 340 different companies spanning 42 countries, including major investments in Islamic banking and investment. In 2008 he was ranked number 12 among the richest Arabs in the world, worth an estimated US$5.3 billion.[4] With ART representing such a small part of the empire built from the Dallah al-Baraka Group that Kamel established in 1969, the question arises as to the benefits he accrued from the ART media project and the network's role in his wider political and economic objectives.

Business in a 'Post-Islamist' Mode?

This chapter explores the possible answers that emerge from an analysis of Kamel's own statements, his business priorities and his relationships. For a start, he might be said to fit Oliver Roy's theory of a privatised, personalised 'post-Islamism' and the 'triumph of the religious self'.[5] Asef Bayat introduced the term 'post-Islamism' in 1996 to connote a change in the Islamist project, towards a focus on 'rights instead of duties, plurality in place of a singular authoritative voice, historicity rather than fixed scriptures, and the future instead of the past'.[6] Bayat sees post-Islamism opening the way to a compromise between Islam and democracy, while Roy uses the concept to focus on the 'privatisation' of Islamisation.[7] Roy argues that several Islamist businessmen personify the privatisation of Islamisation in that they use economic liberalisation to combine business with humanity and altruism in an Islamic framework.[8] In this form of post-Islamism, personal wealth is considered Islamic, as long as money is earned by honest work and all taxes and alms are paid.[9]

Such a conceptualisation allows for Kamel's goal to be perceived in terms of helping to establish an imagined community, whereby a process of re-Islamisation is achieved through the macro spaces and virtual spaces of media and banking. The community thus imagined and invested in is one defined by reference to the time of Prophet Muhammad, where later cultural influences are seen as corrupt.[10] Such a project can also be located in the encounter between a Saudi state wanting to encourage a conservative re-Islamisation and an economically liberal, privately owned media network that promotes individual self-realisation and achievement. Both take as their rationale an alleged state of decay in the West and the rejection of an Islam 'hijacked' by radicals. Here, the question is whether Kamel is actually more media 'baron' than media 'mogul'. While Jeremy Tunstall and Michael Palmer define a media mogul as an owner of major media companies who is willing to take risks and run businesses in a personal or eccentric style, they define a media baron as a chief executive loyal to the sovereign.[11] This latter theorisation suggests that any investigation into Kamel's dealings should also gauge his loyalty to the Saudi ruling elite and his engagement with social rather than political change. It allows for ART to be seen not so much as an instrument for promoting Kamel's own control, either within Saudi Arabia or globally, but as a tool that supports his business, which may have other objectives. Accordingly, ART might appear to operate as just another business among many, most of which are in Islamic banking and finance. In the remainder of this chapter, Kamel's preferred narratives about his rise to prominence and his media acquisitions are therefore set in the context of his links to Saudi Arabia's ruling princes, some apparent contradictions between ART's output and the conservative Islam he claims to espouse, and the way he has deployed media assets in relation to his other business. The chapter concludes by assessing the insights afforded by theories of post-Islamism into Saleh Kamel's dealings and investments.

Accommodations with Saudi Princes

Saleh Kamel was born in 1940. Unlike other Saudi media moguls he was not born into the ruling family, but his family did have royal contacts. For several generations they had been *mutawwifeen*, responsible for guiding pilgrims on *hajj* in Mekkah.[12] For 44 years, Kamel's father was employed under the patronage of Prince Faisal bin Abdel-Aziz, who became king when he forced his profligate half-brother to abdicate, succeeding to the throne in 1964. Kamel's family connections put him at the centre of municipal structures in Mekkah and laid the groundwork for his access to important networks and players of the Saudi state. In this way, his route into Saudi state circles was established from early on.

It was not only a case of being in the right place, but also of starting his businesses at the right time. After graduating with a degree in commerce from Riyadh University and a short career in the Saudi Arabian Ministry of Finance, Kamel created his own company, Dallah Establishment, in the early 1960s. The private mail service he established in that period met a demand in the kingdom, meaning that his personal business interests coincided with the interests of the Saudi state at a time when oil money was driving modernisation of the country's infrastructure. Kamel's company became involved in building Saudi Arabia's roads, airports, pipelines and sewerage networks.

The balance between being in the 'right' place and taking the 'right' initiatives is a theme that runs through Kamel's stories about himself. In some he portrays himself as a self-made man, as in the *halabisa* story already mentioned. In another he reminisces about cleaning sheep bones as a child to make toys to sell to his playmates and, in another, about buying scouts uniforms and sports clothes from a shop in Cairo called Bayt al-Kashaf. Kamel would visit Cairo in the summer, buy the goods, and then sell them on to schools in Jeddah and Mekkah. He recounts how he earned good money from publishing a magazine while still in high school. At university, by his own account, he neglected his studies and devoted all his time to business. One business idea was a photocopying service that Kamel offered to teachers wanting to produce compendiums of reading for students. The venture was such a success and expanded so fast to other faculties that he bought his first car from the proceeds.

When Kamel talks about his family's work as guides for pilgrims in Mekkah, he reveals how he became aware of the potential influence of a well-organised authority.[13] On the one hand, because his family did not run a business as such, Kamel's wealth was built up through his own hard work and ideas and not from a family fortune. This differentiates him strongly from his partners and competitors inside the ruling family. On the other hand, his success was deeply dependent on close links to ruling family members. Cooperation with inner circles of the ruling princes was much in evidence in his media investments. In MBC his partner was King Fahd's brother-in-law, Walid al-Ibrahim.[14] After being bought out of MBC and having established ART, he joined forces with another prince, Fahd's nephew, Alwaleed bin Talal bin Abdel-Aziz, with whom he had worked during the 1980s.[15] Alwaleed owned 30 per cent of the shares in ART, while Kamel owned the rest.[16] Alwaleed bin Talal took charge of ART's five music channels,[17] and in 2003 he transferred them to his newly established satellite network Rotana.[18] At the same time, Alwaleed and Kamel exchanged shares, leaving Alwaleed with a 5 per cent stake in ART and Kamel with an undisclosed share in Rotana after the switch.[19]

Collaboration with members of the ruling family was not without problems. Kamel's manifestly apolitical stance, dependent on good relationships with Saudi princes, was demonstrated when he was forced to sell his beloved mail service company to a prince.[20] On Saudi work ethics, however, Kamel proved more outspoken and was criticised for it. When asked in an interview why he did not employ more Saudi nationals in his different businesses, Kamel attributed the choice to a bad work ethic among Saudis, saying they were not ready or able to work at all levels in a company. He said that all his top executives were Saudi, as were 60 per cent of his middle managers. However, he explained to Turki al-Dakhil on the Al-Arabiya programme *Idaʿat*, Saudis saw themselves only as leaders, which is why his ordinary staff were not Saudi.[21]

With two wives, one Saudi and one Egyptian, Kamel carried his ambivalence about Saudi Arabia over into his private life. He had two sons and three daughters from his Saudi wife and three daughters from his Egyptian wife, actress Safa Abu al-Suʿud. Three of his children play active roles in his business empire. Abdullah, the eldest son from the Saudi wife, is second in command, and Mohi, Abdullah's full brother, also holds a senior executive position, having been responsible for the ART sports channels until they were sold to the Al-Jazeera network. Hadir, eldest daughter of Kamel's Egyptian wife, runs the marketing department within ART. She studied under Abdallah Schleifer,[22] a well-known journalism professor at the American University in Cairo who worked as a private consultant for ART during its early years.

Reconciling TV Entertainment and Islam

Saleh Kamel's media investments are, as already mentioned, only a part of his extensive business interests. With the establishment of Dallah al-Baraka Group, these interests expanded from services into construction and maintenance, with several contracts awarded by the Saudi Ministry of Defence and Aviation under Prince Sultan bin Abdel-Aziz, who was Defence Minister from 1963 until his death in 2011. Besides involvement in ART, Dallah al-Baraka is today mainly involved in insurance, real estate and tourism. Kamel, meanwhile, demonstrated his personal interest in Islamic banking and financing by publishing his writings on the principles of financial operations that accord with Islamic teaching. His concern to uphold Islamic principles resulted not only in his ownership of an Islamic bank through al-Baraka Banking Group but also in the establishment of the Saleh Kamel Centre for Islamic Economy at al-Azhar University in 1992. Kamel became chairman of the General Council for Islamic Banks and Financial Institutions and President of the Islamic Chamber of Commerce & Industry. His engagement in Islamic finance earned him several awards and honorary positions. At first sight, this interest in Islamic ideas and principles seemed lacking in the evolution of ART, which had its origins in the Arab Media Company Kamel formed in 1977 as one of Saudi Arabia's first television, radio and film production companies.

When ART was introduced in 1993, it was the first Arab satellite network to offer niche services.[23] From the beginning it focused on entertainment, and within a few years had grown to encompass some 21 channels. The network became quickly known for its specialised channels broadcasting only sport, only film, only music and so on. It was in turn owned by the Arab Media Corporation (AMC), with start-up capital reportedly amounting to US$300 million.[24] Central offices and marketing were located in Cairo and Jeddah, and transmission was originally from Fucino in Italy but was moved to Jordan Media City in Amman in 2002.[25] Other networks, including MBC, were also moving from Europe to the Middle East at this time, apparently in search of lower costs but also because of some relaxation of restrictions on media in the region and also because of the spread of satellite technology and the establishment of so-called free media cities.[26] ART transmits its programmes to most of the Middle East, the USA and Europe via the Arabsat, Nilesat and Hotbird satellites. As such, it aligns with the regional and global scope of Kamel's businesses.

ART channels are mostly encrypted. Before their sale to Al-Jazeera Group in 2009, the sports channels had special status, because ART had obtained exclusive rights for regional Middle East broadcasting of several popular events, including the four-yearly football World Cup. Kamel, having reportedly paid US$86 million for rights to the 2002 World Cup series, may have paid as much as US$187 million for the 2006 series, calculating that the World Cup would be enough of an attraction to persuade viewers to subscribe to the ART service.[27] Instead, the move backfired, causing negative publicity for ART and forcing its managers to show some matches free-to-air, despite the fee they had paid for exclusivity.[28] The reason given for selling to Al-Jazeera was that the channels were in deficit. Movie channels were always another feature of the ART offering, presented as having the purpose of gathering and preserving Arab movies. After an early deal to secure around 1,000 old Egyptian films, ART claimed to own the largest movie library in the Middle East. Viewers wanting access to these films on ART had to pay.

Iqraa, on the other hand, the region's first Arab Islamic satellite channel, was not encrypted. Its programmes not only on religious teaching, but also lifestyle shows and programmes about society – all have Islam as their common frame of reference. The vast majority may be defined as lifestyle programmes concerned with how to support the identity position of the 'proper' or 'real' Muslim.[29] They include shows such as *Young*

People Want to Marry, aired in 2004, *Comfort House* (2007) and *My Paradise* (2007). By focusing on individual lifestyles, Iqraa can be seen as mainstreaming or popularising Islam.[30] The demonstrable popularity of mediated Islam soon resulted in the launching of other Islamic channels. When Kamel's business partner Prince Alwaleed bin Talal launched his own Islamic satellite channel, Al-Resalah, in 2006, Iqraa seemed to lose viewers. Illustrating the apparently unequal nature of Kamel's dealings with Saudi princes, Al-Resalah hired more than a dozen of Iqraa's most famous and popular preachers.[31]

Kamel's interest in media investment was not limited to ART. When the Lebanese Broadcasting Corporation (LBC) sought to expand from terrestrial into satellite broadcasting, Kamel invested in LBC in a way that allowed it to transmit by satellite from ART's base, at that time in Italy, thereby benefitting from ART's existing deal for transmission via Arabsat.[32] When challenged in 1998 to explain how the 'seductive' behaviour of women on LBC's and ART's film and music channels could be compatible with 'Islamic values', Kamel stressed that he was responsible only for delivery of LBC, not for its content.[33] Those who watched LBC did so of their own free will, he said. Nevertheless, Kamel insisted, he had been able to influence the choice of programming at LBC. Moreover, he continued, there was no 'fundamental contradiction' between Islamic values and competition among satellite channels. ART had tried to counteract the extremes that said media should be 100 per cent 'Islamic' or that Muslims should avoid satellite television altogether. It was 'proud' of offering a children's channel and university channel that were '100 per cent in conformity with Islamic values'. Kamel went on:

> With some 80 per cent of the general content of films and music, we try to introduce content that our viewers will benefit from, and we exercise self-censorship. We are proud of that. If you make a comparison between our film channel and any other Arab film channel, you will see that we are very conservative. The same is true of the music channel.[34]

In March 2001, ART launched Al-Awael bouquet as a platform for pay-TV access to other television networks' channels. These included non-Arab channels such as BBC World, CNN, Eurosport and Animal Planet, as well as channels from other Arabic networks, such as Al-Jazeera and some of the Egyptian Nile Thematic Channels broadcast via Nilesat. In this way, ART moved away from being an 'Arabic-language niche player' to offering a wide and international entertainment programme.[35] The expansion only went so far, however. In 2003, Saleh Kamel declared that his investment group would launch four major media projects: an international news agency, a radio station broadcasting in English, a television channel in all major world languages and a public relations company in the USA.[36] None of these projects materialised. The biggest step towards them was the launching of Iqraa in English as well as Arabic. The aims behind this initiative accord with the motives behind Kamel's media projects more generally.

Motives for Media Involvement

Considering how long ago Saleh Kamel started up in business, his involvement in satellite television came comparatively late. Yet, he was the first to invest in MBC, and MBC was the first Arab satellite channel to exploit satellite broadcasting ostensibly for commercial reasons. Media investment had not been a priority for Kamel before the launch of MBC. So was the move primarily political or commercial, and what did the launch of ART, and later Iqraa, bring to his business empire?

The MBC investment can be explained as either a mere investment or a way to maintain and strengthen ties to relevant members of the ruling family. As Naomi Sakr has shown, the early development of Arab satellite television was deeply influenced by the concentration of resources and cooperation within an enormously rich elite.[37] What Saleh Kamel initially gained from MBC was to become a player in the global media market. He has said himself that it was not so much a matter of earning money from satellite television as presenting Islam 'as it should be presented to the rest of the world'.[38] He made clear that, in the process, he had no intention of jeopardising good relations with Saudi princes. Thus, he sold his 37.5 per cent share in MBC to his co-investors, whose subsequent decision to take MBC's advertising account from Tihama and handle it themselves had a negative impact on profits at Tihama, where Saleh Kamel was a major shareholder.[39] Although MBC started life in London, it quickly earned a reputation for loyalty to Saudi Arabia's ruling princes. Sources close to Kamel said that, when setting up ART, he deliberately rejected the idea of broadcasting news bulletins or including a news channel because of the potential such an activity would have for damaging or complicating his relations with those in power.[40] Since political actors can use media as a space for negotiation with other members of ruling elites, it could be said that, by deciding to stay away from news coverage, Kamel was sending a signal that he was not particularly interested in political negotiation.

Thus, Saleh Kamel's political motives for media investment seem rather subtle. They may have less to do with personal vanity and positioning than with his economic interests, including Islamic financing. According to his private secretary in Egypt, he declined for a long time to appear on his own television channels because, 'unlike other television channel owners', his intention was not to promote himself.[41] It was not until he became president of the Islamic Chamber of Commerce & Industry in 2005 that he introduced a television programme of his own in order to communicate the aims of the chamber. Later, he was interviewed by Mahmoud Saad for *Masr El-Naharda*, an evening talk show on Egyptian state television; this was a turning point in that he was presented not only as a successful businessman but also as someone with ideas and principles.[42]

Indeed, his statements in public interviews indicate that ideas about programme content are central to Kamel's involvement in ART. These include ideas about social and economic responsibility and Islamic finance. One example can be found in a programme featuring Saleh Kamel himself. Called *Al-Suq* (The Market), it highlights and supports the entrepreneurship of young and upcoming businessmen. Kamel described the show as offering everything people needed to know to benefit their business, both big and small.[43] It ran for more than 200 episodes from March 2008,[44] before stopping in 2011 because Saleh Kamel was ill, as well as dealing with his brother's death. After about a year, it resumed with the first programmes of the new season uploaded to YouTube in January 2012. The new version had an even stronger emphasis than the previous one on notions of mentoring and entrepreneurship, popularised through the reality show *The Apprentice*, seen on British and US television.[45] Previously, Kamel had been the key figure and main speaker, sharing his knowledge of Islamic finance and business values. With the revamp he took a backseat, with a role as listener and commentator. Appointed in his place as programme host was Bandar Sami Arab, who has a background in finance. In each programme, two businessmen from the Arab or Islamic world, male or female, participated in sharing ideas, problems and experiences. The focus was still the rules, culture and values of Islamic finance, trade and *zakat* (alms-giving). In Kamel's view, the aim was to convey the experiences of previous generations to future generations, so they could lead future businesses in the Islamic world.[46]

Zakat is an Islamic duty that combines religion and finance and, as such, Kamel made it a centrepiece of his talks, presenting *zakat* as a basis for new business and airing a five-minute slot on *zakat* each day during the fasting month of Ramadan in 2010. His aim was to convince Muslims that *zakat* is a benefit as much for individuals and their businesses as it is for the rest of Muslim society. Addressing a gathering of businessmen and academics in Medina, Saudi Arabia, in 2012, he suggested that housing and land problems in Saudi Arabia could have been solved if Saudis had paid *zakat* based on sales of real estate.[47] He said the global economic crisis would not have happened if the world had followed Prophet Muhammad's instruction 'Don't sell what you don't possess.'[48] On another occasion he presented Islamic financing as offering a variety of innovative products that could provide solutions to the economic crisis and claimed to have communicated this to German Chancellor Angela Merkel.[49]

At the same time, his second stated motivation is to give a more positive and 'truer' picture of Islam to non-Muslims, particularly in the West,
in order to change anti-Islam reactions to 9/11. Interviewed by Reuters
in Kuala Lumpur in the months before the US invasion of Iraq, Kamel
noted a double standard in the bid to disarm Iraq while leaving bombs
in the hands of Israel. This, he said, reinforced anti-Muslim sentiments.
He wanted 'to counter anti-Islam and anti-Arab publicity' and, as well as
correcting Western views of Islam, let Muslims understand that 'Islam
does not allow people to kill'.[50] Such arguments echoed the goal of Iqraa
as it was formulated on the channel's website under 'Our mission'. Key
words included the building of 'a modern Muslim society', helping
Muslims 'to apply the teachings of Islam that call for tolerance and for
addressing others mildly', 'a Muslim society whose members will be able
to positively interact both on the local and international levels', and the
presentation of 'the true moderate face of Islam to people in the West
where media do not present an objective view on the Islamic Law'.[51]
These broad statements point to Islam as a universal value that unites all
Muslims. They also present the channel as a facilitator of knowledge.[52]

Saleh Kamel remained notably silent on the political issues that
arose with the Arab uprisings in 2010–11, parrying questions about
them with answers that dealt only with finance, such as the uprisings'
impact on the general economic situation and on the prices of oil and
other commodities. Shoring up support for the Saudi government's
handling of the new political realities, he told *Business Life* that he
refused to be pessimistic, because one could rely on the cleverness of
political leaders and the business elite.[53] Meanwhile, however, in
response to political instability in Egypt, he moved the planned location
of the head office of a projected new Islamic bank from Egypt to Qatar.[54]

Narratives of Piety

For conservative critics, music videos and films with scantily dressed
women on ART raise questions about Saleh Kamel's sincerity in matters

relating to Islam. Critics find ammunition in films featuring his wife, Safa Abu al-Su'ud, a famous Egyptian actress, singing and dancing in a bikini.[55] Seen in that light, the launching of Iqraa looked like a balancing act between religious convictions and commercial interests. However, Kamel was also forced to deny accusations of supporting and financing terrorism. After the 9/11 attacks in the USA in 2001, he was faced with lawsuits from relatives of the 9/11 victims. Allegations included supporting an Islamic bank in Sudan that held accounts for Al-Qaida members and paying a company salary to an acquaintance of the 9/11 hijackers. Kamel's response was to counter the accusations by pointing to his charity and development work. In an interview in 2010 with presenter Turki al-Dakheel on the Al-Arabiya programme *Ida'aat*, he recounted how he had established a training institute for women in Saudi Arabia some 25 years earlier and how he backed Pakistani hospitals and schools for Afghan refugees, activities that had nothing to do with armed conflict.[56]

Thus, in place of the stereotypical picture of a successful but brutal businessman, the public was presented with another stereotype – that of a true believer standing up for the principles of Islam. Being interviewed by Amr El-Laithy, host of the programme *Ana* (meaning 'I') on Egypt's privately owned commercial channel Dream TV, Kamel refused to rate his own efforts within different fields. The programme, designed to offer close-ups of prominent Arabs, usually asks the guest to assess themselves on a scale from zero to 20 within five categories. The first category relates to basics such as food, sleep and shelter. The second concerns stability and safety, the third love and friendship, the fourth money and fame and the fifth self-realisation. When asked about his achievements on the five scales Kamel answered 'I don't award myself anything. I thank God that he has given me more than I have deserved of the basics in life.'[57] On other public occasions Kamel similarly referred to God's mercy and generosity. In an interview in the online magazine *Business Life*, he attributed his success to the 'blessings of Allah the Almighty', and to the fact that his business is based on the values of

Islam, as taught to him by his mother. He said his very first business contract had been based on Islamic principles for financing.[58]

Kamel's self-identification as a pious Muslim also emerges from interviews with those close to him. His private secretary maintains that her employer is a good listener, who is modest and unpretentious. She believes that he launched ART to promote certain ideas and principles, unlike other television station owners who use their programmes to promote themselves.[59] Whereas Saleh Kamel has been accused of establishing Iqraa to balance the frivolity of ART's entertainment channels, Kamel and his secretary give another reason. His secretary says that Iqraa had always been on the cards. Kamel himself argued in his interview with Turki al-Dakheel on *Ida'aat* that the history of his media activities shows there is no contradiction between Iqraa and ART. This includes regular meetings with respected religious scholars inside and outside Saudi Arabia and an annual seminar on Islamic media held every year for 11 years. The seminar itself was called Iqraa and the aim was to find out how to understand modern media. The aim from the outset was Islamisation of media, he claimed.[60] Kamel's intention was to create channels that would counter the alleged moral decay being endorsed by other media. Asked by Dakheel how far he had succeeded, Kamel conceded that his efforts had not been enough. That, he said, was why he got rid of the music channels and why he could be proud of censorship on ART movie channels.[61]

Conclusion

The significance of the narratives and images discussed above goes beyond any question about whether they are factually accurate or not. Their importance for this chapter lies in the kind of Islam promoted by Kamel and his use of Islam to legitimise investment in media. On the one hand, his Islamisation project is presented as a reaction against a state of decay in the West and an allegedly hijacked Islam, and on the other hand, what is being promoted is an individualised Islam with an element of self-realisation – a form of post-Islamism.[62] The goal is the establishment of an imagined community where spaces are re-Islamised; investment in media and banking is, in effect, investment in this imagined community. In his interview with *Business Life* in 2012, Kamel defined the community by reference to the time of Prophet Muhammad and to Sharia,[63] implying – as discussed by Roy[64] – that later cultural influences are corrupted. While laying claim to a universal Islam, Kamel, as well as owners of other Saudi Islamic channels such as Al-Resalah and Al-Majd, maintain close connections to Saudi Arabia's ruling family. Notwithstanding accusations against Kamel for supporting radical Islamist militants, what Kamel and the Saudi re-Islamisation project agree on is a rejection of radical Islam.

Insofar as Saleh Kamel is loyal to the Saudi elite, engaged in social rather than political change, and a competent businessman with a strong focus on business ethics and success, he can be said to fit Tunstall and Palmer's profile of a media owner who is a baron rather than a mogul. Risk taking and eccentricity are not prominent attributes of Kamel's media operations. Even though he may appear to have absolute authority within his own business empire, his role in the political landscape is more unobtrusive. ART appears less an instrument for the advancement of Kamel's personal power in Saudi Arabia or globally than a tool to underpin his ideas and the Islamic banking and financing ventures seen as closest to his heart. Saleh Kamel ranks as one of the world's richest Arab investors. The contribution made by his media assets to this financial success is difficult to estimate, but there is no doubt that the investment in satellite media served to strengthen existing business connections and opened the way for new ones. His political influence can mostly be summed up as support for, and dissemination of, his own version of an economically liberal post Islamism combined with loyalty towards the political power and conservative system of the Saudi regime.

7

Walid al-Ibrahim: Modernising Mogul of MBC

Najat AlSaied

Walid al-Ibrahim, brother-in-law of Saudi Arabia's late King Fahd and Chief Executive Officer (CEO) of the Middle East Broadcasting Corporation (MBC) Group, has built a US$2.9 billion[1] business empire from his MBC satellite network, which is one of the strongest in the Arab world. MBC's early launch in 1991 made it the first privately-owned Arab broadcasting network to offer free-to-air non-stop programming. As such, it helped to transform television across the Arab world from a traditional nation-based government-censored model to a web of transnational networks, several of which would come to be judged in terms of their contributions to critical and constructive debates on issues facing Arab societies. That process, of building a conglomerate and doing what Walid al-Ibrahim himself calls 'promoting modernity' in Saudi Arabia and the Arab world, forms the focus of this chapter. As defined by Tunstall and Palmer, a media mogul is a person who owns and operates major media companies, who takes entrepreneurial risks and who conducts media business in an 'idiosyncratic or eccentric style'. Media moguls have 'political connections' that lead to 'public controversy' and might also 'face the threat or promise of friendly or damaging new legislation.'[2] Sheikh Walid, this chapter will argue, fits that template rather closely. He may not be quite as eccentric as the definition will have it, but he has been a risk taker, albeit in a different sense from the mostly financial risk taking of the typical Western media mogul.

It is in promoting modernity that the level of risk incurred by Walid al-Ibrahim can be assessed. Abdullah Al-Ghathami, a Saudi literary critic who has written on modernity in Saudi Arabia, describes the development that has occurred in the kingdom to date as *tafra*, meaning 'economic boom'. He sees this boom as the negative face of development, because 'building the place' was achieved much faster than 'building the person'. As a result, he writes, the place has become more modern than the person, meaning that modernity has arrived only in a physical sense, and not in the people's minds.[3] In Ghathami's view, 'the stand towards modernity is the stand towards the new, the stand towards *al-tari*',[4] a concept that Marwan Kraidy translates as 'extraneous, contingent, unforeseen'.[5] For Ghathami, modernity in Saudi Arabia is a form of socio-cultural schizophrenia, remaining incomplete because it is not entirely indigenous. Real modernists, says Ghathami, should not be afraid to get involved in broad-based and contentious social and cultural debates. Otherwise they are part of a 'metaphorical modernism (*hadathiyya majaziyya*)'.[6]

Although it encompasses the development of personal attitudes, Ghathami's understanding of modernity can be readily distinguished from that of US modernisation theorists of the 1950s and 1960s, such as Daniel Lerner, because unlike them he is open to a multiplicity of modernities that are not tied to Western templates. Lerner believed that the 'Western model of modernization exhibits certain components and sequences whose relevance is global' and that it necessarily represented the 'baseline' for modernisation everywhere.[7] As Kraidy shows, Ghathami does 'not restrict modernity to one discourse with no others, since all discourses are necessarily exposed to [renewal]'.[8] Indeed, Ghathami compares the situation in Saudi Arabia with that in advanced societies by pointing out that, in the latter, conservatism is present alongside other 'modes with which it enters into dialogue and with which it can be mutually held accountable' so that the 'proximity of modes leads to a modernisation of society and its ways of thinking through exchanges'. In Saudi Arabia, in contrast, 'the absence of such proximity reinforces the sovereignty of a single mode, and keeps a sensibility of elimination and rejection, which leads to breaking any progress'.[9]

Bearing in mind Ghathami's notion of the symbolic event (*al-hadath al-ramzy*), which Kraidy likens in some degree to the notion of moral panic because it involves an event that elicits strong public opposition and becomes the 'talk of councils and societies' for prolonged periods,[10] Walid al-Ibrahim's real risk taking as a media mogul could be said to depend on whether or not the modernity he claims to promote through MBC is of the real or incomplete and metaphorical kind. To judge that, and his role in the development of Saudi-owned media, this chapter considers the political connections that underpinned the building of MBC, the calculations behind its more controversial programming choices, and the rationale for rapid expansion of the network after 2002.

Family Connections and Political Capital

Walid al-Ibrahim is the brother of Al-Jawhara al-Ibrahim, fourth wife of Fahd, the king of Saudi Arabia who died in 2005. Links between his ancestors and those of Fahd date back to the first half of the nineteenth century. Sheikh Walid's grandfather, Abdul Aziz al-Ibrahim, was Emir of Asir in 1828, Taif in 1830 and Madina in 1833. Sheikh Walid's father, Ibrahim al-Ibrahim, was Emir of Al-Qunfotha in 1888, Deputy of Mekka al-Mukarama in 1898, Deputy of Asir in 1907 and Emir of Al-Baha in 1915. His daughter, Al-Jawhara, was not the only daughter to marry into the House of Saud but was one of five who did so. Sheikh Walid himself did not marry into the Al Saud; instead, he married Hana bint Abdullah Al Shehree, who gave him four children.[11]

After completing his higher education in the USA, Sheikh Walid returned to the Middle East to establish ARA Group International (AGI) in 1985. His assets also included ventures in the USA and UK, notably ANA Radio Television, broadcasting Arabic-language news from Washington, DC, and a stake in Spectrum 558 AM, a radio station serving London and the south-east of England.[12] Less than a year after launching in September 1991, MBC bought the 85-year-old news agency United Press International (UPI) at a bankruptcy hearing in New York in June 1992, outbidding a group of US businessmen. It paid US$3.95 million for the agency and invested a further US$12 million to upgrade its services, with the aim of saving the US$400,000 it was reportedly spending each month in payments to other news services.[13]

It has sometimes been suggested that MBC was directly owned by King Fahd and taken over by Fahd's youngest and favourite son, Abdel-Aziz. A joke in the late 1990s had it that MBC stood for 'My Broadcasting Company', reflecting suspicions of royal ownership. In fact MBC began as a partnership between Walid al-Ibrahim and fellow entrepreneur Saleh Kamel, who seems to have had the initial idea for the channel but withdrew from the partnership in 1993. Walid al-Ibrahim wanted to focus on free-to-air broadcasting supported by revenue from advertising, whereas Saleh Kamel, with his background in banking, was keen on generating revenue through subscriptions.[14] Nevertheless, Shaikh Walid's royal connections undoubtedly secured MBC's future, when it started out with US$300 million in capital and annual running costs of US$60 million.[15] Saudi Arabia's majority shareholding in the Arabsat satellite fleet was deployed to allow MBC to rent a powerful transponder that boosted its signal inside Saudi Arabia, after which MBC-FM was allowed to launch in 1994 as the kingdom's only commercial terrestrial radio station.[16] Through a company called SARAvision, registered in Riyadh in 1995, Walid al-Ibrahim obtained an exclusive licence to deliver a number of thematic channels to a cable network serving Saudi cities. The plan for specialised channels, including an MBC news channel, was dropped in 1998, but was revived at a moment of strategic importance for the Saudi government in 2003, ahead of the Saudi-backed USA-led invasion of Iraq. At that point, the MBC network was being expanded to include not only Al-Arabiya but also additional entertainment channels dominated by Hollywood content.[17]

Evidence like this points to privately owned Arab satellite channels remaining under effective state control, or at least to a blurring of the distinction between private and state ownership whereby private owners benefit from what has been identified as a form of 'political capital'.[18] The existence of such political capital implies that the 'central purpose of creating media organisations is political rather than commercial' and that the majority of satellite television outlets in the Arab region could not afford to rely on commercial revenues alone without the financial and political support of some politically well-connected backer, if not the state itself.[19]

Sheikh Walid's connections with the Saudi ruling family and thus with state institutions are clearly an important factor in assessing the level of risk he took in pursuing his media vision, especially given that he pursued it from a base outside the kingdom, away from its direct jurisdiction. Admirers would say that, through MBC, he introduced a whole new model of doing business in Arab television, complete with new technical solutions, new geopolitical considerations and a new focus on marketing the product. Being the first of its kind, MBC was introduced at a time when viewers were not yet accustomed to receiving via satellite and would have to invest in a dish to receive it. Yet many Arab countries, including Saudi Arabia, had banned satellite dishes to defend their territory from what their governments saw as encroachment by foreign news outlets such as the USA-owned CNN. If Fahd approved of MBC it was at least in part because MBC was envisaged as an Arabic version of CNN.[20] By 1998, however, with Saudi oil income falling and Fahd's health deteriorating, MBC had to revise its strategy. The focus shifted towards entertainment programmes to attract more viewers, UPI was sold off in 2000, and the network moved from London to Dubai to reduce costs.[21] When Sheikh Walid was asked in a press interview why Dubai in particular and not another Arab country, his response was that 'they' (apparently referring to the ruler of Dubai) had done a 'pretty good job in convincing us to move' and the main reason why he was persuaded was 'freedom of speech', which was the 'only thing that made us go to London in the first place'.[22] Saudi observers are aware of the virtuous circle between working environments free from direct control of their country's religious establishment, the ability to attract skilled media professionals and the result in terms of creative output and popularity with viewers.[23]

Sheikh Walid has himself argued in interviews with the Saudi-owned press that governments should not intervene in the management of privately owned media and has called for liberating the media from government dominance, in order to put the viewer in charge and develop the skills and talents of employees.[24] This plea highlights the tension between political capital, in the form of support from those with political power, and financial capital, in the form of advertising money that follows large audiences. When the present author asked Sheikh Walid about the influence of Saudi Arabia's conservative clerics, he used the term 'enemies of development', saying:

> There is nothing that we lack that prevents us from modernity, but there are people who are fighting modernity and development in our society. There are enemies of development and they believe that any change will take away their privileges. They consider themselves guardians of society and any changes to the status quo will be at their expense. Therefore they fight us, especially here in Saudi Arabia.[25]

That fight suggests that, even though Walid al-Ibrahim has clearly benefited from political capital, the benefits are limited. Despite King Abdullah's promises of reform since his succession in 2005, he is just one player in a circle of powerful princes whose divergent and contradictory agendas for the kingdom – some reformist, some deeply conservative – undermine the coherence of the state. Overall power has remained concentrated in the hands of traditionalist princes,[26] which may explain why Ali Jaber, TV

Director of MBC Group, makes it clear that MBC does take government restrictions into consideration when it comes to political and religious sensitivity. In his words, Sheikh Walid's role is 'to abide by the rules but not to the extent that he loses viewers'.[27] This looks more like managing risk than actively taking it.

Promoting Modernity through Programming?

Since launching MBC, Walid al-Ibrahim has said he wants his networks to 'make a difference in the Arab world', with 'one major objective' being to 'get rid of what I call the Taliban mentality'.[28] In 2006, responding to allegations that he was trying to change Saudi customs through the content on his channels, Ibrahim alluded specifically to 'progress and modernity':

> Who says that customs and traditions cannot change or be broken? If our generation believes that it can help in making us more open to the world with all its progress and modernity, then it is our duty to break these obsolete traditions. If we can reconcile between the viewpoints of our society and others, we will. If this is all considered to be breaking customs and traditions, then I welcome it![29]

In 2008, talking to Kai Ryssdal, host of the daily magazine programme *Marketplace* on US public radio WHYY-FM, Ibrahim described himself as an 'Arab Muslim' who is 'looking for change like many people in my generation, who are looking to see this part of the world evolving to become modern, become fit for our children to live in'.[30] 'Everyone tries from his side', he continued. 'And I happen to be in the media.' Asked by this author in 2011 how he defined modernity, Sheikh Walid answered:

> Modernity is to develop humanity first and foremost and our role as media makers is to invest in that through the promotion of knowledge in the Arab world. Our duty as pioneers of modernity lies in our ability to create media content, both recreational and

educational, that builds the viewer's knowledge and that will contribute to social and economic development. We advance towards
modernity steadily and its seeds are sown among the Arab youth,
primarily women. If women were modernised, the whole society
would develop.[31]

Thus, in Sheikh Walid's view, as in Ghathami's, human development is
central to modernity. He told this author:

The term development refers to everything that involves the
development of the person, as wider development in countries
and societies follow on from individual development. We concentrate on human development because it is the backbone of any
development process.[32]

Abdul-Rahman Al-Rashed, General Manager of MBC's news channel
Al-Arabiya, shares this vision. Asked whether achieving modernity is
one of his channel's objectives, he replied 'Absolutely. Without a doubt
this is one of our main goals. We have liberal views, especially about
women, but we need to be supported by the whole of society.'[33] Sheikh
Walid and the entire MBC Group thus appear to constitute a challenge
to the Saudi state's official interpretation of Islam and its social cultural
puritanism. Wahhabi scholars exert strict control over the behaviour
and interaction of men and women inside the kingdom, enforcing
gender segregation and giving strict guidelines for behaviour and
dress. The clerics' condemnation of MBC and other channels was
made explicit during Ramadan 2008 when Saudi Arabia's top judge,
Sheikh Saleh al-Luhaidan, said 'It is lawful to kill […] the apostles of
depravation […] if their evil cannot be easily removed through simple
sanctions.'[34] Everyone knew that by 'apostles of depravation' he was
referring to wealthy Saudi media owners whose channels were broadcasting drama serials specially made for Ramadan, namely Walid
al-Ibrahim of MBC and Alwaleed bin Talal, owner of Rotana. With
local opinions split over this outburst, King Abdullah appeared to take

sides in February 2009, when he sacked Luhaidan as part of his first cabinet reshuffle since taking the throne in 2005. Death threats must be taken seriously, however, and those against Walid al-Ibrahim were a testimony both to deep cleavages in Saudi society and to his willingness to take risks through programmes of various genres and origins, from North America to Turkey and the Arab world.[35]

Luhaidan's ruling about satellite channel owners was prompted by MBC's initiative in airing serialised dramas imported from Turkey. The idea of dubbing Turkish drama serials came from Fadi Ismail, MBC Group Director of Services, who discovered *Noor* (*Gümüş*) at a trade show in Istanbul and brought it to the attention of Adib Khair, the head of Sama Art Productions in Damascus, said to be one of Syria's most innovative drama production companies.[36] Both men realised that the serial was close enough to Arab culture but different enough from day-to-day life in Arab countries to engage Arab audiences, so they dubbed it into colloquial Syrian as an experiment and gained a response that far exceeded their expectations. Romantic relationships portrayed in *Noor* were credited with encouraging Arab women to complain about their husbands' allegedly 'cold' behaviour and to express admiration for the television hero's good looks.[37]

Luhaidan was not alone in condemning MBC's Turkish dramas. Saudi Arabia's Grand Mufti, Sheikh Abdel-Aziz Al Sheikh, issued an edict against the shows on Arab TV, saying they were 'replete with wickedness, evil, moral collapse and war on virtues that only God knows the truth of'.[38] MBC declined to respond, however, and the Turkish serials continued. MBC even launched a pay-to-view television channel in partnership with Showtime Arabia that was entirely dedicated to *Noor* and enabled viewers to watch the show around the clock.

One of the MBC shows that handles sensitive issues in Saudi society is *Tash Ma Tash*, a popular Saudi situation comedy that runs in Ramadan. It began in 1992 and aired on Saudi Channel 1 for 13 seasons before MBC acquired it in 2005. MBC Group bought the show because of its popularity with Saudi audiences. It said it wanted to inject the series with more freedom and professionalism and stand up to the threatened closure of the whole show if it remained on Channel 1.[39] Saudis in general admire *Tash Ma Tash* because it satirises their social, political and economic situation, and women like it in particular because they perceive it as challenging discrimination based on customs and traditions.[40] However, even after transferring to MBC, the show was not immune from political and religious control. In September 2009, for example, MBC1, the channel showing *Tash Ma Tash*, was forced to cancel two episodes that were deemed unacceptable: one dealt with calls to prayer over loudspeakers that were excessively loud, and the other imagined US President Barack Obama growing up in Saudi Arabia.[41] Sheikh Walid is frank about the difficulties of trying to tackle sensitive social topics through popular programme genres:

> The problem of exposing in detail the problems of the disadvantaged, is that we are then accused by the Saudi press of airing our dirty laundry in public. That's why we sometimes try to avoid their problems in drama and talk shows [...] There is no programme that causes us more of headache than *Tash Ma Tash* because of its criticism of society, officials, ministries and the education system in the Kingdom. These issues were presented in dramas and situation comedies because they are more influential than talk shows or any other genres.[42]

Criticism of MBC programmes on religious grounds has also come from Arab countries other than Saudi Arabia. *Al-Ra'is*, the Arabic version of the reality-television format *Big Brother*, was launched on MBC in 2004 from a set in Bahrain and suspended after barely one week on air in the face of Bahraini protests against the mixing of young men and women that was central to the format. According to Marwan Kraidy's research on the affair, MBC sources believed that Saudi clerics had encouraged their counterparts in Bahrain to make a fuss and even that the decision to axe the show had been reached through collaboration between the Saudi Arabian and Bahraini ruling families.[43] Significantly, however, given

Walid al-Ibrahim's subsequently declared willingness to challenge customs and traditions, MBC's own explanation for withdrawing the programme and thereby writing off US$6 million of expenditure spoke directly to the issue of tradition. It said 'MBC does not want to risk, through its programs and broadcasting, being accused of harming Arab traditions and values, because it considers the channel one for the Arab family.'[44] Indeed, Sheikh Walid himself offered his personal apology to any Arab families who were offended by any unintentional 'mistake' that MBC might make in one of its programmes.[45] This response can be evaluated against Ghathami's view that real modernists do not apologise for participating in controversial social and cultural debates.

Controversy over the giving of offence via television highlights the tensions between promoting modernity and heeding the financial imperatives of running a large business. These emerged again during Ramadan 2012, when the television series *Omar*, produced jointly with Qatar Television about Islam's second Caliph Omar ibn al-Khattab, caused a stir even before it was broadcast. Hundreds of Muslims joined Facebook and Twitter campaigns calling for the show to be cancelled because they believed it is forbidden to depict Prophet Muhammad's closest companions. In public, Walid al-Ibrahim gave a rationale for ignoring the opposition that resonated with his interest in progress and modernity. He said:

> Caliph Omar is a very good role model who should be emulated by all Muslims. The main purpose of producing such an important dramatic work is to correct the wrongly understood parts of Islamic history – whether intentionally or unintentionally – at a time when there is controversy globally about all Islamic beliefs and concepts. We are in dire need, now more than at any other time in history, of portraying a character as great as Caliph Omar and presenting him as a good role model for people to follow.[46]

At the same time, however, the financial investment was too major to set aside. MBC claimed *Omar* as the 'biggest drama production ever in the history of Arab television,[47] with an estimated budget of US$67.8 million.

'Institutional Entrepreneurship' and the Imperative of Expansion

According to MBC Group TV Director Ali Jaber, speaking in 2011, Arab satellite channels run at an annual aggregate loss of US$5.5 billion. Jaber told a forum of Arab media academics in London that the channels' combined operational costs amount to US$6.5 billion, but the advertising revenue they generate is only US$1 billion. The calculation underlines how much money political elites are putting into satellite television because they think it is influential. MBC's main general entertainment channel, MBC1, claims privately to have revenues of US$140 million against outgoings of US$100 million. However, the network's news channel, Al-Arabiya, is not profitable. Its general manager, Abdel-Rahman al-Rashed, hinted that the usual equation between bigger audiences and higher advertising revenues could not be relied upon in his channel's case:

> Al-Arabiya is losing money. Its income from advertisements is eight times more than Al-Jazeera. Our income is the highest among news television stations in the Middle East. [...] If you have high ratings, you have lots of advertisements. If you have taken on more issues, you will have more viewers. In theory, high ratings make more money. Covering issues, talking about what matters to people, is supposed to attract more advertisers – but not always.[48]

The question then arises as to why it is that, if the same governments and political elites that are behind state television ultimately also interfere with private satellite channels, the latter still enjoy more latitude in terms of content and larger audiences than state television. What, if anything, distinguishes an owner and investor like Sheikh Walid from others who manage state television? When I put that question to Ali Jaber, he described Sheikh Walid as an 'institutional entrepreneur', a term from organisation studies that refers to someone who has an interest in modifying institutional structures, or in creating new ones, and has the resources to do so.[49] Jaber explained:

> The difference between Sheikh Walid's management and that of state television is what we call 'institutional entrepreneurship'. Institutional entrepreneurs, such as Sheikh Walid, handle things in different ways. They draw up their own regulations, with the main objective of attracting more viewers. Sheikh Walid enjoys a great deal of autonomy although there are limitations when it comes to political and religious sensitivity. His main role here is to abide by the rules but not to the extent that he loses viewers, and this is what defines an institutional entrepreneur. They handle things in different ways. They draft their own regulations.[50]

One way in which Walid al-Ibrahim has handled things differently is through MBC's rapid expansion since 2003. MBC moved from London to Dubai in 2001 to reduce costs, but also, reportedly, to be closer to its Middle Eastern audience. That intention existed in parallel with the hiring of non-Arab executives and with increasingly close relations with UK and US entertainment businesses, driven by an urgent need for content for the rising number of MBC channels. Besides Al-Arabiya, launched in 2003, these include MBC2, also launched in 2003, MBC3 (2004), MBC4 (2005), MBC Action and the music channel Wanasah (both launched 2007), MBC Persia, MBC Max and MBC Plus (all launched in 2008) and MBC Drama (2010). Apart from MBC3, which is aimed at children aged 5–14 years, the added channels are mostly aimed at young people up to the ages of 24 or 35 years. The offering across the whole network is dominated by content that originated in the USA, from films to sitcoms and talk shows. Other expansion has added the MBC-FM and Panorama radio stations, along with Hi FM and Hala FM, introduced between 1994 and 2007. Then there are online services such as

AlArabiya.net, carrying political, economic and cultural news, the entertainment portal mbc.net, and Shahed Online, which offers free on-
demand viewing of MBC programmes. This is in addition to services
such as Jawal MBC and MoBC (started in 2007), which enable users to
download MBC content onto their mobile phones. MBC production
companies O3, Al-Sadaf and Al-Karma meanwhile act as a pipeline for
supplying original Arabic documentaries, drama and other content.[51]

In deciding how to expand, Walid al-Ibrahim has selected some
routes and rejected others. He has invested in film but sees the field as
fraught with difficulties of piracy, censorship, intellectual property protection, a skills shortage and 'substandard production'.[52] He is not in
favour of sports channels because of the high cost of broadcasting
rights, which cannot always be covered by advertising revenue.[53]
Instead, he sees a place for regional versions of MBC, such as the one
launched in Egypt in 2012. Again, the rationale for this is said by MBC
sources to lie in the advertising prospects, because localised MBC channels have the potential not only to generate local content but also to
attract local advertisers.

Despite MBC's expansion into areas other than television, Sheikh
Walid still looks to television as a leading medium in the region. He told
an interviewer in 2007 that 'everyone talks about the death of broadcasting with the web, but I don't think we're anywhere near there in the
Middle East because the technologies aren't here yet'.[54] Television's continuing importance was confirmed by new statistics in 2011 showing that
even the region's youth are still watching in large numbers.[55] Expanding
the number of television channels was MBC's way of maximising the
financial benefits of advertising income, as Sheikh Walid explained:

> We do not look at profits for each individual programme but
> rather as part of a grid. For example, if a programme generates
> little profit, then another programme with lower costs and higher
> profits will compensate for it. Usually in large firms economies of
> scale are used and increased production leads to lower average
> production costs. Also, larger firms have the benefit of being able

to specialise and target specific audiences through different channels, which is what the MBC has done.[56]

He also says his vision was always for the MBC Group to be run according to a decentralised organisational structure:

> I think my role right now is fading. It's not anymore the one man show that it was in the early '90s when we could see less than a metre in front of us. You know, I think today if there's anything I accomplished it's to have a system in place whether I'm there or not; what you see now is there forever. It's not anymore about me.[57]

Conclusion

Even though Walid al-Ibrahim proclaims a personal interest in 'progress and modernity', the socio-political pressures he faces in Saudi Arabia on behalf of MBC Group are such that his efforts are best understood in light of Abdullah Al-Ghathami's work on modernity and development in the kingdom. Given the tug-of-war between two opposing Saudi forces, reformists and traditionalists, it could be argued that launching MBC outside the kingdom may have freed it from the immediate control of conservative clerics who seek to maintain sovereignty for their traditionalist discourse and therefore reject dialogue with alternative modes and discourses. To some degree, therefore, MBC offered those alternatives. However, by operating abroad with non-Arab executives appointed to key positions, Sheikh Walid and MBC perpetuated a form of modernisation that Ghathami might see as incomplete because it is not entirely indigenous.

Sheikh Walid has taken risks outside the scope of those envisaged by Tunstall and Palmer in their work on media moguls in Europe. He has run the risk of death threats and fatwas from senior Saudi clerics. This is the kind of risk that has to be managed. In the absence of governmental or constitutional restraints on clerics, Walid al-Ibrahim has been forced at certain moments to declare his readiness to compromise over controversial programming. This could potentially be perceived as shirking the challenge of direct involvement in contentious social and cultural debates and even encouraging others to avoid them also. However, MBC's need to maximise audiences for the sake of advertising revenue is bound up with the level of risk that Walid al-Ibrahim is prepared to take. Hence, Ali Jaber's thesis is that Sheikh Walid is an institutional entrepreneur, who creates new institutional structures and handles things in new ways. In other words, MBC Group is a relatively complex high-tech Saudi-owned satellite network attempting to operate on capitalist principles in a pre-capitalist traditional society controlled unilaterally by holders of political and religious power. As such, it fits the kind of development that Ghathami describes as *tafra* (economic boom), whereby personal development is left behind and modernity is achieved more in appearance than reality.

8

Alwaleed bin Talal: Media Moguls and Media Capital

Marwan M. Kraidy

In *Playing to the World's Biggest Audience: The Globalization of Chinese Film and Television*, Michael Curtin develops his notion of media capital, inspired by work in cultural geography, to capture the complex interactions surrounding media industries in an era of increasing globalisation. As 'a concept that at once acknowledges the spatial logics of capital, creativity, culture, and polity without privileging one among the four,'[1] media capital enables an understanding of media industries that takes into account global structural forces while remaining sensitive to contextual variations. Arguing that media capital works in three ways, Curtin writes that 'the spatial dynamics of media capital have remained fairly consistent, playing a structuring role in the film and broadcasting industries since the early twentieth century [...] media capital operates according to (1) a logic of accumulation, (2) trajectories of creative migration, and (3) forces of sociocultural variation.'[2]

Although Curtin developed his media capital framework to ana-lyse the globalisation of television and film industries in Greater

China (People's Republic of China, Taiwan, Singapore and Hong Kong) in the late twentieth century, his approach could be helpful in understanding trends in the Arab media industries. In this chapter, I explore the notion that a defining feature of media moguls is their positioning at the intersection of processes inherent in Curtin's three-way logic of media capital. The chapter considers the case of Saudi royal prince and media mogul Alwaleed bin Talal, to explore how a media capital approach enables a new understanding of media moguldom. As is by now well-established, Saudi businessmen were pioneers in the Arab satellite television boom that started in the early 1990s, precisely because of their substantial financial clout and their proximity to political power, which allowed them to pursue accumulation unhindered by economic and political obstacles. Trajectories of creative migration, by which Curtin means the movement of skilled media workers across national boundaries and their concentration in geographical locations where media industries are particularly active, was also central to the rise of Saudi media moguls: media companies that became cornerstones of media empires presided over by moguls did not emerge in Riyadh or Jeddah, but in Rome (Orbit), London and Dubai (MBC and its 24-hour news arm, Al-Arabiya), Beirut and Cairo (Rotana).

Forces of socio-cultural variation, an umbrella concept under which Curtin includes both cultural resistance to foreign media and media policy and content regulation, have been a challenge to Saudi media moguls, especially to Alwaleed bin Talal, who is perceived in his own Saudi backyard as exceedingly liberal. Re-evaluating the notion of the 'Saudi–Lebanese connection',[3] this chapter explores how transnational links give media moguls considerable assets in overcoming what Curtin calls socio-cultural variation. Indeed, a combination of media capital accumulation and creative migration enabled moguls like Alwaleed to overcome, or at least manage, constraints imposed by the forces of socio-cultural variation peculiar to Saudi Arabia.

Accumulation and Creative Migration as Pursued by Alwaleed

Alwaleed bin Talal's peculiar parentage, business acumen, vast media holdings and social and political pronouncements make him arguably the most visible Arab media mogul of his generation, and one of a handful of globally influential media moguls. His father, Talal bin Abdel-Aziz Al Saud, advocated constitutional reforms in Saudi Arabia and rebelled against his brothers and cousins in the 1960s, briefly partaking in Nasser's radio campaign against the House of Saud. His mother, Mona al-Solh, is the daughter of independent Lebanon's first prime minister. Most importantly, unlike his numerous cousins, Alwaleed is an ambitious workaholic not content to live a life of passive luxury on a royal stipend.

Alwaleed moved into the media sector after establishing himself in other sectors, and ventured outside Saudi Arabia after building a strong operational base in the kingdom. Indeed, from relatively modest beginnings in Saudi real-estate development, Alwaleed rose to fame as the investor who rescued Citigroup in the 1990s, consolidated his grip over the Saudi media market, expanded his media holdings to a dominant position in the pan-Arab landscape, became a noted partner and trusted adviser and supporter of Rupert Murdoch, and emerged as a global spokesperson of the Saudi royal family during the Arab uprisings. The prince's fortune increased by 32 per cent in 2011 to US$22.9 billion, cementing his status as the wealthiest Arab, and putting him in 20th position among global billionaires.[4] Alwaleed bin Talal thus positioned himself as an always influential, sometimes decisive player at points of connection between global media and financial forces, pan-Arab media, business and political developments and national Arab polities, especially, although not exclusively, in Saudi Arabia, Egypt, Lebanon and, more recently, Bahrain.

Alwaleed's membership in the royal family of the Al Saud, and his direct ancestral line to the kingdom's founder, gave him the initial financial and political advantage with which to build a business foundation. After a start in construction, in 1993 Alwaleed's company, Kingdom Holding, bought two major Saudi companies and 30 per cent of Arab Radio and Television (ART), the latter for US$240 million. In 1994, Alwaleed bought 25 per cent of Euro Disney. In 1995, he bought 25 per cent of Rotana Audio Visual, 'the largest Saudi soundtrack and music producer',[5] 50 per cent of Silki La Silki (Wire and Wireless), a Saudi telecom company, and 3 per cent of Mediaset S.P.A, affiliate of Italian Fininvest, for more than US$100 million. This was followed in 1997 by acquisitions of stocks in Apple computers, Planet Hollywood, advertising giant Saatchi and Saatchi, Sony Entertainment, Netscape and – most famously – 5 per cent of Rupert Murdoch's News Corporation for US$400 million.[6]

In the following years, Alwaleed focused on building a horizontally and vertically integrated music television conglomerate that became akin to 'MTV, Atlantic Records, and Ticketmaster merged in one entity'.[7] To do this, the prince increased his stake in Rotana from 25 per cent in 1995 to 48 per cent in 2002 and again to 100 per cent in 2003.[8] He also bought ART's music channel and its vast Arabic music archive, which included 2,500 music videos and 5,000 recorded concerts. This enabled him to launch four specialised music channels under the name of Rotana, a company then reputedly worth less than US$1 billion.[9] The deal cemented Alwaleed's position as the dominant player in the pan-Arab music industry, a clout compounded by Rotana's exclusive production, distribution and marketing contracts with leading Arab singers. By the mid-2000s, Rotana had become a monopolistic giant in music and music video production, its roster encompassing leading Gulf, Egyptian and Lebanese stars.

On 8 August 2007, a Rotana press release featuring statements by Alwaleed bin Talal and LBC's Pierre Daher announced a merger with LBCSat. Daher is quoted saying that 'In today's media landscape only groups able to offer a comprehensive package of targeted channels to advertising markets are expected to grow [...] and we intend to be part of that growth.'[10] In the Saudi media, Alwaleed emphasised the merger's expected impact on social and cultural development and on propelling Arab media to an international standing.[11] In the following days, journalists stressed that the joint venture was less than an actual institutional merger, a 'moving in together' rather than a 'marriage', as a Lebanese advertising executive put it,[12] while the Lebanese leftist newspaper *Al-Akhbar* argued that the whole purpose of Rotana's announcement was to give Daher managerial leeway within Rotana.[13]

The global financial recession of late 2008 affected Alwaleed's behaviour in the Arab media sector. In the summer of 2009, production houses in Beirut that had for years churned out music videos for Rotana were complaining that, as one executive put it, 'Alwaleed pulled all his money out of the music video market', with devastating consequences in light of Rotana's size. The pressure of dwindling liquidity exacerbated tensions between Rotana and some of its rivals, with legal proceedings between Rotana and Alam El Phan in Cairo.[14] In the meantime, Rotana was bleeding talent, with numerous singers complaining about the company's alleged monopolistic practices and breaking or not renewing their contracts, encouraged by a trend of self-production and by the distribution and marketing opportunities afforded by the online media environment.[15] By late 2010, rumours increasingly suggested that Rotana was undergoing a deep restructuring and shutting down its Beirut offices.[16]

In spite of the financial crisis, Alwaleed increased his media holdings. In 2009, Alwaleed's share of Saudi Research and Marketing Group (SRMG), the mother company of the pan-Arab daily newspaper *Al-Sharq al-Awsat* and one of the largest Arab media companies, was reported to have risen to 35 per cent.[17] Alwaleed also grew closer to Rupert Murdoch and, by 2010, the Saudi prince and Australian tycoon were notable investors in each other's companies, with Alwaleed owning 7 per cent of News Corporation stock, worth around US$3 billion, and Murdoch owning 9 per cent of Rotana Group, worth around US$70 million. In December 2011, Alwaleed made a US$300 million investment in the San Francisco-based, micro-blogging company Twitter Inc. At the time, the company was valued at US$8.4 billion, making Alwaleed's stake about 3.6 per cent of the company.[18] Kingdom Holding sent a release to the media emphasising both the expected investment pay-off and the growing influence of Twitter, which had been touted as an important factor in the Arab uprisings that began in Tunisia in December 2010.

Alwaleed's logic of accumulation took full advantage of what Curtin labelled 'trajectories of creative migration'. It is now well-established that the growth of Arabic-language satellite television during the last two decades followed a peripatetic industry that first germinated in London and Rome, before sprouting in Dubai, Beirut, Cairo, Abu Dhabi, Riyadh and Manama.[19] In Curtin's framework, 'trajectories of creative migration' give 'access to reservoirs of specialised labour that replenish themselves on a regular basis, which is why media companies tend to cluster in particular cities'.[20] European capitals were attractive for several reasons, including their infrastructure, a concentration of specialised human resources, and distance from political interference. However, they were also more costly in terms of rent and salaries. By giving favourable operational terms and insulating media operations from direct political interference, the advent of media cities, especially in Dubai, attracted Arab media moguls back to the Arab world.

Alwaleed's expansion strategy took full advantage of the mobility of media labour and production within the Arab world. His initial partnership with Saleh Kamel, which launched Arab Radio and Television (ART) as a subsidiary of Arab Media Corporation, began broadcasting in Arabic and English, first from Fucino and then from Avezzano, Italy, in 1993. While based in Italy, ART was producing in Cairo, Beirut and Jeddah. After Alwaleed bin Talal bought ART's music archive in 2002 and launched Rotana in 2003, ART relocated to Jordan's Free Media City at a cost of US$8 million, paid by the Arab Media Holding Company.[21] Although Rotana's headquarters were initially in Riyadh, until 2008 production was centred in Lebanon, specifically in Naqqash (the location of Michel el-Murr's Studiovision), and to a lesser extent in Cairo, allowing it to sign the Lebanese and Egyptian pop singers who have traditionally dominated Arab airwaves and concert halls. In contrast to Saudi Arabian locations, Beirut provided a more liberal feel to Rotana programmes, which have systematically attempted to graft Arab sensibilities onto a Western style by including poetry programmes, announcing prayer times five times a day, and ordering video jockeys to dress conservatively during the holy month of Ramadan.[22]

With costs rising and security conditions declining, Beirut grew less desirable as a location for Rotana, which by 2008 had moved most of its production work to Cairo. Within a couple of years, plans for a 24-hour news channel called Al-Arab, a channel owned by Alwaleed but technically independent from both Kingdom Holding and Rotana, occupied the Arab press. To be headed by Jamal al-Khashoggi and headquartered in the Bahraini capital of Manama, Al-Arab had still not started normal broadcasting by late 2013, having officially deferred its launch to mid-2014. Nonetheless, it reflected Alwaleed's practice of capitalising on, or creating, felicitous synergies between his logic of accumulation and strategies of creative migration. Indeed, Bahrain's rulers offered such highly beneficial conditions, including rent-free facilities and US$15 million, that Alwaleed decided to move the headquarters for Rotana to Manama's Media City.[23]

Alwaleed and the Forces of Socio-Cultural Variation

Curtin understands 'forces of socio-cultural variation' to encompass a wide gamut of issues, including social values and cultural identities that in turn influence politics and shape policy at local and national levels. Curtin reminds us that '[n]ational and local institutions have remained significant actors despite the spatial tendencies of production and distribution'[24] which undergird the global and transnational scale of operations of contemporary media industries. Indeed, Curtin emphasises that social and cultural issues are often instrumentalised for political expediency. '[T]he forces of sociocultural variation', Curtin writes, 'were often influenced by assertions of political will, which no doubt is one of the reasons that Hollywood film companies go to such great lengths to present themselves as apolitical institutions.'[25]

The constellation of social, cultural, religious and political factors that constitute forces of socio-cultural variation in Saudi Arabia and the broader Arab world have often shaped Alwaleed's media operations. Saudi Arabia is a peculiar country, politically mediaeval, socially conservative and religiously strict. The country's regime, based on a foundational alliance between the Al-Saud clan of rulers and the Al-Shaykh family of religious clerics, has historically been sensitive to media and popular culture. Reactionary elements opposed photography and television, which were allowed only after decades of struggle and royal pressure to introduce them for modernisation purposes. Cinema remains a contested art in the kingdom, with Alwaleed himself spearheading efforts to develop a Saudi film industry.[26]

The prince's own cultural and political outlook has over the years been reflected in his media outlets, including Rotana and Al-Resalah, a hip, youth-oriented alternative to Iqraa and Al-Majd. This can be clearly seen in the programming content. *Rotana Café*, a daily hour-long programme, is a revealing example of Alwaleed's outlook. Showcasing a motley crew of Gulf and Levantine teenage hosts who casually discuss film, celebrity, music and fashion and provide general social commentary, the conversation is fuelled by calls from viewers, and set in a studio arranged as a coffee shop. The show reflects Alwaleed's liberal – in a Saudi context – leanings by featuring female presenters. Nonetheless, during the Holy Month of Ramadan the hosts' dress and song selections take a decisively more conservative turn, and prayer times are announced during the programme. As such, Rotana is typical of an Alwaleed media operation, overall staying within the socio-political bounds of the Saudi mainstream while introducing new elements from both the global media industry and global youth culture to lure audiences.[27]

Nonetheless, Alwaleed's increasing prominence and ever closer association with LBCSat (discussed in the following pages) was becoming a liability *vis-à-vis* conservative Saudi elements. The reality television controversies of the mid-2000s generated hostile pronouncements and fatwas (religious rulings) that sometimes included clear, if not explicitly phrased, criticism of Alwaleed. It was perhaps to fend off such criticisms that Alwaleed launched Al-Resalah. Established in 2006 with a youth focus as part of the Rotana network,[28] its programming grid mixes films, music, talk shows and prayer, striking a balance between hipness and morality. In a press release, Tarek al-Suwaidan, the channel's general manager at the time, said that 40 per cent of the programmes would be youth-oriented, 30 per cent would target women and families, and 10 per cent would focus on children. The cartoons are produced in Turkey, Egypt and Jordan. Alwaleed made the channel's priority to present 'Arab heritage through a modern medium' and to counteract the misconceptions of Islam in other societies, with al-Suwaidan stating that the channel was part and parcel of the prince's 'mission to serve Islam and to change the ideas of the youth about terrorism'.[29] Like some of Rotana's programmes, Al-Resalah is positioned as a bridge between East and West.[30] As such, it fits Alwaleed's agenda to help bring about a more fashionable, flexible and 'moderate' Islam, and reflected the use of his media empire to promote his own socio-cultural variation for Saudi society.

Thus, the forces of socio-cultural variation impinging on Alwaleed, as well as the opportunities for him to circumvent constraints, are jointly manifest in the Saudi–Lebanese connection, especially with Saudi involvement in LBC. Indeed, Saudi moguls have been major investors in LBC since the company launched a satellite channel in 1996. Saleh Kamel initially owned 49 per cent of the shares of LBCSat, but his involvement did not endure, precisely because of what Curtin called forces of socio-cultural variation. Ostensibly, Kamel's personal religious convictions made him ambivalent about his stake in the socially-liberal and Christian-managed Lebanese channel. When an interviewer asked Kamel how he reconciled his 'dedication to Islamic principles' with his 'investment in LBC', Kamel equivocated:

> Our investment in LBC involves the delivery system; we are not responsible for content. Whoever subscribes to it does so of his own free will. We have, nevertheless, *been able to influence the*

*choice of programming at LBC, especially that having to do with
their aims concerning the Islamic faith* [emphasis added].[31]

Before long, Alwaleed acquired Kamel's shares in LBC, and exploited this
investment to circumvent the constraints of Saudi conservatism, leverag-
ing LBC's liberal ethos for the prince's commercial and political agendas.

When in 2000 Alwaleed paid US$100 million to acquire Kamel's
shares in LBCSat, he benefitted the Lebanese company commercially, by
flushing it with liquidity, and politically, due to his excellent relationship
with then Lebanese President Emile Lahoud, a Lebanese client of Syria's
Assad, which made LBC less vulnerable to Syrian intervention and
Lebanese censorship. Coming on the heels of multiple media ventures
by Alwaleed, the transaction also confirmed the Saudi prince as a major
player in Arab media industries.

Depicting himself as a 'Muslim businessman' – a strategic rhetorical
arrow lobbed at the heart of Saudi 'socio-cultural variation' – Alwaleed
also regularly reminds his interlocutors of his commitment to Lebanon
and the Lebanese.[32] Half-Lebanese by birth (through his mother), the
prince acquired Lebanese citizenship and regularly made rhetorical
interventions in Lebanese public discourse, often to criticise Hariri's
economic policies. For a while, this fuelled a rumour that the prince
was interested in the Lebanese prime minstership, which, following
Lebanese political tradition, is usually reserved for a Sunni Muslim.
Alwaleed's portfolio of Lebanese media encompasses interests in Murr
Television (MTV) and the *Al-Nahar* newspaper, among others.

LBCSat's decision to add Saudi media personalities and Saudi programmes to its schedule attracted negative attention, with one media
critic, for example, chiding LBCSat for airing a Saudi version of the US
comedic ambush show *Candid Camera*, which he described as 'primi-
tive', 'incoherent', 'devoid of ideas' and featuring 'poor acting'.[33] As a
result, the media critic argued, LBCSat harmed its own reputation by
not contributing to an improvement in the quality of Gulf productions,
while trying to define itself as 'more Saudi than MBC'.[34]

Important 'forces of socio-cultural variation' were behind the increasing imbrication of Saudi interests and agendas in Lebanese media. These forces include the USA–UK invasion of Iraq and the geopolitical shifts it created, most notably a scrambling of the power equation between Iran and Saudi Arabia as Iraqi Shia ascended to power at the expense of their Sunni compatriots. The effect of the invasion in terms of the peculiar dynamics of conservative versus liberal politics in Saudi Arabia could be seen in the summer of 2004, when Saudi authorities contacted LBC, asking the channel to feature Muhammad Hussain Fadlallah, the now-deceased Lebanese Shia *marjaa al-taqlid* [source of emulation], who would then, upon the Saudi authorities' urging, call upon Saudi Shia to remain peaceful and not follow in the militant footsteps of their co-religionists in Iraq. Through the convoluted Saudi–Lebanese connection, Saudi princes who rule in the name of Sunni Wahhabiyya were able to circumvent forces of socio-cultural variation by asking a Christian Lebanese channel to feature a Shia Lebanese religious scholar to appease Saudi Shia.[35]

Such byzantine manoeuvres are needed because of the fierce battle between liberals and conservatives in Saudi Arabia and because of the royal family's precarious balancing role in that conflict. Because LBCSat is nominally a Lebanese channel with a history of Christian ownership, it could host the prominent Lebanese Shia cleric and his message of 'peace' addressed to Saudi Shias, without provoking the ire of Saudi Sunni clerics, who hold sway over the Kingdom's domestic media and are loath to provide a platform for a leading Shia figure. Tawfiq Rabahi, a media critic for *Al-Quds al-Arabi*, captured the roundabout communication practices of the Saudi elite without mentioning LBC by name:

> To break the chains imposed by religious institutions, the Saudi approach relies on channels of foreign origin but of Saudi affiliation, the most prominent of which is a Lebanese channel that manages the scheduling and content of its programs according to Saudi timing. Here Saudis, hosts and participants, say what is prohibited in their country's channels because of the power of

religious groups, or maybe because the ruling institution hides behind the putative power of these groups.[36]

The author went on to call LBC's hiring of Saudi film maker Haifa Mansour in April 2007 to host a show a 'taboo breaker', through which LBC 'prepared a 100 per cent Saudi dish on Lebanese land, out of the reach of the Commission to Promote Virtue and Combat Vice',[37] the feared Saudi religious police. Replaying a role the Lebanese press performed in the 1970s and 1980s, when it provided a pulpit for many Arab dissenters, Lebanese satellite channels today provide a platform for various Arab 'reformers'. 'The difference now', Rabahi wrote ominously, 'is that both the Saudi government and the opposition practice reform from the outside', through channels like LBC.[38]

Saudi Arabia has long supported the Sunni community in Lebanon, represented at the highest political level in the office of prime minister, a post by tradition reserved for a Sunni. Saudi interest and involvement in Lebanese affairs has grown tremendously over recent years, in parallel with the tightening Saudi–Lebanese connection in the media industry. On 5 July 2008, Alwaleed bin Talal increased his stake in LBCSat to 'more than 85 per cent and less than 90'.[39] Growing Saudi involvement in Lebanon cannot be reduced simply to the kingdom's desire to protect the Sunni community there; if this were the case, the Saudis would be involved in Iraqi politics in the same way, which they are not. Rather, as leading historian of Saudi Arabia, Madawi al-Rasheed, argued in *Al-Quds al-Arabi*:

> [Lebanon] is an intermediary on which Saudi Arabia relies in various fields, a role that no other Arab country, large or small, is able to play. Lebanon, state and people, plays this role in different realms including culture, media, politics, economics, and even religion.[40]

As a tourist destination, Lebanon 'provides Saudi Arabia a social and entertainment space, a mediator between internal Saudi isolation and external Western openness'.[41] In addition, Lebanese historians, journalists and media institutions were historically able to promote Saudi agendas, regionally and internationally, and in several languages. As Al-Rasheed proceeds to explain, various Saudi 'reform' projects about hot-button issues such as women, religion and politics (discussion of which does not exist in Saudi media) find their way to the Saudi sphere through the Lebanese intercessor, which helps mitigate the impact of domestic socio-cultural variations peculiar to the Saudi environment.[42] Thus, the author argues:

> [Television] programs that focus on the internal Saudi situation have become a Lebanese specialty, while (many) Saudis are kept away from these dialogues by the state. The Saudi person comes to this open, Saudi-owned, media space, carrying his concerns, sharing his private life and the secrets of his society with a Lebanese dialogue partner, on screens that appear to be Lebanese though in fact they are Saudi in both inclination and ownership.[43]

Since the assassination of Rafik Hariri in 2005, the Saudis have expanded their influence in Lebanon by backing the March 14 political block, led by the Future Movement (founded by Hariri), in its confrontation with the Hezbollah-led March 8 coalition. Concurrently, Alwaleed has boosted his share in LBCSat, which he now controls, as Pierre Daher remains engaged in a protracted battle with Samir Geagea, the leader of the Lebanese Forces, who founded LBC in the 1980s and has been attempting to regain the channel.

The global financial crisis that began in late 1998 had a major impact on Alwaleed's media empire, including its Lebanese components. *Al-Nahar*, Lebanon's veteran daily, owned by the Tueini family, in addition to Alwaleed, faced a severe crisis and initiated deep cuts, which entailed laying off more than 50 members of staff.[44] As the crisis spread to other media outlets, including Murr Television and LBC, in which Alwaleed had a stake, one newspaper published an article in which it compared *Al-Nahar*'s problems spreading to other institutions to 'influenza'.[45] It soon became apparent that the layoffs had been driven by Alwaleed's cost cutting at his Rotana conglomerate after his Kingdom Holding Company incurred losses in the global financial markets, and that the prince was interested in bringing in his old friend Rupert Murdoch as an investor in Rotana.

Mediating between Global Capital and National Media

Using Curtin's media capital framework, this chapter has attempted to understand a prominent Arab media mogul at the intersection of logics of accumulation, trajectories of creative migration, and forces of socio-cultural variation. Over the years, Alwaleed bin Talal has used his vast cash reserves, global connections and political status to expand his business empire (including his vast media holdings) across national boundaries and media platforms. Through business acquisitions, partnerships with global and local players, and a willingness to extract creative media labour at the best price and under the best conditions from different Arab countries at different times, Alwaleed's case illuminates what it means to be an Arab media mogul.

The partnership between LBCSat, Rotana and News Corporation is a telling example of how a local sectarian outlet has shifted to being a national television station, then morphed into a major pan-Arab channel, attracting Saudi audiences and investors, including Alwaleed, who eventually bent LBC to his business strategy to attract global investors like Murdoch. Indeed, this can be viewed as a microcosm of the local–regional–global entanglements of Arab television. As Curtin put it:

> on the one hand capital must concentrate and integrate sites of production to reduce the amount of time and resources expended in manufacture, and on the other hand it must increase the speed of distribution to reduce the time it takes to bring distant locales into the orbit of its operations. These centripetal tendencies in the sphere of production and centrifugal tendencies in

distribution were observed by Karl Marx more than a century ago when he trenchantly explained that capital must 'annihilate space with time' if it is to overcome barriers to accumulation [...] [E]ven though a film or TV program may be founded with the aim of serving particular national cultures and local markets, it must over time redeploy its creative resources and reshape its terrain of operations if it is to survive competition and enhance profitability.[46]

Most importantly for our discussion, the fact that Alwaleed bin Talal is the linchpin of such a national–regional–global partnership highlights the importance of Arab media tycoons as mediators between global capital and national media, and this mogul's particularly developed ability to take advantage of the time–space dynamics described by Curtin above.

Nonetheless, even a financially dominant and politically connected media mogul like Alwaleed will encounter resistance when venturing outside of Saudi Arabia, and the ensuing struggles are revealing of media moguls' twinned business and political considerations. From the beginning, Alwaleed's Lebanese ventures were not trouble-free:[47] in the late 1990s, the prince lost a legal battle over shares in Al-Sayyad publishing group with its owners, the Frayhas. The more recent spat between Alwaleed and LBCI CEO Pierre Daher had business and political ingredients. In terms of business, with Alwaleed controlling LBCSat and production house PAC and Daher controlling LBCI and maintaining some influence over PAC employees, the two found themselves fighting over ownership of specific programmes, including the highly lucrative *Star Academy*.[48] Politically, it is interesting to observe that tensions between the two men increased dramatically after Samir Geagea, leader of the Lebanese Forces and recently a legal foe of Daher over the control of LBCI, visited Saudi Arabia to bolster his political domestic status in Lebanon and undoubtedly to seek financial support from the kingdom's ruler. It is also important to mention in that regard Geagea was firmly ensconced in March 14, the Hariri-led, Saudi-funded and Saudi-supported Lebanese political coalition, whereas Daher was increasingly seen to be closer to Michel Aoun's Free Patriotic Movement, whose alliance with Hezbollah created the foundation of the Iran-supported March 8 political block in Lebanon. On balance, Alwaleed's continued involvement in this Saudi–Lebanese connection appears to have brought the prince more benefits than handicaps.

Alwaleed's decision to move Rotana headquarters to Manama and base his Al-Arab news channel in the Bahraini capital also has clear political overtones. It arose against a background of Saudi troops having entered Bahrain in 2011 under the Peninsula Shield Gulf Security Council arrangement, and the Saudi royal family providing aggressive support to Bahrain's Sunni royal family. As one Lebanese journalist wrote of Alwaleed's decision, 'The Saudi tycoon expands his business with a news channel planted in the Bahraini wound.'[49] The move looked like a masterful convergence of Alwaleed's own business interests with the national interest of Saudi Arabia. Although he has had no qualms about building his media empire on the backs of Egyptian, Lebanese, Kuwaiti and other Arabs, Alwaleed has recently emerged as a high-profile backer of Saudi-isation, even supporting a new regulatory regime in Saudi Arabia that imposes financial penalties on companies who employ more foreigners than Saudis.[50] The prince's vocal support of Saudiisation reveals an important feature of this powerful Arab media mogul – that no matter how global his profile, transnational his outlook, and pan-Arab his customers, his fealty to the Saudi nation state and the royal family of which he is part is a paramount consideration. The case of Alwaleed tells us that financial clout and political connections notwithstanding, media moguls have to remain loyal citizens to their nation states to continue to thrive. To conclude, with Curtin, that '[t]he centripetal and centrifugal tendencies of media capital unfolded within the context of national broadcasting systems, allowing the state to exercise influence over flows of information and culture in public as well as private contexts'[51] enables us to think of media moguls as national agents in addition to being businessmen and political players.

9

Tarek Ben Ammar:
The Networked Entrepreneur

Donatella Della Ratta

'The ultimate networker in an industry founded on personal relationships, discreet backroom deals and a capillary system of famous names.'[1] This is how the *Financial Times* portrayed Tarek Ben Ammar, the Franco-Tunisian entrepreneur who started working as a film producer by 'literally renting sand to Hollywood'[2] and later succeeded in attracting to his home country, Tunisia, the filming of US or US-distributed movies such as Monty Python's *Life of Brian* and George Lucas' *Star Wars*.

From the start of his decades-long career to the Tunisian uprising in 2010–11, Ben Ammar produced more than 70 feature films. Yet his prominent position in global media industries during the latter part of that period was mostly due to the key role he played as personal advisor to multibillionaires such as Rupert Murdoch and Silvio Berlusconi. Ben Ammar's financial assets, estimated in 2006 at up to €550 million[3] (US$726 million), pale in comparison with the wealth amassed by those whose money he has helped to invest. For example, according to Prince Alwaleed bin Talal, *Forbes* underestimated Alwaleed's fortune by US$9.6

billion when they put it at up to US$20 billion in March 2013.[4] Ben Ammar's real assets, in contrast, can be located in the extensive network of personal relationships that he cultivated with moguls, politicians and financiers over several decades, capitalising on what the Italian financial daily *Il Sole 24ore* dubbed the 'art'[5] of creating connections. This definition matches Ben Ammar's own description of himself: 'I am an adviser to a few big boys who couldn't solve their problems through the big investment banks.'[6] 'It's easy for them [the moguls] to deal with other moguls through me directly.'[7]

By looking at his personal and professional biography and his way of conducting financial deals and planning business strategies across multiple territories and industries, this chapter agrees with Tarek Ben Ammar's own assessment, quoted above, that he does not correspond to the mogul as defined by Tunstall and Palmer.[8] Nor can he be described as a 'baron',[9] in Tunstall and Palmer's sense of a competent executive who is loyal to the supreme leader, and who might be eligible as the mogul's successor. Both definitions, in fact, refer to preindustrial institutions, recalling a sense of absolute power combined with an eccentric, unpredictable behaviour from the mogul[10] and implying obedience and a type of feudal loyalty from the baron. Instead, the present research attempts to read Ben Ammar's personal and professional biography in light of the idea of a modern entrepreneur as described by Joseph Schumpeter[11] – that is to say, somebody who carries out a creative act that drives economic development and growth, yet not necessarily generating profit in the short term. Discussing Schumpeter's definition of enterprise, Hans Landström, quoting Richard Swedberg's work on entrepreneurship, stresses that:

> entrepreneurs are characterized by the desire to found private kingdoms, the will to conquer, and the joy of creating, or in more modern parlance [...] (i) the desire for power and independence, (ii) the will to succeed, and (iii) the satisfaction of getting things done – money *per se* is not the driving force behind the entrepreneur.[12]

In Schumpeter's view, in fact, economic development is driven not by capital accumulation but rather by innovations, described by the Austrian-born economist in terms of 'new combinations', meaning 'a new product, process, or method of production; a new market or source of supply; a new form of commercial, business, or financial organisation'.[13] The entrepreneur is the one who carries out these 'new combinations we call "enterprise"'.[14] Ben Ammar's dealings fit with those of the Schumpeterian entepreneur who is able to bring new combinations into a business. However, Ben Ammar is also a networked entepreneur, in the sense of operating in the context of a 'networked economy'[15] where productivity is generated by a global web of interactions among several business networks and where the capacity to expand one's network and exponentially link it to others becomes a key asset.

'New Combinations' for Old Media Patterns

This chapter argues that Tarek Ben Ammar has introduced the Schumpeterian 'new combinations' in a variety of domains, from film making to financing and banking activities. It explores the Franco-Tunisian entrepreneur's innovative strategy of buying up non-core assets from mergers and acquisition deals in order to create new transnational media businesses in the Euro-Arab audiovisual market,[16] by reference to specific cases selected from Ben Ammar's media portfolio. Examples include the purchase of Italian television channels, Europa TV and Prima TV, following Murdoch's investment in Italy's audio-visual market in the early 2000s. The analysis will reflect on this business method and attempt to read it in light of the political and economic framework that helped to shape Ben Ammar's rise. It will discuss his activities as a networked entrepreneur, connecting people and providing them with business platforms and products to connect and reconnect in the framework of a global, networked economy.

Despite these innovative features, however, in some other ways Ben Ammar's strategy does not appear novel. Indeed, his method of using the mergers and acquisitions that he himself facilitated and oversaw in order to buy up non-core assets involved in the 'production, distribution, exhibition, and sale of a single type of media product'[17] can equally be seen as part of a vertical integration process that is very traditional in the media business. In the early 1990s a belief existed that the increasing accessibility of information technology would accelerate vertical disintegration, bringing more flexibility and pluralism to the media sector.[18] Yet, even if mass diffusion of the internet and new media technologies seemed at times to have lessened the importance of specific audio-visual delivery platforms,[19] being in control of distribution channels still appears to be key in contemporary media industries.[20] The development of such control over the past decade has proved to what extent 'integration and globalization'[21] are still the dominant forces shaping the media landscape. As economist Eli Noam has underlined, the trend to expand vertically in media industries has been consolidated by the 'relaxation of regulatory restrictions' at work in the new millennium, and boosted by emerging possibilities to create 'new synergies' within a vertically integrated company. That is to say, there are 'cross-business opportunities' whereby one part of a business can be used to 'promote or benefit from another'.[22] The 'economic dynamics of digital media'[23] show that the concentration trend is on the rise even within this emerging sector, and proves that the sentence once pronounced by media mogul Ted Turner remains valid: 'Today, the only way for media companies to survive is to own everything up and down the media chain [...] Big media today wants to own the faucet, pipeline, water, and the reservoir.'[24] Within this perspective, Ben Ammar's innovative business method has been applied in a context where the traditional strategy of 'creating a small, vertically integrated media company'[25] is still key.

With this in mind, the aim is to reflect upon the features of Tarek Ben Ammar as a globally-connected, networked entrepreneur introducing new combinations to audio-visual business in the Euro-Arab area, while at the same time underlining how these new combinations emerge in parallel with and *because of* the consolidation of the traditional, vertical integration process in global media industries. This confirms an ownership pattern where power and control stay firmly in the hands of a few moguls, often linked together in stable alliances by mutual interests, personal friendships, business and family ties. In this context, Ben Ammar's role as a people connector and mogul networker helps to strengthen these ties.

The analysis entails a focus on Nessma TV, the Tunisian television channel owned by Ben Ammar in partnership with media mogul Silvio Berlusconi and local businessmen Nebil and Ghazi Keroui. The joint media project is examined chronologically, from its launch with the support of former president Ben Ali until the ousting of the latter's regime, which resulted in a reshaping of the channel's identity and its politics. The examination is framed in a wider regional and cross-regional perspective, where both Nessma TV and Ben Ammar's acquisition of Egyptian TV channel ONTV in 2012 hint at his ambitious project of creating a joint North African–Egyptian conglomerate that, linked to his European assets located in France and Italy, would counterbalance the Gulf's hegemony over Arab media and generate a self-sustaining Euro-Arab audio-visual network.

Personal Connections and a 'Boutique' Advisory Company

When once interviewed by Bloomberg news agency, Tarek Ben Ammar claimed that 'two things have won him clients and made him rich: connections and coincidence'.[26] Yet there is no coincidence in the fact that connections, a key concept underlying Ben Ammar's striking career in media, financing and investment banking, form the very basis of the modern 'networked economy'.[27] Being born into the Bourguiba family, which gave Tunisia its first post-independence president, Habib, Ben Ammar had connections by default. His father was ambassador to Italy, which granted Ben Ammar the opportunity to grow up between two continents, Europe and Africa, and to speak several different languages

(Italian, French, English and his native Arabic). Furthermore, Ben Ammar's education was truly multi-faith and multi-cultural. He was raised by a Muslim father and a Catholic mother of Corsican descent, and married a Catholic Pole. When in Rome, he attended an American Catholic high school. He then moved across the Atlantic to get his degree at Georgetown University, the oldest Catholic and Jesuit institution of higher education in the USA.[28]

This background granted Ben Ammar direct access to many prominent, wealthy families in the Arab world, including Saudi princes. Prince Talal bin Abdel-Aziz, father of Prince Alwaleed bin Talal, was very close to the Bourguibas, which is how the young Tarek first met one of the most valuable names to be added later to his business portfolio. His family connections also played a major role in his decision to invest in the film business in Tunisia, a sector that was not organised as an industry in 1974, when he first built a film studio called Carthago Films. 'Though I was still a young man without a big reputation in the film business, I had access, thanks to my family, to some of the most important people in this region',[29] Ben Ammar revealed to *Screen International*. His early interest in the movie industry was consolidated through a strategy that first consisted of making Tunisia a film destination for Hollywood directors in search of cheap, exotic locations for their movies. Working with directors such as George Lucas on *Star Wars* and Steven Spielberg on *Raiders of the Lost Ark* eventually opened the doors to big studios and to the wealthy financiers behind them. At this point, Ben Ammar understood the strategic importance of financing in the film business. 'I learned that financing is really the center. You get people together and instead of doing a movie you do deals. I became an adviser, an investment banker, and I learned financing.'[30]

The focus on financing lies at the core of Ben Ammar's business strategy. In keeping with the Schumpeterian 'new combination', the mix of high finance, film production and investment banking, framed in a complex nexus of personal connections with global moguls like Murdoch and Berlusconi, was truly unprecedented in the Euro-Arab area. Ben Ammar's intuition was to understand that, in 'a European financial world dominated by family-held companies and Byzantine alliances that Wall Street investment banks find hard to penetrate',[31] personal connections would be at the core of the business. Hence, in 1989 he launched, in association with Silvio Berlusconi, his boutique investment business Quinta Communications S.A., linking his passion for the media industry to financing. This small firm would provide advisory services to media groups, and be a consultant on investments, mergers and acquisitions. At the time of their first meeting, in 1983, Berlusconi was a powerful businessman and the owner of Italy's first private national television network, which was made up of three channels – Canale 5, Italia 1, and Rete 4 – which had *de facto* broken the state television's monopoly on nationwide television broadcasting. The channels were legalised in 1984, thanks to an emergency decree passed by Bettino Craxi, secretary-general of the Italian Socialist Party, Italy's prime minister from 1983 until 1987 and a politician with strong ties to Berlusconi. Berlusconi introduced Craxi to Ben Ammar and new financial bonds and political alliances were formed between Tunisia and Italy. Berlusconi and Ben Ammar started working together producing television mini series' until they launched Quinta Communications S.A., headquartered in Paris.[32] The former Italian prime minister's holding company, Fininvest Spa, still owns a 22 per cent stake in this.[33]

Because of its emphasis on personal connections, boutique advice plays a strategic role in global finance and media industries. Speaking of Ben Ammar, media mogul Rupert Murdoch has been quoted as noting: 'He knows more people than investment banks do [...] It's not hard to call up a big bank – they all love your business – but someone telling you who to trust? He's extremely valuable as a negotiator.'[34] Ben Ammar's talent in this domain has pushed several big names to ask for his advice in investment and financial deals. In 1997, Prince Alwaleed's US$400 million investment in Murdoch's News Corp was reportedly Ben Ammar's brainchild. Similarly, two years before, the Franco-Tunisian businessman had convinced the Saudi billionaire to buy stakes in

Berlusconi's media group Mediaset for US$100 million. In total, during 1995, Ben Ammar helped to arrange US$1 billion of investments in Mediaset, including purchases by another media magnate, the German Leo Kirch.[35]

Sometimes Ben Ammar has worked to advise two different parties in related business transactions – something he apparently never regarded as a conflict of interest – as when he advised Murdoch on a US$1.4 billion investment in Kirch's pay-TV unit in 1999. In the same year, Ben Ammar says, Kirch paid him to put together a US$1.3 billion investment in KirchMedia GmbH by Lehman Brothers Holdings, Alwaleed, Berlusconi and others.[36]

Probably the most profitable business deal Ben Ammar facilitated during his career was the acquisition of Italian pay-TV platforms Telepiù (owned by French group Vivendi Universal) and Stream (owned by Italian telecommunications company Telecom Italia) on behalf of Murdoch, which was instrumental in granting the Australian-born magnate a monopoly over the Italian satellite market. It took Ben Ammar three years, from 2000 to 2003, to broker a deal worth US$7 to US$8 billion, for which Murdoch's News Corp paid less than US$1 billion.[37] At present, Sky Italia controls the Italian satellite market, with over 5 million subscribers.

The success of the Sky Italia deal opened the doors to a new business for Ben Ammar, in the form of national television broadcasting. He purchased the frequencies of two Italian television channels from News Corp, which had to sell them in order to obtain anti-trust regulatory approval to finalise the merger between Telepiù and Stream. The French media group TF1 later acquired 49 per cent of both television stations, Europa TV and Prima TV. The first, despite being originally licensed to provide only encrypted television services, was turned into a free-to-air terrestrial and satellite sport channel, Sportitalia, after Ben Ammar successfully used his political connections in Italy to obtain a new decree allowing him to convert the pay-TV licence into a licence for free-to-air TV. The controversial law was issued in 2004 by Maurizio Gasparri, at the time Minister of Communications of the second Berlusconi-led government, which lasted for five years, until April 2005. Today, Sportitalia provides three digital terrestrial free-to-air sport channels, initially distributed by Murdoch's Sky Italia platform, and now handled by Telecom Italia Media Broadcasting, whose ownership can be tracked back to Telecom Italia, the Italian incumbent telecommunications company where Ben Ammar holds the official position of member of the board.[38]

Prima TV, the second Italian channel he acquired, controls Dfree,[39] a digital multiplex distributing a variety of premium movie channels produced by Mediaset-controlled RTI. In December 2012 Prima TV acquired the private Egyptian channel ONTV,[40] formerly owned by another wealthy Arab entrepreneur, Naguib Sawiris, an Egyptian Copt who became a prominent player in the Italian business scene in 2006 when he purchased Wind, a national telecommunications company. The ONTV acquisition was the latest addition to Prima TV's rich media portfolio, which could by then already rely on a strong multi-territory distribution arm including Italian film distributor Eagle Pictures and Tunisian private channel Nessma TV, Ben Ammar's first ever investment in his native country's television broadcast business.

Nessma TV: Political Ambitions and the Dream of a Grand Maghreb

In their analysis of media moguls, Tunstall and Palmer shed light on a very important aspect of moguldom, namely the close link between moguls and politics. On the one hand, a mogul might try to influence national politics by exploiting his media power; on the other, he can opt for a direct political involvement in return of some sort of (legal, economic) support to run his business.[41] However, Tarek Ben Ammar's case seems to move away from this pattern, at least where his native Tunisia is concerned. During his career, in fact, the entrepreneur has been much more actively involved politically in Italy, a country where he holds the key position of board member in important institutions such as the telecommunications company Telecom Italia and Mediobanca, a leading investment bank. Despite claiming to have only one goal in mind, namely to 'develop a veritable industry of the seventh art in his country',[42] Ben Ammar has lived most of his life outside Tunisia, particularly in France where, in 1985, he went into exile with his family when his aunt was repudiated by her husband, former president Habib Bourguiba. Later in his career he was harshly criticised by several Tunisian film makers for never producing any Tunisian-made films.[43] Yet Ben Ammar has publicly declared that he invested in his country in a different way, by giving it 'a name, a brand, a label'[44] in order to attract foreign investments.

In 2008 Tarek Ben Ammar seemed to have slightly revised this strategy of avoiding political involvement in Tunisia. A policy of a more direct commitment in his country's media scene was inaugurated with the acquisition of a 25 per cent share in Nessma TV (meaning 'gentle breeze' in Arabic), a private Tunisian entertainment channel launched in 2007 by Nebil and Ghazi Keroui, two Tunisian businessmen who had worked in the advertising sector since 1996.[45] Ben Ammar had convinced his long-time business partner and friend Silvio Berlusconi to have his media group, Mediaset, acquire another 25 per cent share in the channel. The remaining 50 per cent was left to the original owners, the Keroui brothers. Both Ben Ammar and Mediaset agreed to buy shares in a capital increase operation: the acquisition, supported by a €5 million investment from each side,[46] was announced on 21 May 2008 at the Cannes Film Festival.[47] At the time of the launch, Mediaset chairman Fedele Confalonieri declared: 'We have in southern Europe ten million immigrants arriving from this region [...] This channel will allow them to feel less uprooted living in our countries.'[48] On his website, Ben Ammar described Nessma TV as having 'the ambition to become the channel of the tolerant Maghreb countries'.[49]

However, rather than a mere joint Tunisian–Italian commercial media venture with half-hearted cultural aspirations, Nessma TV seemed to become the expression of a wider network of political alliances with different private interests and businesses at stake. Berlusconi was offered the deal not simply for his talent in launching successful private media ventures in Italy, experience that could have been an asset in establishing Nessma's brand as a commercially-oriented entertainment channel. Being a powerful politician, at the time leading the Italian government for his fourth term in office, the Italian magnate had strong international leverage and an expanded network of political and business ties. Berlusconi's long-time friend Ben Ammar apparently used these ties to get Ben Ali's green light for Nessma TV to gain official status in Tunisia; until presidential approval was received on 20 March 2009, the station had operated without a licence. For his part, Ben Ali was in constant need of international support for his regime, and Italy had been a long-time political ally since the 1980s. In 1987, when Ben Ali seized power through a bloodless coup that deposed Bourguiba, Bettino Craxi was the first international politician to officially recognise his legitimacy. Some rumours at the time even suggested that former prime minister Craxi played an active role in the transfer of power.[50]

Many journalists and media experts agree that Ben Ammar convinced Ben Ali that Tunisia's international alliances could be strengthened through media, as a way to help the country gain a more prominent role within the Euro-Mediterranean area and attract foreign investment.[51] Nebil Keroui describes his own attempts to find partners with international leverage, such as Ben Ammar and Berlusconi, as directed to 'protect Nessma from Ben Ali and his arbitrariness in dealing with media'.[52] As for Berlusconi, he probably wanted 'just to do a favour to a longtime friend',[53] perhaps as a form of payback for Ben Ammar's proven loyalty and the many business deals that he had helped the Italian mogul to secure during his career.

However, the Ben Ammar–Ben Ali–Berlusconi connection suggests something more complex than these quite evident mutual benefits. In June 2009, the Libyan investment company Lafitrade Holding BV, based in the Netherlands but owned by the state-controlled Libyan Arab Foreign Investment Company (LAFICO),[54] acquired a 10 per cent stake in

Tarek Ben Ammar's Quinta Communications, approximately 22 per cent of which is held by 'a Luxembourg-registered investment company owned by the Berlusconi family investment vehicle, Fininvest'.[55] As a result of this financial operation, Berlusconi, at the time serving as Italian prime minister, openly engaged in a private business with another head of state, albeit through subsidiary companies. Despite joint attempts by Ben Ammar[56] and Berlusconi's PR offices to stress that 'there are no relations whatsoever between the prime minister and the business group he created with President Qaddafi or with the Libyan state',[57] many details suggested a close political and financial cooperation between the two leaders, facilitated by Ben Ammar.

The Franco-Tunisian entrepreneur, in fact, was referred to as the main mastermind[58] behind a new political and financial alliance between Italy and Libya, inaugurated with the signature of the Treaty on Friendship, Partnership and Cooperation, formalised in Benghazi on August 2008. The agreement acknowledged Italy's responsibilities during the colonial period in Libya and agreed to pay compensation to the tune of €5 billion for the loss and damages inflicted on the country. In exchange, Libya undertook to toughen its security measures in order to fight illegal immigration coming into Europe from its shores, boost investments in Italian companies, and help Italian enterprises in establishing their businesses in Libya. However, even prior to the agreement, Libya already had a number of relevant investments in Italian companies, including prominent banking group Unicredit[59] and Finmeccanica, Italy's largest defence company.[60] For his part, Berlusconi exploited the Libya treaty for the benefit of his domestic political strategy. For example, he backed the candidature of Impregilo, an Italian building group, to win the bid to lead a billion-dollar construction project for a coastal highway in Libya. At the time, the group was managed by Massimo Ponzellini,[61] politically affiliated to Berlusconi's closest ally in the government, the Lega Nord Party.

As for Nessma TV's role as a tool of political liaison between the Italian and Libyan leaders, in August 2009, just one year after the treaty,

Berlusconi stopped at the channel's studios during a visit to Tunisia to record a 40-minute exclusive interview covering many topics, from immigration to media. Speaking of Libya and the friendship treaty, he won the studio audience's applause by declaring 'I did not apologise; I asked, in front of the Libyan Parliament, to be excused for having oppressed free people as the Libyans are, something that we shall not accept or replicate in the future.'[62] In the same interview, he also paid tribute to Ben Ali, whom he described as 'a true friend [...] and a real democrat.'[63] In light of these connections it is no coincidence that Nessma TV was the only channel to get an exclusive interview with Qaddafi immediately after he gave a speech condemning the Tunisian revolution, on 15 January 2011.[64] Jamel Arfaoui, a Nessma TV journalist and Libya expert, said of the event:

> If one thinks about the friendly relation between Berlusconi and Qaddafi, and their common business interests, it is clear why Nessma was allowed to see the Libyan leader and get an exclusive interview aiming at calming down the tense atmosphere between Libya and neighbouring Tunisia immediately after Ben Ali's fall.[65]

It is very likely that this media diplomacy operation between Tunisia and Libya, conducted using Berlusconi as a privileged channel to get access to Qaddafi, was the brainchild of Tarek Ben Ammar. Until that moment, the Franco-Tunisian businessman had officially supported Ben Ali and his regime.[66] However, once the Tunisian uprising started, and particularly after its success in ousting Ben Ali, the entrepreneur found himself in a much more ambiguous position.

A specific episode illustrates Ben Ammar's ambivalence *vis-à-vis* Ben Ali and his regime, showing to what extent the Franco-Tunisian entrepreneur has managed to comply with the authorities in order to conduct media business in the country, at the same time using his media outlets to follow a personal political and business agenda. Different sources[67] have reported that, a few days after the unrest started in

Sidi Bouzid on 17 December 2010, with information and videos spreading all over Facebook and becoming news items broadcast on satellite television by Al-Jazeera, Ben Ali got in touch with Ben Ammar asking for his advice on how to use media to calm the situation.[68] Ben Ammar reportedly suggested that local media should tell their own version of the Sidi Bouzid story to Tunisian audiences, who up to then had been exclusively informed about the events through the Qatari news channel, given the general silence of Tunisian news outlets. He allegedly proposed that Nessma TV could film a short documentary in Sidi Bouzid and then air it during a live show, which would openly discuss the issue with journalists and experts at the channel's studios. Being a private station, Ben Ammar seemingly suggested, Nessma would be more credible than any government television station in dealing with the Sidi Bouzid case. It would signal that the Tunisian regime was ready to grant more freedom of speech and, at the same time, function as a safety valve, a practice referred to in Arabic as *tanfis*.

Nebil Keroui recalls that, on 30 December 2011, when the talk show was about to go on air together with the short feature filmed in Sidi Bouzid,

> nobody would ever imagine what was about to happen. Tarek Ben Ammar had given his blessings […] I personally thought Ben Ali would have stayed two, three years more, yet allowing some reforms, opening up a bit.[69]

However, the show (which was, according to many of those who worked on it, uncensored and sidestepped the official censorship channels[70]) apparently opened up real debate among Tunisian audiences. According to Keroui, 'many people thought it was Ben Ali wanting to allow them to talk more about certain issues: they thought it was the right time for *tanazulat* (concessions)'.[71] For Jamel Arfaoui it was rather the bravery demonstrated by those present at the studio talk show – who openly addressed hot issues such as corruption and unemployment – that encouraged more people to talk about the unrest in Sidi Bouzid and catalysed the revolution, at least at a media level.

Debating the Tunisian case of 'authoritarian upgrading'[72] (a process by which authoritarian regimes reorganise 'strategies of governance to adjust to new global, regional, and domestic circumstances'[73] and seemingly promote reforms in several fields, including media), Rikke Hostrup Haugbolle and Francesco Cavatorta have argued that, even if it resulted from what looked like cosmetic change,

> the reform has permitted the arrival on the media scene of new social voices and actors that never had the opportunity to discuss taboo topics and this transforms public debate. While political discussions were excluded and political pluralism absent, the new private media managed to challenge previously prevailing notions of national unity and homogeneity.[74]

This may be what happened with the Sidi Bouzid talk show aired by Nessma TV and the reported mobilisation of the Tunisian public that followed immediately after its broadcast. Whether intentionally provoked by the journalists who took part in the programme, or indirectly engineered by the channel's management, as Hostrup Haugbolle and Cavatorta have put it,

> society does not remain exclusively passive and supine, but generates a set of responses that can moderate the top-down upgrading of authoritarianism and provide social and political actors with new instruments for creating autonomous publics where dissent might be generated.[75]

Both Nessma TV's management and Ben Ammar himself later exploited this episode to testify to the channel's claimed revolutionary identity even before the revolution itself had succeeded. There is no evidence of this prior to January 2011; on the contrary, several times before the regime was toppled Nebil Keroui had publicly called Ben Ali *notre père* (our father). However, immediately after 14 January 2011, Nessma started to reshape its schedule (previously tailored to cater to a wider North African audience with entertainment programmes) towards more political debates and talk shows. As Nebil Keroui stressed several months later:

> We became a truly political channel, hired new staff and gained lots of audience inside Tunisia. But, at the same time, we lost most of our Moroccan and Algerian audiences, which we usually rely on for advertising revenues.[76]

According to its director general, 40 per cent of Nessma TV's advertising revenue comes from Algeria. In contrast, Ben Ammar and Berlusconi's contribution to the business would be minimal: 'I would love to have them investing more in Nessma and being more around.'[77] In fact, Mediaset, after having sent some of its Milan-based executives to train local staff and manage the business on the ground, recalled everyone home. By October 2011, no one from Mediaset was left at Nessma, and only local staff were employed, including in executive positions. Elias Gharbi, who was employed at Nessma as programme host and also used to deal with format acquisitions prior to 2011, speaks of a 'privileged agreement'[78] with Mediaset and its subsidiaries when Nessma had to acquire the television rights of shows licensed by the Italian media group, such as *Jiak el marsoum* ('C'e posta per te'). Other than this, and the fact that Berlusconi's group still holds its 25 per cent share, nothing else indicates any direct involvement by Mediaset in Nessma.

Nevertheless, Berlusconi's presence, as seen in the Qaddafi case, remains key to affording Nessma TV privileged access to international alliances, business groups and networks of political protection. In this framework, Ben Ammar acts and acted as a networked entepreneur or, better, as a networker of moguls, as seen in previous cases analysed in this chapter. In mid-2012, after experiencing a brief phase of direct political engagement, culminating in protests that exploded over the nationwide television broadcast of the movie *Persepolis*, deemed blasphemous by many because of a scene in which God is depicted talking to a young girl,[79] Nessma TV returned to its original mix of entertainment programmes. These were characterised by relative openness and a liberal approach in the selected topics, which mostly appeal to secular, relatively progressive elites. The variety of language spoken by the anchors, a quite sophisticated mix between French and Tunisian, seems also to confirm this to be the channel's primary target group.

Nessma's return to a predominantly entertainment-oriented strategy aligned with Tarek Ben Ammar's December 2012 acquisition of the Egyptian private channel ONTV. The station, previously owned by Egyptian businessman Naguib Sawiris, strongly tied, like Ben Ammar, to the Italian political and business scene, was bought by Prima TV, the Italy-based group that holds all of Ben Ammar's media assets. Ben Ammar stressed that ONTV, which had become well known in Egypt for its edgy shows dealing with current affairs and politics, would not carry any political agenda:

> I come from the entertainment world [...] I have no ties to any political party, even in my own country, Tunisia. I am solely focused on providing audiences with the best, most relevant content possible.[80]

However, it is apparent that the acquisition of ONTV was another step towards expanding Ben Ammar's vertically integrated media mini-empire, which could already rely on strategic transnational assets, from nationwide broadcasting frequencies in Italy, Tunisia, Egypt and possibly also France, where negotiations were under way with Canal+ and TF1 (itself a stakeholder in Prima TV), to production studios in Tunisia and France, to media deals with international distributors. As Ben Ammar himself explained, he had an entire supply chain: 'I can make movies, post-produce them and develop them in my lab. I have studios in France and Tunisia. I have film channels I can put them on. I have media deals with Sky and RAI.'[81]

Seen from that perspective, the combination of Nessma TV and ONTV seemed to confirm Ben Ammar's ambitions to use his extensive regional and global networks of moguls and politicians to create what he called a 'North African media empire'.[82] His aim, expressed at the time of the ONTV acquisition, could be seen as a Euro-Arab media group with a strong presence in North Africa and Egypt, as well as Italy and France, which could eventually compete with big pan-Arab Gulf-owned ventures such as the MBC Group or the Al-Jazeera network.

Conclusion

This analysis has framed Tarek Ben Ammar as a modern entepreneur *à la* Schumpeter, someone who is able to introduce a certain degree of innovation in a given environment through new combinations of products, markets and business models. At the same time it has looked at Ben Ammar as a networker among moguls, a broker of connections and relationships, who has capitalised on the networked structure of the modern economy in order to provide moguls with platforms and products that connect and reconnect them, one to another. As the chapter has noted, these new combinations emerged and were pushed forward in the framework of a vertical integration process that has the effect of consolidating global media industries. It reproposes a firm control over the media distribution chain and an ownership pattern built around the power of a few moguls linked together by business and personal interests, family ties and political alliances.

This trend seemed even to be reconfirmed in the aftermath of the Arab uprisings. Looking at his investments in Tunisia and Egypt, Nessma TV and ONTV, Ben Ammar's strategy seemed to be directed towards yet more vertical integration of his media assets, and consolidating his business ties and political alliances with Arab and European magnates and politicians, such as Berlusconi and Sawiris.

10

Naguib Sawiris: Global Capitalist, Egyptian Media Investor

Naomi Sakr

It has long been routine for Naguib Sawiris to be labelled in terms that refer to his wealth and power. A 'whale' of the Nile was the term used in an article about Egypt's business networks in the 1990s, translating the word *hout*, applied colloquially in Egypt in the plural (*hitan*) to the very wealthy.[1] 'The New Pharaohs' was how *The Economist* described the Sawiris family in a headline in 2005.[2] A penchant for alliteration among sub-editors often produces the phrase 'telecom tycoon', while 'billionaire' is an equally safe bet, given that *Forbes'* annual 'Rich List' regularly estimates Naguib Sawiris' wealth at between US$2.5 and US$3 billion. To think of Naguib Sawiris as a 'media mogul', however, is to switch the spotlight onto a specific aspect of his financial dealings and power base. It invites potentially unflattering comparisons with a particular type of entrepreneur – a type that came to prominence in the USA in the late nineteenth century, as advances in transport extended circulation possibilities for newspapers and thereby seemed to promise increasing political influence to their owners. The expansionism and eccentricities of such people were captured in Orson Welles' 1941 film *Citizen Kane*, based on the real-life magnate William Randolph Hearst.

The examples of Hearst and Joseph Pulitzer, as well as US movie moguls such as Jack Warner of Warner Brothers or Louis B. Mayer of MGM, illustrate how media moguls can become household names. In the process, the name directs attention to the individual and draws it away from the particular combination of circumstances, events and relationships in which the individual's fortunes flourished. Yet the limited theoretical literature on moguldom touches on interactions of personality with family and the wider political economy of media in ways that, if applied to the case of Naguib Sawiris, may yield insights about the nature of his wealth and power. For example, by linking between the rise of European media moguls and the shift from state-controlled to privately owned commercial broadcasting in the 1980s and 1990s, Jeremy Tunstall and Michael Palmer hint at the impact of regulatory policies on the individual owner-operator's scope for building a media empire, and thus, in turn, the way those policies may permit an investor to indulge an 'eccentric personal management style' and pursue a 'distinctive political stance'.[3]

Capital Personified?

It is the fine balance between two elements of Tunstall and Palmer's theorisation of the media mogul – between a focus on individual character traits and an awareness of an historically specific context conducive to individual aggrandisement – that makes this theorisation interesting to test. Where common ground exists among observers of the media mogul phenomenon, it tends to be in recognising that, where moguls are concerned, personality and personal achievement are overstated and context is downplayed. In *The Curse of the Mogul*, three Columbia University law professors blame moguls for spreading disinformation about the workings of the media industries. They identify three 'characteristics' that give cause for concern. One is the extent to which moguls exercise, or appear to exercise, 'absolute power' over their business. The second is the extent to which they acquire mythic status through undiscerning labels like 'visionary' or 'genius' based on one or two episodes in which they made money out of creativity or successfully forecast consumption trends. The third is what Knee and his co-authors see as an 'unhealthy but relentless interest in expanding the scope of their domains', usually through acquisition.[4] Citing examples of moguls who allegedly lost their bearings over time, these authors argue that shareholders and the public have allowed themselves to be 'seduced by the often incoherent visions spun by the most out-of-control moguls'. The curse of the mogul, they write, is that, after initially creating value for shareholders, moguls 'somehow lose the thread of what the actual source of that initial value creation was'.[5]

Journalism professor and blogger Jeff Jarvis similarly locates the essence of the media mogul not only in the mogul's personal characteristics but also in perceptions within the society in which they operate. Accordingly, the mogul is characterised by control over a company, control over a market, hunger for influence and attention, and a combination of narcissism with a lack of self-awareness that 'inspires endless anecdotes about his ego'.[6] Jarvis' allegation about narcissism, like the point made by Knee and colleagues about seduction, implies the existence of a legal and institutional setting in which an individual who extends their media ownership and control may win acclaim for doing so. It could be argued, drawing on Marxist theories of capital, that individual investors who expand their business empires win plaudits from capitalist media, including their own, because they 'personify the power of capital'.[7] In Marxist theory, capital is not a thing but, as David Harvey puts it, a 'process'. It is a process of 'putting money into circulation to make more money', one that 'cannot abide limits'.[8] Evidence suggests that US-based media with a global reach have been eager to portray certain Arab billionaire investors, notably Saudi Arabia's Prince Alwaleed bin Talal and Naguib Sawiris, as 'citizens of the world', who share the allegedly liberal free market values of a transnational capitalist elite and are somehow helping to spread business-friendly practices to countries in the Global South.[9]

Timothy Mitchell cites Egyptian entrepreneur Ahmad Abbud as an example of someone who should be understood not as an agent in his own right but as a personification of the power of capital. Abbud, one of the most powerful figures in Egyptian business and politics in the 1930s and 1940s, was ranked by the international press after World War II as one of the ten richest men in the world.[10] He was not a media mogul; he expanded from irrigation and construction into sugar, shipping, real estate and banking. The potential parallel with Naguib Sawiris is that Mitchell refuses to attribute Abbud's power and wealth to the man himself or his 'skill as a calculating agent'. To do so, Mitchell argues, is to neglect entirely those arrangements of 'law, property, political economy, engineering, irrigation and much more' that 'made such calculation possible'. It likewise overlooks the agencies that kept those arrangements in place.[11] Instead, Mitchell sees Abbud as the 'conscious representative of [capital's] power to reproduce and expand', involved not only in the 'movements and metamorphoses of capital' but in a 'whole series of interconnected circuits' whereby 'nonhuman things or processes' form a 'hybrid' with the consciousness of humans.[12] Seen this way, the issue of Abbud's power and agency becomes a question, 'instead of an answer known in advance'.[13] Mitchell demonstrates what that means for analysis by tracing the intricate interweaving of Abbud's fortunes with the multiplicity of human and non-human factors that influenced decisions on agriculture, public health and engineering in postwar Egypt.

Following that example, the present chapter seeks to problematise power and agency in relation to Naguib Sawiris' media investments in a way that similarly interrogates the personalisation and concentration of Sawiris' media ownership, with reference to ideas about the special characteristics of media moguls. It explores these aspects in light of processes of capital circulation and accumulation of the kind identified by Mitchell. The focus here is on interconnected circuits of people, resources and technology, and on processes affecting the flow of capital, notably legal processes and regulation. It considers possible slippage between the reality of those circuits and processes on the one hand and rationales offered by Sawiris for his various media initiatives on the other. It looks in turn at Sawiris' dealings in cinema, newspapers and television, and concludes with some observations about the underlying aspects of his fluctuating fortunes, including the interaction of individual and context.

'Love' and Profit in the Film Industry

Egyptian film production dates from the 1920s.[14] Its growth was associated with 'Egyptianisation' of the economy in the 1930s, as exemplified by funding for Studio Misr by Bank Misr, launched by nationalist industrialist and businessman Talaat Harb.[15] After army officers overthrew the monarchy in 1952, the government became heavily involved in the cinema industry with the creation of public bodies for film production, distribution and movie theatres. Annual film production averaged 30 to 50 films per year between the 1960s and 1970s. It then soared in the 1980s as the video distribution of films encouraged advertisers to spend heavily on this medium, before declining in the 1990s as the regional growth of satellite television exerted its own pull on advertising spend.[16] Even allowing for vagaries in data collection, the downward trend in film production in the 1990s is clear. According to the Egyptian Chamber of Cinema Industry, a mere 24 films were produced in 1996, the lowest figure in 30 years and a mere fraction of the numbers being produced annually just ten years earlier.[17]

Apparently responding to the downturn, the government of President Hosni Mubarak passed Law No. 8 of 1997, offering financial incentives and tax exemptions to film industry companies, provided they had a minimum capital of 200 million Egyptian pounds (then roughly equivalent to US$57 million). Two companies emerged quickly to benefit from the new law. One was the Egyptian Renaissance Cinema

Company, founded in February 1998 by the Sawiris family through its Orascom Group, together with a number of minority shareholders including two state-owned banks. Renaissance Cinema was capitalised at 500 million Egyptian pounds, fuelling protest from smaller investors at what they said was blatant government discrimination in favour of big firms.[18] Perceptions were rife that Orascom's backers had actually persuaded the government to offer them a tax holiday for film industry investment.[19]

Orascom Group had its origins in the construction company formed by Onsi Sawiris, Naguib's father, in the 1950s, and nationalised under Egypt's President Nasser in 1961.[20] After a period of self-imposed exile in Libya, Onsi returned to Egypt to rebuild his business under Nasser's successor, Anwar Sadat, who had started in the mid-1970s to reopen the Egyptian economy to private investment and renew ties with the USA. Over the next 30 years the Orascom group grew into a global empire worth US$12 billion, controlled by Onsi's three sons. With Orascom operating a military technology import subsidiary close to the Pentagon in the USA and acting in Egypt for US firms such as Hewlett Packard, IBM and AT&T,[21] the empire stretched literally, as *The Economist* put it, 'from America to Bangladesh via Iraq – and from tourism to cement and mobile telephony'.[22]

Renaissance Cinema benefited from government-introduced investment incentives in 1998 at the same time as OTH, Orascom's telecommunications subsidiary headed by Naguib Sawiris, was benefiting from government liberalisation of Egypt's mobile telephone market. State-owned Telecom Egypt had launched the country's first and only global system for mobiles (GSM) in November 1996, and in 1998 it passed the business to the Egyptian Company for Mobile Services, MobiNil, Egypt's new private mobile phone monopoly, majority owned by OTH in a consortium with France Telecom and Systel, the local agent for US operator Motorola. MobiNil inherited 83,500 subscribers from Telecom Egypt, with a waiting list of 25,000.[23] MobiNil had the field to itself until the second GSM licence was awarded a few months later.

Renaissance Cinema was interested as much, if not more, in refurbishing Egypt's movie theatres as in creating new films. It immediately opened the first Renaissance cinema in Cairo, with Naguib Sawiris representing the company at the launch.[24] Egypt's stock of cinemas had shrunk from 238 in 1970 to 138 in 1994, while cinema seats per 1,000 inhabitants had plummeted over the same period from 6.1 to 1.7.[25] Upon receiving its licence Renaissance announced that it planned to build 100 new cinemas, starting with ten in the first year, four of which would be in Alexandria and six in Cairo.[26] In this way it gained additional benefits from a government decision to cut the tax on cinema tickets from 40 to 15 per cent for foreign films and from 20 to 5 per cent for Egyptian films. When the tax cut, ostensibly intended to encourage film-going, had little reported effect on ticket prices, suspicions mounted that investors were simply pocketing the tax savings.[27] Ticket prices of 15 Egyptian pounds at that time were beyond the reach of most ordinary would-be cinema goers. Yet EFG-Hermes, a minority shareholder in Renaissance Cinema, felt confident that cinemas and the film industry were now among the most promising investment sectors in Egypt.[28]

Speaking at the inauguration of the first Renaissance cinema in May 1998, Naguib Sawiris conceded that 'people may be sceptical as to our intentions'. 'But', he said, 'we actually want the good of our country.' Declaring that 'we are dedicated to fine art', he pledged that 100 new movie theatres would open within five years and that Renaissance would also produce films. He noted that the new cinema had chosen an Egyptian movie rather than a foreign one for its first showing but warned that the 'problem we have to contend with is the scarcity of local production. Egyptian films are not enough to keep one cinema going, not to mention 100.'[29] Two years later, Renaissance had opened 35 cinemas but not produced a single film. Challenged as to why his company had taken all the privileges offered by the 1997 law but never actually invested in film production, Sawiris claimed his move in this direction 'was actually emotional'. He continued 'I love the cinema and I love the Egyptian movie industry. I wanted to do something people would thank you and remember you for.'[30] He blamed his company's failure to produce films on a lack of production finance resulting from a 'cash squeeze.'[31]

Sawiris' love for cinema was not so strong that it stopped him from selling Renaissance to a Jordanian board member of OTH, who was part of the OTH consortium that won the licence to provide a cell phone service (called Iraqna) for central Iraq after the USA-led invasion of Iraq in 2003.[32] OTH nevertheless maintained its association with film and the Egyptian government by sponsoring the Cairo International Film Festival in 2006 and 2007, giving Naguib Sawiris a forum for launching and publicising his new television channel, OTV (see below). This sponsorship had its critics among certain Egyptian journalists, who complained loudly that Sawiris now 'owned' the festival and had tried to keep Egyptian reporters away from the event.[33] By 2008 Sawiris was venturing again into film production, through Misr Cinema, a US$90 million joint venture with tourism investor Kamel Abu Ali, with distribution provided by Al-Arabia Cinema Production and Distribution, purchasers of the Renaissance Cinema chain. One of Misr Cinema's first films in 2009, the high-grossing *Dukkan Shehata* (*Shehata's Shop*) attracted attention by featuring Lebanese star Haifa Wehbe.

Risks and Rewards in Television

Whatever the extent of private-sector pressure on the Egyptian government to make investment in cinema more lucrative, pressure on the government to liberalise the terrestrial television market was vocal but less successful. Naguib Sawiris was initially scornful of the government initiative in 2000 to allow private Egyptian broadcasting by satellite only, aware that satellite penetration was too low at that point to make locally based satellite channels seriously appealing to advertisers.[34] 'Why does the government keep the monopoly of terrestrial broadcasting to itself?' he complained.[35] From 2000 to 2006 Sawiris left other Egyptian investors to take the political and financial risks of launching satellite channels that would handle local controversies and thereby help to push the spread of satellite reception among viewers hungry for such content.[36] During that time he had a presence in safer pastures of the Egyptian satellite television industry, through majority ownership of Melody Entertainment, a network that began with music television and added a film channel in early 2006. Melody TV and MobiNil were partners in the first Virgin Megastore to open in Cairo in September 2003, reportedly with involvement from the son of Safwat Sharif,[37] Egypt's information minister for 23 years until he moved to a party political role in 2004. Commercial synergies between pan-Arab satellite television, music labels and the mobile phone sector became self-evident when reality television formats for singing contests started to take off in the Arab region in 2003–4.[38]

In order to follow through on his interest in terrestrial television, Sawiris had to turn his attention to Iraq, where his mobile phone operation, Iraqna, was rapidly building a customer base. In April 2004, while the USA-led Coalition Provisional Authority still had executive, legislative and judicial control over Iraq,[39] Sawiris won a licence to operate a private terrestrial television station in Iraq. Originally called Hawa (Air) but later renamed Nahrain (Two Rivers), the channel was a joint enterprise with Muhammad Gohar, head of Video Cairo Sat, Egyptian veteran of broadcast transmission cooperation with providers of international news. Sawiris, who said he was investing US$25 million in Nahrain, apparently calculated that, at the very least, it would carry advertisements for Iraqna and its evening schedules could carry Egyptian movies.[40] The channel's stated purpose was to convey public opinion to the Iraqi government. Equally, however, Nahrain's parent company Hawa Media was intended to spawn terrestrial channels in other Arab countries. In 2006, with Nahrain said to be proving popular with Iraqi viewers, Sawiris told the press that, just as OTH had been conceived as a regional activity, he wanted to 'replicate the [regional] story in media'.[41]

According to some narratives, Sawiris' Egyptian satellite channel OTV, launched in January 2007, grew out of the collaboration in Iraq with Gohar and his team. Albert Shafik worked for Video Cairo Sat before being involved in the launch of Nahrain and, when OTV was planned in 2006, he joined the channel as its technical director. By that time roughly half of all Egyptian households with a television had acquired satellite reception, up from just over 7 per cent in 2002,[42] and the programming landscape was evolving rapidly in the wake of political developments triggered by presidential and parliamentary elections in 2005. Sawiris professed to have non-pecuniary reasons for introducing OTV, a project capitalised at US$17 million (96.8 million Egyptian pounds at the time). He denied that the name reflected an association with Orascom, asserting that the 'O' could stand for whatever viewers wanted it to.[43] He said he regarded media as the real catalyst for change in any society[44] and he envisaged OTV as a channel for 'young people, without religious or loud content [...] [able to] attract the public's attention onto itself and make people reflect on who they are'.[45] When Sawiris added the news and current affairs channel ONTV in 2008–9, he presented it as a move for enlightenment through its slogan 'Stay in the Light'. It lived up to the billing through talk shows about Egyptian national issues that were geared to compete with the most outspoken counterparts on rival channels. In Ramadan 2009, Sawiris himself hosted an ONTV talk show called *Naguib Sawiris Yohawer* (*Naguib Sawiris Interviews*).

At the same time, the profit motive was not absent. Sawiris himself argued that economic progress achieved in Egypt in the past few years meant that early 2007 was the right time to start a new television station, while his plan to show Hollywood movies uncut seemed to be aimed at outflanking existing entertainment channels.[46] Arrangements to stream OTV online via LINKdotNET, an internet service provider owned by Sawiris, also promised to widen the potential for advertising revenue. Three years into the project, financial concerns about ONTV surfaced in an interview Sawiris gave to a French researcher. 'I'm losing a lot of money', he said. 'It's the most unsuccessful venture I have done until now financially speaking.'[47] Given the extent of OTH involvement in high-risk markets such as North Korea and Zimbabwe, Sawiris had earned himself a reputation outside Egypt as someone with the know-how to make money in 'emerging markets' and able to share the 'secrets of success'.[48] 'When the risks are high the rewards are high', he was quoted as saying in 2010,[49] in defence of an OTH investment in Algeria, where an Algerian government dispute with the construction company headed by his brother was being blamed for pressure on OTH to sell its Algerian subsidiary. OTH had created a company in Algeria with revenues of US$2 billion in six years, Sawiris boasted. 'Where else can you do that? You can't do that in the UK. We don't go to these places because we like trouble', he said.[50] The limits to Sawiris' tolerance of 'trouble' were demonstrated in December 2007 when, despite its profitability, he sold Iraqna for US$1.2 billion to a Kuwaiti firm. The Iraqi operation had been subject to so many attacks and kidnappings that the overall costs of keeping the licence were deemed too high.

Tensions and contradictions between two facets of the persona of Naguib Sawiris – patriot entrepreneur and profit-seeking global capitalist – came to the fore during and after Egypt's revolutionary uprising of 2011. In the early days of the mass protests, Sawiris was cautious in his dealings with the Mubarak regime and, even in the aftermath of Mubarak's removal, was ready to put in a good word for the dictator in interviews with US television stations, commending Mubarak for economic advances, peacefulness *vis-à-vis* Egypt's neighbours and a 'balanced relationship with the US'.[51] Having been one of the 18-strong 'Committee of Wise Men' who tried to negotiate the transition, Sawiris formed his own Free Egyptians Party in April 2011 as a 'liberal, secular' party supporting 'equality, freedom, democracy and capitalism', saying his main aim in doing so was to prevent Egypt becoming like Iran.[52] In May 2011 he stepped down from his position as OTH executive chairman and in June made a very expensive momentary miscalculation when he re-tweeted a cartoon, showing a bearded Mickey Mouse and Minnie Mouse wearing a face veil, which reflected his concerns about Islamisation. Some in Egypt took offence at the joke, calling on Sawiris as a Christian to show more sensitivity. Faced with lawsuits accusing him of contempt for Islam, along with a threatened consumer boycott of his companies, Sawiris apologised.

The incident seemed to mark a watershed in Sawiris' financial relationship with Egypt, eventually leading to the surprise sale of ONTV at the end of 2012. For most of 2011–12, ONTV had appeared to provide Sawiris with a platform for his political objectives. At the start of March 2011 the channel hosted the Mubarak-appointed premier, Ahmad Shafik, on a talk show in which Naguib Sawiris himself also took part and which was credited with prompting Shafik's resignation.[53] Although OTV stopped broadcasting in 2011, ONTV's parent company Hawa chose September 2011 to challenge the broadcast licensing regulations in force under the post-Mubarak military-led regime by launching both ONTV-Live, a 24-hour news channel designed to compete with Al-Jazeera, and ONTVRamadan, a special vehicle for drama series during the month of Ramadan. It was ONTV that hosted the first season on mainstream television of *Al-Bernameg* (*The Programme*), the widely acclaimed show of surgeon-turned-satirist Bassem Youssef. However, as Islamist parties swept to victory in the parliament that opened in January 2012 and a Muslim Brotherhood candidate won the presidency six months later, the Sawiris brothers started moving their families and capital abroad. In May 2012 Naguib Sawiris sold most of his remaining shares in MobiNil to France Telecom, despite having indicated to Bloomberg just a few months earlier that he was emotionally attached to 'my first asset and the reason for my success'.[54] MobiNil's management later admitted that, after the damage caused to its image during the 2011 boycott and a three-year tussle over the share price for France Telecom's buyout, its first priority in 2013 was to return to profitability.[55]

When the news broke in December 2012 that Sawiris had sold ONTV to Tunisian Tarek Ben Ammar,[56] it triggered questions about his future plans for investing in Egypt. A travel ban and legal case, raised by the Muslim Brotherhood-run government against Nassif and Onsi Sawiris for alleged non-payment of tax, intensified the doubts. Prominent Egyptian journalist Wael Ibrashi quizzed Naguib Sawiris about his intentions in March 2013 in an interview on the Cairo-based satellite channel Dream 2, owned by another leading Egyptian business magnate, Ahmad Bahgat. Bahgat had by then also been involved in a standoff with the Morsi government over uplinking arrangements for the Dream network. Conducted in London, Ibrashi's interview drew attention to Sawiris' decision to remain outside Egypt. Ibrashi returned repeatedly during the interview to the sale of ONTV, which Naguib Sawiris said had been a painful decision taken as a result of pressure from his family, who perceived ONTV's editorial line as having provoked the government's actions against them.[57] He revealed that he had warned his family that selling ONTV would not solve their problem with the incumbent regime, which he compared to Mussolini's rise to power in Fascist Italy. Asked whether he planned to move all his business abroad, Sawiris drew a distinction between the location of his assets and his relationship to Egypt. Declaring himself deeply homesick, he said that outside Egypt he was like a fish out of water and would 'never liquidate [his] assets in Egypt'.[58] He had always had businesses abroad, he said, and no-one had questioned this before.

Two months later, with investor confidence badly dented by the treatment of Orascom companies and trading in Orascom shares suspended from 23 April, pressure to end the tax dispute led to a compromise deal and the lifting of the travel ban. A private jet carried members of the Sawiris family, including Naguib, to Cairo, where they were welcomed with flowers by an emissary of the president and headed to the Red Sea resort of Gouna in time for the Coptic Easter celebration in early May. Trading of Orascom shares resumed and the slide in the Egyptian stock exchange was reversed.

Business Rationale for a 'Free Press'

Naguib Sawiris has often made it clear in press interviews that he favours a certain kind of environment for investment. Efficient communication and what he calls 'media freedom' are priorities. Asked about the Mubarak government's decision at the end of January 2011 to suspend internet and mobile phone connections, Sawiris warned that the suspension was 'paralyzing all the business correspondents'. Business could not continue as usual, he said, because 'in today's world you cannot do any business without your emails'.[59] Challenged about his opposition to the Egyptian Constitution that the Muslim Brotherhood-led government put to a referendum at the end of 2012, he stressed his insistence on a democratic framework that would not stifle the press.[60] Under Mubarak, Sawiris took steps with other investors in local media to push the boundaries of press freedom a few years before he repeated the exercise in television with the launch of ONTV. In 2002–3, when Egypt's only daily newspapers were run by the government or opposition parties, three entrepreneurs with established businesses recruited Egypt's most daring newspaper editor to start an independent daily. The entrepreneurs were led by Salah Diab, who made his fortune with PICO Group, Egypt's first oil services company, and, besides Sawiris, included Ahmad Bahgat, owner of a consumer electronics and real estate empire, as well as Dream TV.[61]

Named *Al-Masry al-Youm* (*The Egyptian Today*), their newspaper was run by Hisham Kassem, former editor of the outspoken English-language weekly *Cairo Times*, which had used the internet to circulate stories censored from its print edition. Kassem's vision for *Al-Masry al-Youm* was for 80 per cent of the news to be local, with issues relating to civil liberties, human rights and political reform to be considered front-page material.[62] He sacked two editors who showed they did not share his vision for human rights or financial independence before hiring Magdy al-Galad, who stayed in the position until March 2012. US approval for the newspaper venture was demonstrated when Kassem received an award from the National Endowment for Democracy in Washington in September 2007. Having launched in June 2004, *Al-Masry al-Youm* had by that time built its circulation by exposing election fraud in late 2005 as well as other evidence of Egyptian government corruption.

Kassem left the paper in early 2008 to start a new venture, after reportedly clashing several times with the owners of *Al-Masry al-Youm*. As the paper's managing editor Muhammad Samir explained to a US journalist in June 2008, the government still essentially ruled business coverage because 'leaders of private business shy away from challenging official perspectives in print' for fear of financially painful retribution. 'We are our own censors', he said, 'to uphold high journalistic standards and avoid breaking laws or taboos'.[63] Editor-in-chief Magdy al-Galad subsequently gave observers reason to believe that he was not averse to self-censorship, especially in matters that could harm relations between the newspapers' owners and the ruling elite, the military and security forces. After presiding over the launch of an English version of *Al-Masry al-Youm* in 2009, Galad oversaw the start-up of a full-scale English-language sister paper named *Egypt Independent* at the end of 2011, but stepped in after only its second week in circulation to censor it. Objecting to an article by an American academic, Robert Springborg, discussing the possibility that 'discontented' army officers might decide to remove Field Marshal Muhammad Tantawi, head of the Supreme Council of the Armed Forces that took over from Mubarak, Galad ordered the entire print run of *Egypt Independent* to be shelved.[64]

Despite editorial costs associated with sourcing original content for the more outspoken English-language paper, the lion's share of advertising revenues was reportedly always allocated to the Arabic edition of *Al-Masry al-Youm*.[65] In 2013, in a surprising move for a publishing venture that had once aimed for accurate and honest reporting, the former chairman of Al-Ahram Press Organization, Abdel-Moneim Said, was brought onto the board of *Al-Masry al-Youm*. In his previous post, Said, who was also a member of the Higher Policy Council of Mubarak's ruling National Democratic Party, had expressed approval for editorial decisions that showed Al-Ahram's full support for Mubarak. These included celebrating Mubarak's birthday on the newspaper's front page in 2008 and doctoring a photograph of Mubarak and four other leaders at Middle East peace talks in Washington in September 2010 so as to show Mubarak walking ahead of the group on the red carpet, whereas the real picture showed US President Barack Obama in the lead.

No sooner had Said joined the Al-Masry al-Youm Group than he closed the *Egypt Independent* website and weekly paper, as well as the group's recently established weekly *Al-Siyassi*, ostensibly for financial reasons. In a blog post entitled 'Goodbye *Al-Masry al-Youm*', *Egypt Independent* staff member Sarah Carr declared 'that is the risk of linking fortunes with giant profit-led corporations led by men from another era whose leadership style is based on the hubris and hierarchy model that dominates large organisations in Egypt'.[66]

Conclusion

This study, following Mitchell,[67] set out to interrogate the power and agency enjoyed by Naguib Sawiris in the media industry through an exploration of the interweaving of Sawiris' fortunes with a multiplicity of human and non-human factors. Analysis of his investments in film, television and the press over the 15 years from 1998 to 2013 showed how tightly interwoven these were with the investments and interests of multiple other human agents. Most influential in this nexus were other family members, whose business interests in construction and tourism underpinned plans to build new cinemas but also constrained the whole family's dealings with the government of the day in ways that affected editorial policy in Sawiris-owned newspapers under the regimes of both Hosni Mubarak and Muhammad Morsi and, according to Naguib Sawiris himself, persuaded him to sell off his television interests in 2012. Other investors, both Egyptian and non-Egyptian, were also critical to his undertakings, not least in purchasing the cinema, television and telecommunications assets he chose to sell at strategic moments. Partners like Muhammad Gohar, Kamel Abu Ali, Salah Diab and Ahmad Bahgat shared the risk of certain media ventures in Iraq and

Egypt, the most prominent of which aligned with the US Administration's policy in both countries. Professionals like Albert Shafik and Hisham Kassem were deployed to lend their own credibility to the brand image of Sawiris-owned media businesses. Those businesses also developed as they did because of technological factors, notably innovations in telephony, the convergence of mobile phones, television and internet, online streaming of television and online publication of newspapers.

The story of Naguib Sawiris' media investments is thus one of circulating capital, in which interconnected networks of investors have the power to move obstacles so as to shift capital around, within and between countries, to protect it and make it grow. Together, Sawiris and his family or allies had the leverage to control cinema and film assets in Egypt, benefit from first-mover advantages in the mobile phone business in Egypt and Iraq, and come through a battle of wills over taxation with the Egyptian government under the presidency of Muhammad Morsi. Sawiris articulated the trade-off in his mind between risk and reward when he acknowledged that the level of profit his company had achieved in Algeria would never have been possible in a stable economic environment. In other words, laws and regulations in authoritarian and politically unstable countries are an important element in explaining Sawiris' power and agency generally. As representatives of capital, or 'capital personified',[68] Naguib Sawiris and his allies and proxies invested in media to safeguard other business assets. A vague commitment to revive Egyptian film production opened the door to control over the hardware of the movie industry, in the form of cinema screens and seats. Having newspapers and television channels poised to investigate ministerial failings created a vantage point from which to bargain with ruling officials over investment policy.

Inasmuch as capital is, by definition, expansionist, Sawiris can be said to share the trait of expansionism with archetypal media moguls. By investing in 'free' media, expansionist entrepreneurs can hope to put their own visions, policy preferences and even favourable interpretations of their eccentricities into circulation in parallel with their capital. Ultimately, this activity may be better explained by theories around the personification of capital rather than the nature of the media mogul. Theories of moguldom, as explored in this chapter and book, certainly highlight the ego-driven individualism and narcissism of the archetypal media mogul. But, in doing so, they also encourage us to look beyond the individual, to uncover the web of interactions that enable an individual to accumulate wealth and power.

11

Broadcasting and Businessmen in Egypt: Revolution is Business

Tourya Guaaybess

Revolution is business. Such a subtitle seems gratuitously provocative as it suggests that the so-called 25 January revolution, driven by an astonishing popular movement in the subsequently highly symbolic Tahrir Square, was good news for business. It might be more accurate to assert that 'revolution is *also* business', in the sense that businessmen in the field of media, wherever they are in the world, know how to adapt to new situations and, often, to take advantage of them. However, not all powerful actors in the Egyptian media arena are businessmen. Accordingly, it makes sense to distinguish Egypt's predominant media tycoons from other media players to assess their real weight. The aim of this chapter is to review the main actors in Egypt's privately owned media sector, and to consider their relationship with the state and centres of power in order to explore their role in political liberalisation of the media sector. These businessmen did not put themselves forward as vocal opponents of the regime; in fact, they maintained close relationships with the ruling elite. This poses the question of whether media owners stay close to the centres of political power as a way of preserving their economic interests, or as a covert way of doing politics. The question is difficult because the boundary between politics and business is often blurred.

This chapter draws on a methodology borrowed from sociology, which focuses on specific actors and their political and economic environment and opportunities. French sociologists Pierre Bourdieu and Jean-Claude Passeron developed the paradigm of social reproduction and showed how heirs or inheritors (*héritiers*) are privileged in terms of social capital (professional networks), economic capital and cultural capital (education).[1] A sociological focus on such powerful individual actors in the media means analysing the constraints they face in order to make sense of their actions within a given political and social environment. In turn, these actions have an impact on the sector as a whole. Thus, instead of adopting a 'top-down' approach (analysing society to understand actors), I opt for a structuralist view to understand the evolution of a system as the consequence of individuals' behaviours and decisions. Such an analysis is close to the concept of methodological individualism borrowed from economics (notably the Austrian school of Ludwig von Mises or Friedrich von Hayek). Arising from this methodological choice is an important question: what does the sociological evolution of actors in the media sector tell us about the sector's general dynamics?

The chapter does not claim to be a definitive synthesis of 'businessmen in Egypt', nor an exhaustive list of every business person involved in the media field. Rather, the aim is to highlight the main logics that structure the relationship between businessmen and the Egyptian state in order to arrive at some clues as to their role in the evolution of media. Moreover, Egypt provides a telling example of the ultimate test of any media mogul: how to reconcile established links to political power with a fast-changing political situation. The chapter's title, 'Broadcasting and businessmen', reflects its focus on television, but the chapter will demonstrate television's intricate relationships with other media, particularly the press, in terms of content, personnel and, indeed, owners.[2] After briefly recalling some of the repercussions of the 25 January revolution on the media sector, the study will describe the main Egyptian media tycoons according to their main motives, be they political or economic, from which a loose typology will be compiled. It will be shown in particular that some businessmen in this field were already in a good position, before the revolution, to take advantage and reap benefits from it.

Broadcasting in the Aftermath of the Revolution

One of the first effects seen in the media sector in Egypt and other Arab countries where a dictator was suddenly ousted was a mushrooming of new outlets, from the printed press to broadcasting. In this context of rapid change, which may be expected to last for years to come, the nature of the relationship between the businessmen of the Mubarak era and the Mubarak government starts to emerge more clearly. The current situation and its outcomes allow the analyst to ascertain how robust were the links between businessmen and the former rulers, their interdependence and the consequences of political change on the economics of the private sector. Are moguls a product of the authoritarian state that controls the economy, or are they a variable independent from the state? By shedding light on the relationship that prevailed, the revolution also reveals the usefulness, or otherwise, of previous analyses.

When Mubarak was forced to step down on 11 February 2011, changes occurred in the media sector with striking speed. The head of the Egyptian Radio and Television Union (ERTU) was still Osama el-Sheikh, but the Minister of Information, Anas el-Fiqqi, resigned and a few days later both men were put into custody. In March 2011 the Ministry of Information was replaced by a Ministry of Communication. The end of March seemed to introduce a crucial phase in the restructuring and reorganisation of the state-owned press and printing houses, with decree 451/2011 changing the overall management at Dar al-Tahrir, Dar el-Hilal, Rose el-Yousef Publishers, Al-Ahram Press Organization, *Al-Akhbar* and Egypt's state-run Middle East News Agency (MENA).

However, many hopes were dashed when the Ministry of Information was reinstated in July and the heads of the state-owned newspapers were chosen by the upper chamber of parliament, the Shura Council, as under the old regime. Muhammad Morsi, newly elected as president in June 2013, retained the post of information minister, appointing Salah Abdel-Maksoud to the post.

The Businessman, the Entrepreneur and the Media

Under the previous system, the 'millionaire businessmen', as they were often called, were part of the system as media tycoons, not only because making profit is an attractive activity but also because the law made them a necessity. Journalists were barred by the regulation of their government-controlled syndicate (union) from owning a press organ, so they had to be backed, financed, sponsored and thus controlled by seasoned businessmen. Thus the definition of 'businessman' was already somewhat blurred. For example, when Salah Diab, Naguib Sawiris and others hired Hisham Kassem in 2003 to set up the daily newspaper *Al-Masry al-Youm*, which of these people was the businessman? One was the financier, bringing the money, while the other was the entrepreneur, bringing the know-how. It is important to introduce this specific actor – the entrepreneur – who can be at the same time a media professional and a businessman. Importantly, the distinction we make between financier and entrepreneur does not mean that the financier is free from political motivations, only that both partners will not respond equally to the constraints placed on them. The political motivation (determining the nature of the relationship with the state), or the lack of it, can be inferred *a priori* in the media to be funded or launched. This will be illustrated in this chapter.

For example, consider Emad Eddin Adeeb, chairman and Chief Executive Officer (CEO) of Good News Group, a 'media and entertainment company' that he founded in 1987 and whose website lists as key objectives the production of first-class entertainment and the adoption of 'new content distribution practices' to grow the customer base.[3] The group is active in film, newspapers and magazines, television and radio, digital content, theatres and cafés. Its publications include *Al-Alam al-Youm*, a leading daily newspaper dedicated to financial news and founded by Emad Eddin Adeeb, *Kol al-Nas*, a weekly family magazine, and a more recent daily, *Nahdet Misr*, described as 'liberal'. Among Adeeb's achievements is the portal *gn4me*, a leading platform for digital content. There is no satellite channel in Good News Group. All this might lead one to say that Adeeb is simply a businessman out to make money, leaving the political arena to others.

Adeeb himself furnished the evidence for such a conclusion in August 2005, when he produced a much-criticised seven-hour interview with Hosni Mubarak, in which he focused on Mubarak's personal life, with no mention of corruption, lack of democracy or Egypt's dire social conditions. The interview took place amid rumours that Adeeb might buy a share in state television channels, until the information minister at the time, Anas el-Fiqi, declared that the channels would not be sold. Moreover, the interview took place while Lamees el-Hadidi, managing editor of *Al-Alam al-Youm*, was also head of media relations for Mubarak's 2005 presidential election campaign. One might add that Adeeb has been present in the media for quite a long time. After starting his career at Al-Ahram, he held several editorial positions, the main one being in the Saudi-financed newspaper *Al-Sharq al-Awsat*. He is well renowned for having hosted the groundbreaking '*Ala al-Hawa*' (*On Air*) on Orbit TV,[4] a political talk show that pushed the boundaries of the politically acceptable for 11 years until Adeeb resigned from both the show and the newspaper in 2005. The following year he produced *The Yacoubian Building*, a somewhat dissident movie based on Ala al-Aswani's famous novel. The film's political content, which seems to be in accordance with some statements from Adeeb, sits ill with his continued service to Mubarak. The daily *Nahdet Masr*, also owned by Good News Group, was even praised by the Cairo Institute for Human Rights Studies, along with *Al-Masry al-Youm*, for providing 'excellent service both at the level of information and analysis' during the elections of both 2005 and 2010.[5] It is rather awkward, then, to make a judgement about the announcement by Ahmad Shafik, head of Egypt's interim government, two days after Mubarak's removal, that Emad Eddin Adeeb was likely to be nominated as Minister of Information.[6]

Emad Adeeb is the brother of Amr Adeeb, host of the first show to be aired live on Orbit, *Al-Qahira al-Youm*, and husband of *Al-Alam al-Youm* managing editor and Mubarak campaign manager Lamees el-Hadidi. A dispute between Orbit and the majority state-owned Media Production City (MPC) led to the MPC twice closing the Orbit offices and studios on its premises, first in September 2009 and again a year later, shortly before the 2010 elections, supposedly for an unpaid debt. As the settlement of the financial dispute seemed to drag on, speculation arose that the real reason lay in criticism made by Amr Adeeb about Egypt's metal fence along its border with Gaza,[7] which is a sensitive political issue, or about his criticism of the state press for being overly flattering about Gamal Mubarak. After the initial dispute was settled towards the end of December 2009, the show went back on air with Amr Adeeb thanking Hosni Mubarak for intervening to save Orbit and *Al-Qahira al-Youm*.[8] It is impossible to confirm that Mubarak himself had intervened to save Orbit and the show, but intervention would have had to come from the very top, because Amr Adeeb had been known for harsh criticism of the government and certain figures in Mubarak's ruling National Democratic Party (NDP). *Al-Qahira al-Youm* was a very popular show, and press freedom had then made some undeniable progress, so it would have been costly in political terms to keep it off the air. It may also be surmised that the help provided by Emad Adeeb to Mubarak back in 2005, during Egypt's first multi-candidate presidential election campaign, may have convinced the latter to help Amr Adeeb return to the airwaves.

Amr Adeeb, then, is a prime example of a type of businessman who neither opposes the ruler, nor is entirely on his side, but is close enough to guarantee his own survival should trouble occur. Such behaviour is not necessarily cynical; one has to consider the Adeeb brothers' trajectory and take account of the context of 2005, when very few media organs within Egypt were really independent. As mentioned above, the choice of media to be established may give *a priori* hints as to the political motivations of a particular businessman. The Adeeb brothers never set up a satellite channel. They largely focused on entertainment and other digital content. Emad Adeeb set up a financial daily not really interested in politics, which may explain its success. Meanwhile, their presence on air remained under the umbrella of an existing, stable and large group – the Orbit network. On the other hand, the daily *Nahdet Masr* contradicts any suggestion that the Adeebs were either mere 'loyalists'[9] or mere businessmen.

Salah Diab, another media owner, represents another model. When, in 2002, Diab, in partnership with Naguib Sawiris and Ahmad Bahgat, hired a professional like Hisham Kassem to set up a new independent daily, *Al-Masry al-Youm*, the intention seemed rather clear. With dozens of newspapers and magazines already published in Egypt, the goal of these businessmen was certainly not to create more of the same. Salah Diab, the leader of the project, is of a different generation from Emad Adeeb. He is Chief Executive Officer and Chairman of PICO group, which he founded in 1974. PICO is a diversified conglomerate, initially focusing on petroleum services, then diversifying to oil extraction, construction, agriculture and real estate. Diab admits that he did not create *Al-Masry al-Youm* as a businessman, but because he 'was raised in the house of Tawfiq Diab'.[10] Tawfiq Diab, Salah's grandfather, was a prominent and respected journalist who founded *Al-Jehad* newspaper in the first half of the twentieth century. Owing to the often non-conformist tone of his columns, Tawfiq Diab was sentenced to nine months in prison and a fine for defaming the government, a sentence that came as a shock to people then, all the more so as the prison term was compounded with hard labour, the first such sentence for a journalist.

It is likely that nostalgia and prestige played a part in Salah Diab creating *Al-Masry al-Youm*. This may be why Diab teamed up with another leading businessman of the 'older' generation, and hired Hisham Kassem, a well-respected editor. Kassem is not a broadcaster but a publisher, which is how he defines himself.[11] Besides being President of the Egyptian Organization for Human Rights, he founded and edited the independent weekly newspaper *Cairo Times* in 1997.[12] *Cairo Times* was published abroad, in Cyprus, and imported to Egypt in order to bypass licensing constraints and reduce censorship. Even so, a page on the website of the pioneering newspaper provided uncensored versions of the articles that were cut in the hard copy. Given his background, Diab's choice of Kassem could not be neutral. Kassem had a very precise idea of what he wanted to do. He said he wanted to give readers independent coverage on matters important to Egyptians and news that would be independent from political influence.[13] He wanted the news to be mostly domestic, focusing on human rights, political participation, political reforms and social issues. He introduced investigative journalism, excluded political or religious partisans, and would hire only young university graduates who had not yet been 'formatted' by the state press tradition.[14]

The first issue of *Al-Masry al-Youm* came out in July 2004. Parliamentary and presidential elections were due in 2005. As mentioned earlier, the Cairo Institute for Human Rights Studies documented the quality of the paper's coverage of the presidential election, but it was its coverage of the parliamentary elections that saw the paper really take off. On 24 November 2005, after the first round saw the Muslim Brotherhood win a large number of seats, Noha el-Zeiny, the judge supervising the elections in Damanhur, wrote an article exposing fraud that occurred in that polling station, and *Al-Masry al-Youm* published the article on its front page. Copies sold so fast that issues had to be reprinted for three days in a row. After this, 120 judges signed a statement confirming the veracity of El-Zeiny's allegations. This was a milestone in *Al-Masry al-Youm*'s development and its circulation quickly rose to 200,000 copies per day, placing it among Egypt's top four dailies and making it a paper of record, not least because it was one of the very few to cover the political opposition movement Kefaya ('Enough') from its inception in 2004, even setting the agenda for other newspapers.

Despite this success, Kassem left his post in October 2006. According to him, *Al-Masry al-Youm* was hiring more people than necessary, doubling the staff in less than two years. Much to his own regret, he says he felt compelled to withdraw in protest against the continued meddling of the newspaper's owners.[15] He decided to start a new media outlet from scratch, believing it would be easier than changing the culture of the existing one, even though he had been responsible for setting it up. After Kassem left, Salah Diab became CEO of *Al-Masry al-Youm*, and from then on the management began to interfere more heavily in the editorial content. This was a period of fresh restrictions on press freedom, including a new law in 2006 making it an offence to insult a foreign head of state, and making editors-in-chief responsible for the offences of journalists serving under them.[16] A plausible hypothesis is that Kassem had become persona non grata to the shareholders of *Al-Masry al-Youm* for being too liberal and independent – at least more than they as businessmen required to protect their interests. Kassem found investors to back his new multimedia news project, inspired by the same spirit behind the initial success of *Al-Masry al-Youm*, but the economic downturn that followed the 2011 uprising left the project stalled. Diab's refusal to remain a passive shareholder may also have prompted Kassem to leave. As CEO of *Al-Masry al-Youm*, Diab led the creation of its English website, and later an English version of the paper.

The paper did not lose its independence under Diab, as shown by its coverage of the 2010 elections. On the other hand, his presence could also be seen as reassurance that the person in charge would be careful not to challenge the president directly. It seems that newly cordial relations were being established with the centre of power; in 2007, Diab praised Gamal Mubarak warmly for helping to bring 'new' thinking, in the form of pro-market economics, to national policy making, even though such ideas were far from new. Diab also said he 'wouldn't mind at all' if Gamal became president, even though it seemed that the population was hardly thrilled at this prospect. He did warn however that 'if he [Gamal] thinks he's coming to be the fourth pharaoh in a row, I don't think that's going to be acceptable to anyone'.[17] This could be called a soft opposition to the ruler, contrasting with the rather neutral stance of the Adeeb brothers. In this case, Diab carefully managed his position *vis-à-vis* the regime, using his prestige, his financial weight and his visibility to distance himself just enough to appear credible as a politically committed or at least ethically acceptable media tycoon. However, Diab is someone who ultimately knows who sets the rules, and hence would not hesitate to be tough with any journalist who thought that true independence and opposition had become possible.

This leads us to our third model. The journalist Ibrahim Eissa knows a lot about the limits to press freedom in the last year of the Mubarak presidency. Eissa was sacked in October 2010 from the independent daily *Al-Dostour* by its new owner, El-Sayyid El-Badawi, another prominent businessman and owner of Sigma Pharmaceuticals, which is among the ten largest pharmaceutical companies in Egypt. El-Badawi was elected president of the Wafd Party in May 2010. In August that year he bought *Al-Dostour*, which had Ibrahim Eissa as its editor-in-chief. The paper's other large Wafd Party shareholder was Reda Edward. For a man like El-Badawi, with ambitions in both business and politics, a personality like Eissa was not really an asset. He had been one of the most constant critics of the government and the NDP. He was also one of the few journalists who would regularly cover the Muslim Brotherhood, publish their views and defend those of its members who were arrested and faced trial. He did not do so out of sympathy with their political programme, but because it was a matter of 'honour as a journalist'; he considered that the 'the Brotherhood represents 20 per cent of parliament [...]. It is the foremost opposition in the parliament, which [in itself] is insignificant and bare. It is like a semi parliament.'[18] Last but not least, Eissa accepted to publish an article submitted by Muhammad El-Baradei against the wishes of El-Badawi. Indeed, El-Badawi was one of the toughest opponents of El-Baradei's appeal for a boycott of the 2010 elections in the absence of a government guarantee that they would be free and fair.[19] El-Badawi was no doubt working to strengthen the Wafd Party by bringing it closer to the government, so a close association with the 'real' opposition posed by people like Eissa and El-Baradei was inconvenient.

Like Salah Diab, El-Badawi fits into the 'soft opposition' category, comprising those with too many interests at stake to be able to afford to criticise the government too strongly. However, if we compare El-Badawi's situation with that of Diab, we see that his business was smaller (Diab owns a conglomerate), he did not come from a wealthy or renowned family, and his political ambitions were clearly stated. That is to say he was vulnerable to government action on both fronts. Interestingly, even though the decision to fire Eissa came at a time – the end of 2010 – when the crackdown on media by the government was getting particularly tough because elections were close, at no point did El-Badawi suggest that the decision was imposed on him. A few weeks later, he announced that he had sold his shares in *Al-Dostour* to his partner Reda Edward, probably out of fear that sacking Eissa would hurt his image and the Wafd Party. Edward then asserted that Eissa was no longer welcome at the paper because his editorial line alienated advertisers. It is useful to recall here that newspapers are also economic ventures: advertising is a vital revenue source, especially for independent newspapers, which makes it a discreet but powerful lever in the hands of authorities.

After Mubarak's downfall in 2011, Eissa and two business partners launched Al-Tahrir television channel. As months passed, shares changed hands,[20] and in December 2011 businessman Samer Soleiman acquired 84 per cent of the channel's capital.[21] Many famous journalists had to leave the channel, including Eissa himself, host of the channel's show *Fi'l-Midan* (*In the Square*), as well as Mahmoud Saad, Hamdy Kandil and Dina Abdel-Rahman. Al-Tahrir channel gradually began to diversify its programmes away from a concern with the revolution, no doubt to comply with the expectations of the new interim rulers, the Supreme Council of the Armed Forces (SCAF).[22] Ibrahim Eissa was more successful as the editor of the newspaper *Al-Tahrir*, which he co-founded in July 2011 with publisher Ibrahim Moallem (also the owner of the independent daily *Al-Shorouk*). Al-Moallem is an entrepreneur, belonging to the new generation, known for being independent, with diversified economic interests in the publishing and media sectors. His profile hence contrasts strongly with that of El-Badawi.

It is important to note that El-Badawi owns the Al-Hayat satellite channels, which were launched in 2008, a period when the government was intensifying its clampdown on media in general while promoting broadcasting channels carrying sport, entertainment and movie channels. By launching this type of media El-Badawi demonstrated his willingness to abide strictly by the wishes of the ruler, and to stay clear of any political ambition in the playground set aside for private media. One can speculate about his freedom of movement as president of the Wafd Party when not one of his four channels established a political show.

The Egyptian billionaire Naguib Sawiris offers a further example. Sawiris, the richest man in Egypt, comes, like Diab, from a successful business family. The family's main company, Orascom, was established in the 1950s by his father Onsi Sawiris – himself the son of a lawyer.[23] Orascom's activities were split into three distinct companies: Naguib's brothers led Orascom Construction and Orascom Development and Hotels, while Naguib, holder of a diploma from the Swiss Federal Institute of Technology in Zurich, made his fortune through Orascom Telecom Holding. He was one of the pioneers in betting on emerging market companies, often investing in risky markets. He was not present in the news sector until 2002 when he and others teamed up with Salah Diab to launch *Al-Masry al-Youm*.

When Naguib Sawiris launched his satellite channel OTV in January 2007 he gave it a regional perspective from the start, in line with his achievements with Orascom Telecom. Speaking in 2006 as a majority shareholder in the Melody music and film channels, Sawiris explained that he had started in the media business to contribute to 'a change in education to combat religious fundamentalism and extremism'.[24] OTV would be his third entertainment channel, and he had already applied by then for a licence to launch a 24-hour satellite news channel (OnTV) for Egypt's domestic market. Sawiris talked about this channel as a businessman: his goal was to attract high-end advertisers, such as real estate companies, keen to display their products to 'class-A' viewers. The political agenda was not the type to offend the president but to 'build bridges between Egypt and the West, including America'.[25] In September 2010, after the management of OnTV cancelled a show in which Ibrahim Eissa was scheduled to speak, Sawiris told *Al-Masry al-Youm* that he had to be careful: 'I don't want to upset anybody because someone might come and say "something went wrong with your station", and this will have repercussions'.[26] Like Salah Diab, he did not want to engage in head-on opposition to the Mubarak regime. Even so, there was undeniably a political content to both OTV and OnTV, although not the one Egyptians might have expected: US serials were aired uncut, and there were educational programmes and popular political talk shows. It is actually very difficult to measure the long-term impact of shows like those of Emad Adeeb, or others, in raising the level of expectation of the population little by little, and gradually lowering public tolerance thresholds *vis-à-vis* the regime.

In a show hosted by the American journalist Charlie Rose after the fall of Mubarak, Sawiris gave an interesting account of his relationship with the former leader.[27] He admitted that he did not really see Mubarak's departure as a necessity, and described his initiative in setting up a group called the 'Council of Wise Men' as an attempt to mediate between an angry crowd and an isolated president. In doing so, Sawiris revealed the distance between himself (as well as other businessmen of his generation) and the young people (the 'kids' as he called them) on the streets, demanding the changes that he saw as legitimate.

On 4 April 2011 Sawiris announced that he was creating the Free Egyptians Party (*Hizb al-Masriyīn ul-Ahrār*) to contest the promised parliamentary elections,[28] with the stated principles of democracy, freedom, a civil state, equality between all citizens, the empowerment of women to participate in all fields, an independent judiciary and separation between the executive and legislature. He declined to take the helm, saying that the party was not 'his' and that the youth should be left to play their role, which they started on 25 January. It is noteworthy that Sawiris did not try to launch such a party while Mubarak was still in power. As a businessman investing in broadcasting, Naguib Sawiris appears closer to the Salah Diab model than to that of El-Sayyid El-Badawi. Without obvious political connections or a clear political agenda, he owed his position mainly to the economic scene. Despite his ideals in terms of media, society and political power, he remained essentially a businessman: without actively seeking the patronage of the ruler, he remained pragmatic enough to know who has the ability to pull the plug.

Among the founding shareholders of *Al-Masry al-Youm*, along with Diab and Sawiris, was Ahmad Bahgat. Bahgat began his career as an engineer before turning to real estate and then creating a large conglomerate, Bahgat Group, with a wide range of businesses. He launched Egypt's first private satellite channel, Dream TV, in November 2001. According to its website, Dream TV is 'dedicated to create well-being for the audience by providing useful advice, interactive cooperation, entertainment with the latest songs, video clips and interviews with the most famous superstars of Egypt's entertainment scene'.[29] Bahgat freely admitted during Mubarak's 2010 clampdown on the media that the government was in control and that there was a very real possibility it would intervene. He said 'If I get a phone call telling me to shut Dream TV, I will do so. Am I going to fight the state? I can't.'[30] He had to take this risk into account when managing his channels, as apparently the state's priorities were not up for discussion.

In an interview with the author, Dream TV executive manager Muhammad Kedr confirmed that the channel had freedom only as long as it did not cross the red lines surrounding the president and his family. Like all large conglomerates in Egypt, the Bahgat Group was doing business with the state, and Dream was dependent on the state as an advertiser. The ramifications of this situation emerged in a conflict with Mona El-Shazly, host of the show *Al-Ashera Masaan* (*10pm*) after she described how the NDP chose its candidates for the parliamentary elections. Dream TV denied the statement, saying that El-Shazly was on vacation. After a complaint by the NDP, the parliamentary Media Standards Review Committee issued a report saying that El-Shazly had denied the NDP fair treatment and that she was also under scrutiny after interviewing the new leader of the Muslim Brotherhood in April 2010. Dream TV had banned veteran commentator Muhammad Hassanein Heikal back in 2004 for stating that power should not be inherited in a democracy, a remark clearly referring to Hosni Mubarak and his son Gamal.[31]

Another key businessman in the Egyptian media landscape is Muhammad Gohar, who began his career in the early 1970s as a cameraman and producer for Egyptian television and then NBC. Between 1973 and 1981, Gohar was the main producer covering the appearances of Anwar Al-Sadat and, through his work as a cameraman and producer, he gradually established partnerships with many broadcasters and news agencies. His independent media production company, Video Cairo, set up in 1973, later became one of the leading news production and gathering agencies in the Middle East. Gohar sees media as playing a social and political role, as demonstrated by his 2008 documentary *The Bridge*, to 'bridge the growing divide between American and Arab Islamic societies, counter misconceptions and stereotypes.'[32]

Gohar was involved in Al-Mehwar, which went on air in February 2002 as Egypt's second private satellite channel. His partner on the project was Hassan Rateb, who made his fortune in land development, tourism and cement. Rateb appeared to be moved by a political and social vision, arguing that the private sector needed a voice to gain legitimacy and to counter the 'socialist way of thinking' that caused the collapse of the Soviet Union but was still 'very evident' in the Arab region. He was quoted as saying 'The space for democracy in our society is changing. This is a new sphere. With private ownership of such a powerful tool the public sphere is much wider.'[33] The channel had a difficult start, as it faced competition from pan-Arab channels that had a decade of experience and a loyal viewership. Rateb handed the whole production of the channel to Gohar, but then, after an inconclusive experience with entertainment, asked him to focus on a news service that would avoid the region's regular diet of 'offensive, sensational news or protocol news reflecting the comings and goings of state leaders'.[34] This was an attractive project, but Gohar pulled out, apparently for financial reasons, as did some of the original investors, leaving Rateb to continue. Yet it would be erroneous to consider Al-Mehwar an independent channel. As the heads of three government-controlled bodies (ERTU, Nilesat and MPC) all sat on its board, it was clearly a loyalist operation.

Gohar meanwhile went on with his Video Cairo Sat venture and used it in April 2011 to launch a new television channel, called 25TV because it was said to be based on the principles of democracy, freedom and social justice that underpinned the 25 January uprising. On the channel's website, Gohar stated that 25TV is 'committed to honest and non-biased programming that is independent of any ideological, religious or political affiliations'. He said it was 'inspired by, and targets, change seekers and catalysts for change, regardless of age, ideology or personal beliefs'.[35] Following licensing obstacles under SCAF, however, and alleged jamming of the 25TV signal under the government of Muhammad Morsi, the channel was suspended in September 2012. A year later Gohar himself left Egypt for Canada after reportedly receiving death threats.

Mapping Businessmen's Motives and Power Relations

To clarify the structure of the media sector in the Mubarak era, and the motivations of its main actors, we can now establish a loose typology of the businessmen and entrepreneurs in the sector in terms of their relationship to the regime. These relations were very often, but not always, conciliatory. As we saw, it would be simplistic and incorrect to view them as mere clientelism, or a stable, and mutually recognised, if asymmetrical, relation of power. Rather, the relationships described here seem more ephemeral, and are characterised by pragmatism or even cautiousness. This preliminary study does not claim to be 'objective', as any classification of people should be done and read with great care. Nor is it exhaustive. However, it may be useful in opening a new research path in the study of Egyptian, and other, media – one that, by using economic actors and their motives as the main analytical prism, provides tools to help understand how the media sector is structured and how it relates to the economic sphere. It is an attempt to deploy the methodology of political science or sociology in scrutinising media. Identifying the most salient and visible actors of the Egyptian media sector allows the construction of ideal-types (as defined in Weberian sociology), from which the ideal-type of 'media mogul' may be drawn, which in turn provides keys to establish a similar classification for other Arab countries.

The various actors we selected, the most visible ones in the public space, are classified in Table 11.1 according to the following criteria:

- Are they businessmen or entrepreneurs?
- Are they media professionals; in other words are they directly involved in the sector with a specific know-how?
- Are they heirs or not? When Diab refers to his grandfather, it is also to assert a certain legitimacy in the Egyptian media field and reap some kind of benefit from this legitimacy. This can be easily analysed through the paradigm defined by Bourdieu.
- Another important criterion is their formal political commitment: do they have an identifiable political position?
- Do they have a political ambition or vision, either for themselves, or for the media they launch?
- Do their media investments form their main activity?

When key actors in Egypt's media sector are analysed according to these criteria, they fall into three groups. The first group consists of typical businessmen. They are not so much men of media as financiers. Almost all inherited a situation from their parents, and most lack a

Table 11.1: Typology of key Egyptian media actors

Who?	Businessman (B) Entrepreneur (E)	Man of media	Heirs?	Formal political commitment	Political or social ambition for media	Business owned / Media outlet
First group: businessmen						
Ahmad Bahgat	B	No	Yes	No	No	Bahgat Group (diversified)/ Dream TV (2001); shareholder of Al-Masry al-Youm
Salah Diab	B	No	Yes	No	Unclear, but co-founded Al-Masry al-Youm, hiring Hisham Kassem	PICO group (diversified)/ Al-Masry al-Youm
Naguib Sawiris	B	No	Yes	No	Co-founded Al-Masry al-Youm; many statements (OnTV); created the Group of Wise Men; created a political party	Orascom Telecom Holding/ Melody Channel, OTV/OnTV (2007–9, sold 2012); shareholder in Al-Masry al-Youm
Sayyid El-Badawi	B	No	No	President of the Wafd Party	No	Sigma Pharmaceutical/was co-owner of Al-Dostour; Al-Hayat satellite channels (2008)
Hassan Rateb	B	No	Yes	No	No	Various (Sinai Cement, etc.)/ Mehwar TV
Second group: media professionals						
Muhammad Gohar	B/E	Yes	No	No	Yes	Video Cairo (1973)/25TV (2011)
Tarek Nour	B/E	Yes	No	No	No	Tarek Nour Communications/ Al-Qahira Wal-Nass

Ibrahim Al Moallem	B/E	Yes	No	Son of Mohamad al-Moallem, founder of Dar El Shorouk publishers	No	Founder and chairman of al-Shorouk group: Dar El Shorouk publishers, the National Printing Company, *Al Shorouk* daily newspaper, *Weghat Nazar* magazine, Shorouk Bookstores, Shorouk Media Production (TV), CLIP Solutions (digital media production)
Emad Eddin Adeeb	B/E	Yes	No	No	Yes: *'Ala al-Hawa'* (Orbit TV); political talk shows for 11 years; daily *Nahdet Misr*	Good News Group (press, broadcasting, digital content)/ *Al-Alam al-Youm*, *Kol Al-Nas*, *Nahdet Misr*; portal – gn4me.com
Third group: independent journalists/media professionals						
Hisham Kassem	E	Yes	No	Formerly president of the Egyptian Organisation for Human Rights, Vice-President for International Affairs of Al-Ghad Party	Stated need for freedom of speech, media independence and more professional journalism; acted accordingly	Editor of *Cairo Times* (closed); built *Al-Masry al-Youm*; building a news website/platform
Ibrahim Eissa	E	Yes	No	No	Stated need for freedom of speech and media independence; acted accordingly (and lost several editorial positions)	One of the founders and owners of Al-Tahrir TV when it launched in 2011; founder and editor-in-chief of the newspaper *Al-Tahrir*

Source: Author's compilation

clear political position. They have built diversified industrial groups, to which they add media (*Al-Masry al-Youm*, Dream TV, Al-Mehwar, Al-Hayat channels). Interestingly, the media represented here are not openly pro-government, probably because that sort of media fails the business test in that it does not meet the audience's needs.

The second group hails from a younger generation. They are more entrepreneurs, often entirely focused on the media sector, in which they have developed a recognised expertise. They are mostly self-made, having built up their businesses from scratch. They often base their success on a technical know-how that they used to fill a gap in the market, but they can also be journalists or talk show hosts. With regard to this last category, they are well aware of state controls and see neither need nor scope for media to venture too deeply into criticising those who hold political power.

The final group comprises an emerging type, represented by the entrepreneur who is also typically a media professional, a journalist, calling for real autonomy of the news media segment *vis-à-vis* all interests and powers, whether in government or business, because they have sometimes had conflicts with these interests in the past. They base their involvement in the media sector on what they perceive as the journalist's role in society, and they call for increased professionalisation of journalists. This last group appears more clearly aligned with the ideals of the 25 January uprising in terms of content and use of new technologies. Personalities such as Hisham Kassem or Ibrahim Eissa best embody this group. They actually keep this category alive in an intellectual and journalistic tradition dating back to the late nineteenth and early twentieth centuries, keeping the door open for newcomers to the group.

Analysing the media sector's evolution through the prism of the sector's key actors makes it obvious that the weight of the system set up by Mubarak continues to hamper a true liberalisation of the sector, whereby the actions of numerous individuals would be allowed to compete to shape the media regardless of government interests. First, there is a reason inherent to the centralisation of political power in the presidency and/or the military. A reason more specific to the sociology of the media sector is the lack, so far, of strong successors able to take over from the businessmen in terms of influence and ability to change things. It would be misleading to present these businessmen as if they were the 'old guard' holding onto their power: they want to survive as businessmen leading large international groups, as they wished to do before. Under the Mubarak regime they were careful (or maybe ethical[36]) enough to avoid being the mouthpiece of the government, so they retained enough credibility once the regime changed to remain key actors in the arena. Subsequently, several signs they gave hinted at a desire to be a catalyst for change (stronger involvement with youth movements for instance, or launching of satellite channels). The actors of the second group – the media professionals who successfully set up their own ventures – are also careful to appear as catalysts for change, and their actions are close to those of the businessmen.

Members of the third group remain relatively limited in number, and the most prominent members are Hisham Kassem and Ibrahim Eissa. The fact that they have failed so far to come back to centre stage in the media sector, despite their prestigious past, and also the fact that no new personality has emerged so far in this third group, seems to indicate that change is slow. Even with the passage of new laws, structural change takes time (with new habits and competencies to be acquired, generational change, and so on).[37] This can also be a symptom of some segments of the media sector (or of the public space) remaining closed to newcomers, which suggests that there are limits to what a revolution can achieve within a given timeframe.

Conclusion

In the Mubarak era, all the major media businessmen tended to be close to the regime. However, being close does not mean that they approved of the regime or that they actively sought its patronage. Rather, it was often an inevitable consequence of the economic importance of the groups they were heading. Some of the entrepreneurs were critical *and* at the same time tolerated by the president, or even encouraged by him, as in the case of the Adeeb brothers. These businessmen represented a sort of safety valve, or a soft opposition, akin to an alibi for those in power. There was a constant negotiation with those in power to find the right balance between, on the one hand, their intention to achieve success in the economic arena and, on the other, their reluctance to be assimilated by the regime, whether for reasons of personal conviction or financial pragmatism. As the balance moved with the priorities of the state, the leading media investors had to move and adapt. This is what they are still doing now. With all that happened in Egypt in the three years after the 2011 uprising, media censorship was not removed. One may surmise that actors of the 'independent journalist' type will eventually gain in influence given the public's need for information in a situation of political turmoil, and it is possible that their number will grow during a faltering and protracted process of media liberalisation.

Notes

Chapter 1

1 Curran's phrase appeared in media coverage of his response to the November 2012 *Leveson Report into the Culture, Practices and Ethics of the Press* in the UK.

2 Tunstall, Jeremy, and Palmer, Michael, *Media Moguls* (Routledge, London, 1991), p. 105.

3 Dodge, Toby, 'Bringing the bourgeoisie back in: Globalization and the birth of liberal authoritarianism in the Middle East', in T. Dodge and R. Higgott (eds), *Globalization and the Middle East: Islam, Economy, Society and Politics* (Royal Institute of International Affairs, London, 2002), p. 175.

4 Dodge, 'Bringing the bourgeoisie back in', p. 186.

5 BBC, 'Saudi prince sacks TV chief for Muslim Brotherhood ties', 18 August 2013, http://www.bbc.co.uk/news/world-middle-east-23747381 (last accessed 30 January 2015).

Chapter 2

1 Tunstall, Jeremy, and Palmer, Michael, *Media Moguls* (Routledge, London, 1991), p. 12.

2 Cooke, Philip, 'Regional innovation systems: competitive regulation in the New Europe', *Geoforum* 23 (1992), pp. 365–82.

3 Curtin, Michael, *Playing to the World's Biggest Audience: The Globalization of Chinese Film and TV* (University of California Press, Berkeley, CA, 2007), p. 286.

4 Giddens, Anthony, 'The globalizing of modernity', in A. Sreberny (ed.), *Media in Global Context: A Reader* (Arnold, London, 1997), pp. 19–26.

5 Hamelink, Cees J., and Nordenstreng, Kaarle, 'Towards democratic media governance', in E. de Bens and C. J. Hamelink (eds), *Media between Culture and Commerce* (Intellect Books, Bristol, 2007), p. 232.

6 Freedman, Des, *The Politics of Media Policy* (Polity, Cambridge, 2008), p. 14.

7 McQuail, Dennis, 'Introduction: The current state of media governance in Europe', in G. Terzis (ed.), *European Media Governance: National and Regional Dimensions* (Intellect Books, Bristol, 2007), pp. 17–18.

8 Heidenreich, Martin, Cooke, Philip, and Braczyk, Hans-Joachim, *Regional Innovation Systems: The Role of Governances in a Globalized World* (Routledge, London, 1998), p. 15.

9 Siebert, Fred S., *Four Theories of the Press: The Authoritarian, Libertarian, Social Responsibility, and Soviet Communist Concepts of What the Press Should Be and Do* (University of Illinois Press, Urbana, IL, 1956), p. 2.

10 Rugh, William A., *Arab Mass Media: Newspapers, Radio, and Television in Arab Politics* (Praeger Publishers, Westport, CT, 2004), p. 254.

11 Ayish, Muhammad, *Arab World Television in the Age of Globalization: An Analysis of Emerging Political, Economic, Cultural and Technological Patterns* (Deutsches Orient-Institut, Hamburg, 2003), p. 41.

12 The term 'private' is itself problematic, as many contributors in this volume show.

13 For more on this topic, see Sakr, Naomi, *Satellite Realms: Transnational Television, Globalization and the Middle East* (I.B.Tauris, London, 2001); Zayani, Muhammad, *The Al-Jazeera Phenomenon: Critical Perspectives on New Arab Media* (Paradigm Publishers, Boulder, CO, 2005); Sakr, Naomi, *Arab Television Today* (I.B.Tauris, London, 2007); Kraidy, Marwan M., and Khalil, Joe F., *Arab Television Industries* (Palgrave Macmillan, Basingstoke, 2009); Mellor, Noha, Rinnawi, Khalil, Dajani, Nabil, and Ayish, Muhammad I., *Arab Media: Globalization and Emerging Media Industries* (Polity Press, Cambridge, 2011).

14 Seib, Philip M., *The Al Jazeera Effect: How the New Global Media Are Reshaping World Politics* (Potomac Books, Washington, DC, 2008), p. 191.

15 Kraidy and Khalil, *Arab Television Industries*, p. 146.

16 It can also be argued that events surrounding the so-called Arab Spring in Tunisia, Egypt, Libya and Syria fall under this category.

17 For analyses of the situation in Mediterranean countries, also in terms of their media systems, see Mancini, Paolo, 'Political complexity and alternative models of journalism: The Italian case', in M. Park and J. Curran (eds), *De-Westernizing Media Studies* (Routledge, London, 2000), pp. 265–78; Papatheodorou, Fotini, and Machin, David, 'The umbilical cord that was never cut: the post-dictatorial intimacy between the political elite and the mass media in Greece and Spain', *European Journal of Communication* 18(1) (2003), pp. 31–54; Statham, Paul, and Trenz, Hans-Jörg, *The Politicization of Europe: Contesting the Constitution in the Mass Media* (Routledge, New York, NY, 2012).

18 For analysis of the development of the television production scene in Syria see Della Ratta, Donatella, *Dramas of the Authoritarian State: The Politics of Syrian TV Serials in the Pan Arab Market* (Department of Cross-Cultural and Regional Studies, Copenhagen University, Copenhagen, 2013).

19 Karlsson, Charlie, and Picard, Robert G., *Media Clusters: Spatial Agglomeration and Content Capabilities* (Edward Elgar, Cheltenham, 2011), p. 381.

20 Ibid. p. 376.

21 See Chapter 3 in this book, on Antoine Choueiri.

22 Interestingly, Melody Group's owner Ashraf Marwan has failed to weather the political and economic changes of Egypt's post-January 25 revolution. After several attempts to rescue the group, the channels were shut down in 2013.

Chapter 3

1 For example, *Arabian Business*, 9 March 2010; *The Daily Star*, 10 March 2010.

2 Tunstall, Jeremy, and Palmer, Michael, *Media Moguls* (Routledge, London, 1991), p. 105.

3 Al-Awar, Nada, 'Antoine Choueiri: Grandfather or godfather?', *ArabAd*, January (1998), p. 9.

4 International Advertising Association obituary, http://www.iaauae.org/en/special-feature/antoine-choueiri-dies.html (last accessed 4 August 2014).

5 Antoine Choueiri married Rose Salameh, the mother of his two children, Pierre and Lena, in 1961. The author interviewed Rose and Lena in Beirut, 24 July 2012.

6 Ibid.

7 Ibid.

8 According to Abu Zahr, quoted by Kutschera, Chris, 'France: The rise and fall of the Arab press', *Middle East Magazine*, April (1997).

9 Ibid.

10 The sale is discussed in Chapter 5 in this book, on Rafik Hariri.

11 Quoted by Sakr, Naomi, *Walls of Silence: Media and Censorship in Syria* (ARTICLE 19, London, 1998), p. 76.

12 Author's interview, 24 July 2012.

13 Hagey, Keach, 'Antoine Choueiri: An advertising man to remember', *The National*, 11 March 2010, http://www.thenational.ae/business/antoine-choueiri-an-advertising-man-to-remember (last accessed 17 August 2012).

14 *Kippreport*, 2010. Available at www.kippreport.com (last accessed 1 September 2012).

15 Ibid.

16 Ibid.

17 Author's interview, 24 July 2012.

18 Al-Awar, 'Antoine Choueiri: Grandfather or godfather?', p. 10.

19 Author's interview, 24 July 2012.

20 According to a media expert who preferred to remain anonymous, interviewed by the author in Beirut, 27 April 2012.

21 Author's interview, 24 July 2012.

22 Al-Awar, 'Antoine Choueiri: Grandfather or godfather?', p. 12.

23 Author's interview with Talal Salman, *Al-Safir* newspaper offices, in Hamra, Beirut, 11 April 2012.

24 Ibid.

25 Ibid.

26 Author's interview with Salman, 13 April 2012.

27 Ibid.

28 Harb, Zahera, *Channels of Resistance in Lebanon: Liberation Propaganda, Hezbollah and the Media* (I.B.Tauris, London, 2011), Ch. 5.

29 The author heard these concerns expressed frequently when she worked at Télé-Liban during that period.

30 In 1992, LBC became LBCI. See Koubiasi, Faten, 'Oudwan: LBCI court case goes around who owns the company' (Oudwan: qadiyat LBCI tadur hawla man yamluk al-sharikah), *Al-Safir*, 15 October 2010.

31 Author's interview.

32 Author's interview. For more on the dispute, see Chapter 4 of this book, on Pierre Daher.

33 Koubiasi, 'Oudwan'.

34 Author's interview.

35 Author's interview.

36 Fahd, Saud , 'Walid al-Ibrahim: Choueiri is gone, but left with us who can steer the boat' (Walid al-Ibrahim: Antoine Choueiri Rahala lakinnahu taraka man yaqud al-safinah), AlArabiya.net, 9 March 2010, http://www.alarabiya.net/articles/2010/03/09/102605.html (last accessed 12 June 2012).

37 al-Rashed, Abdul Rahman, 'Finance, media and the new Arab reality', 18 March 2010, http://www.alarabiya.net/views/2010/03/18/103435.html (last accessed 12 June 2012).

38 The Choueiri Group stopped representing LBCSat after it was acquired by Alwaleed bin Talal, but continued representing LBCI's terrestrial channel.

39 *ArabAd* 1(8) January (1998).

40 See http://www.chroueirigroup.com/SubPage.aspx?pageid=303&PID=302&FPID=254 (last accessed 24 August 2012).

41 Author's interview with Rose Choueiri. Also see Lahamag.com, 27 March 2010; www. Choueirigroup.com (last accessed 2 August 2012).

42 Choueiri Group.com (last accessed 2 August 2012).

43 Ibid.

44 Author's interview with Lena Nahas.

45 Ibid.

46 Author's interview with Rose Choueiri.

47 See 'Choueiri group invading the Egyptian media' (Mu'assasat Choueiri al-lubnaniyya tajzu al-I'lam al-misri), *Al-Fagr,* 19 January 2012; Mohamad,

Mohsen, 'Choueiri's ghost surrounds Egypt' (Shabah Choueiri yukhayem 'ala Misr), *Al-Akhbar,* 30 January 2012.

48 Hagey, 'Antoine Choueiri: An advertising man to remember'.

49 Ibid.

50 Ibid.

51 Doyle, Gillian, *Understanding Media Economics* (Sage, London, 2002), p. 31.

52 Author's interview with Rose Choueiri.

53 Author's interview with Lena Nahas.

54 Al-Awar, 'Antoine Choueiri: Grandfather or godfather?', p. 10.

55 Fahd, 'Choueiri is gone'.

56 For details, see Chapter 4 of this book, on Pierre Daher.

57 Author's interview.

58 Author's interview.

59 Hagey, 'Antoine Choueiri: An advertising man to remember'.

60 Author's interview with Rose Choueiri.

61 Ibid.

62 Ibid.

63 Tunstall and Palmer, *Media Moguls*, p. 105.

64 Al-Awar, 'Antoine Choueiri: Grandfather or godfather?', p. 10.

65 See Choueirigroup.com for a long list of obituaries.

Chapter 4

1 Several interviews in this chapter are taken from a larger forthcoming work on the Lebanese media system from a comparative perspective.

2 Daher is the son of Sheikh Youssef el Daher, one of the main founders of the Kata'eb (Phalange) Party and himself the son of Butrus Khury, whose prominent family was granted the title of 'Sheikh' by Prince Melhem Al Shahabi in 1750.

3 Although LBC was transformed into LBCI after it was allegedly sold to Pierre Daher, LBCI and its satellite operations are commonly referred to as LBC. Therefore, unless otherwise specified as LBCI, or LBC Group, the acronym LBC is used.

4 Rugh, William. A., *Arab Mass Media: Newspapers, Radio, and Television in Arab Politics* (Praeger, Westport, CT, 2004), pp. 195–8.

5 Hirst, David, 'With Syria in turmoil, Lebanon remains at risk', the *Guardian,* 15 August 2012, http://www.guardian.co.uk/commentisfree/2012/aug/15/syria-lebanon-proxy-war (last accessed 7 October 2013).

6 Siebert, Frederick. S., Peterson, Theodore, and Schramm, Wilbur, *Four Theories of the Press* (University of Illinois Press, Chicago, IL, London, 1956), pp. 1–2.

7 External pluralism refers to the diversity that is represented on the level of the media system. The contrary term, internal pluralism, refers to pluralism

achieved within each individual media outlet or organization; Hallin, Daniel C., and Mancini, Paolo, *Comparing Media Systems: Three Models of Media and Politics* (Cambridge University Press, Cambridge, 2004), p. 14.

8 al-Zubaidi, Layla, *Walking a Tightrope. News Media and Freedom of Expression in the Arab Middle East* (Heinrich Böll Foundation Middle East Office, Beirut, 2004), pp. 64–5.

9 With this the Sunni Muslims were represented by Future TV, the Shi'a Muslims by Al-Manar TV (although the licence for Al-Manar was granted later) and NBN, Greek Orthodox by MTV, the Maronites by LBCI and the Catholic Church by Télé-Lumière.

10 Rugh, *Arab Mass Media*, pp. 202–4.

11 Political parallelism refers to the extent to which the media system reflects the major political divisions in a given society; Hallin and Mancini, *Comparing Media Systems,* pp. 21–2.

12 Nötzold, Katharina, *Defining the Nation? Lebanese TV Stations: The Political Elites' Dominance over the Visual Space: Lebanese Television and Political Elites, 1990–2005* (Frank & Timme, Berlin, 2009), p. 345.

13 Video recording of LBC inauguration on 30 August 1985 in the presence of Elie Hobeika, among other Phalange and Lebanese Forces' operatives, http://www.youtube.com/watch?v=fqtVC3kbWOc (last accessed 8 October 2013).

14 Rugh, *Arab Mass Media*, pp. 202–4.

15 The Lebanese Forces party was dissolved in 1994 (and their leader incarcerated) after they were blamed for an explosion targeting a church. This was used to try Geagea for assassinations committed during the war, despite the general amnesty that was passed.

16 The communiqué was released on 24 March 1994 after the Lebanese Forces party was dissolved for allegedly bombing a church; Nötzold, *Defining the Nation?*, pp. 137–8.

17 Ibid.

18 Author's interview with *Al-Hayat* newspaper columnist Hazem Saghieh in Beirut, 2 February 2011.

19 Shortly after Choueiri's death in 2010, Daher said that while Choueiri often described himself as a 'good ad salesman', he was actually much more, because the revenues he secured insulated LBC from political interference and instrumentalisation. 'Antoine moved from being an ad salesman to a defender of freedoms and media independence.' A tribute to Antoine Choueri was broadcast on LBC's show *Kalam El Nas* on 11 March 2010, http://www.youtube.com/watch?v=EvpLmDLCr44&feature=related (last accessed 8 October 2013).

20 See Chapter 3 of this book, on Antoine Choueiri. The Choueiri Group has controlled the advertising of eight of the most watched pan-Arab channels, including MBC, Dubai TV and LBCSat until 2008, which has translated into

a revenue of US$2.4 billion; Kraidy, Marwan M., and Khalil, Joe F., *Arab Television Industries* (Palgrave Macmillan, Basingstoke/British Film Institute, London, 2009), pp. 116–21.

21 It should be noted that in 2008, after LBC's merger with Rotana, the satellite operation opted for in-house advertising representatives, whereas LBCI was to remain represented by the Choueiri media group. In addition to financial considerations in light of the merger, some political considerations may have come into play as Choueiri had weighed into the ownership dispute in favour of the Lebanese Forces.

22 Author's interview with Marcel Ghanem, *Kalam el Nas* host, in Beirut, 27 May 2011.

23 Author's interview with the Choueiri Media Group in Beirut, 6 June 2011.

24 Author's interview with Arafat Hijazi, Journalists Syndicate board member, in Beirut, 25 January 2011.

25 Stat-IPSOS figures published in 'Evening newscast viewership statistics' (*ihsā'āt nisbat mushāhadat al-nasharāt al-masā'ya*), *Al-Akhbar*, revealed that, between 20 July and 17 August, *Al-Jadeed* was leading. See http://al-akhbar.com/node/167310 (last accessed 8 October 2013).

26 Author's interview with Dr Jad Melki, media professor at the American University of Beirut, in Beirut, 3 February 2011.

27 LBCSat's news was subject to prior censorship in 1997, and was also stopped alongside Future TV in 1998; Nötzold, *Defining the Nation?*, pp. 139–44.

28 In an interview with the author conducted on 14 September 2011 in Adma, Lebanon, Daher recounted how 'Hezbollah boycotted us several times, the Syrians threatened us, not only boycotted us'. Meanwhile, senior reporter Tania Mehanna, whom the author interviewed on 28 May 2011, recounted how at one point five censors were stationed in the newsroom as well as armed men. 'They were there, they were controlling everything, every story that we were trying to do,' she said.

29 Author's interview with Pierre Daher in Adma, 14 September 2011.

30 *Za'im* refers to political leaders and patrons of communities. Arnold Hottinger captures the peculiarities of this type of Lebanese leader in Hottinger, Arnold, 'Zu'ama and Parties in the Lebanese crisis of 1958', *The Middle East Journal* 15(2) (1961), pp. 128–9.

31 Frangieh, in an interview published in *Al-Nahar* newspaper on 1 October 2000; LBCI, 'Timeline, Milestones and Dates', internal report, p. 19.

32 Nötzold, *Defining the Nation?*, pp. 139–44.

33 Despite having met all the stated requirements, New TV, later rebranded as Al Jadeed, was denied a licence and shut down in 1996. Four years later, in 2000, the State Council ruled in their favour, and the station was finally granted a licence.

34 Sakr, Naomi, *Arab Television Today* (I.B.Tauris, London, 2007), p. 184.

35 Interview with Professor Nabil Dajani in Beirut, 26 January 2011.

36 According to a content analysis conducted in 2002, Al-Manar and LBCI emerged as the two channels that identify most with the sect of their majority holders; Nötzold, *Defining the Nation?*, p. 340.

37 Chantal Mouffe refers to the consumption of media that reinforces one's views and beliefs as 'autism'. Quoted in El-Richani, Sarah, 'The Lebanese broadcasting system; a battle between political parallelism, commercialisation and de-facto liberalism', in T. Guaaybess (ed.), *National Broadcasting and State Policy in Arab Countries* (Palgrave Macmillan, Basingstoke, 2013), pp. 68–82.

38 LBCI's 'vision and mission' consists in 'extending our reach to as wide an audience as possible as consistently as possible, while remaining accountable to them'. See http://www.lbcgroup.tv/about-lbci (last accessed 8 October 2013).

39 March 8 refers to a coalition of pro-Syrian parties and political actors in Lebanon and takes its name from a protest held on 8 March 2005 in support of Syria following the assassination of former Prime Minister Rafik Hariri and amidst intensified pressure to withdraw Syria's troops from Lebanon. March 14, meanwhile, refers to a coalition of what is considered anti-Syrian and pro-Western political parties including the Future Movement, the Phalange and Lebanese Forces amongst others. The coalition also takes its name from the massive protest held on March 14, 2005, demanding the withdrawal of Syrian troops from Lebanon.

40 Several interviewees, including former and current LBC staff members, spoke of an 'identity crisis' or 'confusion', which may have been due to 'marketing problems' to explain the new LBC. In the author's interview with Marcel Ghanem, LBC talk-show host, in Beirut on 27 May 2011, Ghanem said 'Both March 14 and March 8 want us in their direction, I cannot tell you how difficult this task was and how difficult it is. Yes we did endure falls and some mistakes, yes. But, our goal is not to be here nor there. In a meeting, Pierre Daher is said to have said that "I am not March 14 nor 8, I am March 18 and I am ahead of them and we ought to be before them".'

41 Author's interview with Pierre Daher held on 14 September 2011 in Adma, Lebanon.

42 Ibid.

43 Pierre Daher spoke on LBC's *Kalam el Nas* show entitled 'LBC for whom' on 21 October 2010. He claimed the total amount paid to Samir Geagea to be around US$11 million.

44 Arabic for 'with a drop of musk', to mean plus a little bit extra/bonus. Here, Daher means he paid the entire fee to the last cent.

45 Samir Geagea in an interview on Murr TV's *Bi Mawdou'yeh* on 27 October 2009. See http://www.youtube.com/watch?v=2agzyfXEqME&NR=1 (last accessed 8 October 2013).

46 Author's interview with Lebanese Forces media department director in Maarab, Lebanon, on 11 October 2010.

47 Wikileaks cable entitled '*Ja'Ja' frustrated by failures, seeks better relations with Sunni ally*'. The cable was penned on 15 May 2006, and classified as confidential by the then-ambassador to Lebanon, Jeffrey Feltman. It was republished by *Al-Akhbar English*. See http://english.al-akhbar.com/node/279 (last accessed 8 October 2013).

48 Following Samir Geagea's release from prison, the Lebanese Forces leadership had several meetings with Daher, which finally broke down in 2007, resulting in the calling off of an interview with Geagea on LBCI and the lawsuit.

49 Television show host anchor May Chidiac resigned on air on 3 February 2009. See http://www.youtube.com/watch?v=6tSbClrBeIY (last accessed 8 October 2013).

50 Rizk, Carol, 'Indictment backs LF lawsuit against LBC, seeks jail for Daher', *The Daily Star*, 15 October 2010, http://www.dailystar.com.lb/News/Local-News/Oct/15/Indictment-backs-LF-lawsuit-against-LBC-seeks-jail-for-Daher.ashx (last accessed 8 October 2013).

51 Author's interview with Magda Abu-Fadil, media analyst, in Beirut on 19 January 2011.

52 'LF's court case against Pierre Daher dismissed', *The Daily Star*, 2 March 2012, http://www.dailystar.com.lb/News/Local-News/2012/Mar-02/165240-lfs-court-case-against-pierre-daher-dismissed.ashx#axzz254bwcrz5 (last accessed 8 October 2013).

53 Another leaked US cable entitled 'Boutros Harb urges independent list, even absent official presidential backing', filed on 5 November 2008 by then-ambassador Michele Sison in the run up to the 2009 parliamentary elections, reveals how a March 14 politician lamented his coalition's failure in swaying LBCI 'previously neutral but recently opposition-slanted back to an unbiased reporting line' referring to 'Geagea's attempt to repossess LBC [as] a "big mistake"'. Quoted in *Al-Akhbar*, http://www.al-akhbar.com/node/1076 (last accessed 8 October 2013).

54 Samir Geagea in an interview on MTV's *Bi Mawdou'yeh* on 27 October 2009, http://www.youtube.com/watch?v=2agzyfXEqME&NR=1 (last accessed 8 October 2013).

55 Diab, Youssef, 'Court decision opens way for LBC ownership trial', *The Daily Star*, 24 October 2012, http://www.dailystar.com.lb/News/Local-News/2012/Oct-24/192567-court-decision-opens-way-for-lbc-ownership-trial. (last accessed 8 October 2013).

56 Author's interview with Pierre Daher, Adma, 14 September 2011.

57 Kraidy and Khalil, *Arab Television Industries*, pp. 149–51.

58 See Chapter 6 in this book, on Saleh Kamel.

59 LBC timeline provided to the author by LBC.

60 Kraidy and Khalil, *Arab Television Industries*, pp. 149–51.

61 See Chapter 8 in this book, on Alwaleed bin Talal.

62 Kraidy and Khalil, *Arab Television Industries*, pp. 43–4.

63 Wikileaks, 'Bin Talal takes over LBC/satellite', 14 July 2008, http://leaks.hohesc.us/?view=08BEIRUT1017 (last accessed 8 October 2013).

64 Zawya, 'LBC SAT and Rotana television channels merge to form media powerhouse', 8 August 2007, https://www.zawya.com/story/ZAWYA20070809064547/ http://leaks.hohesc.us/?view=08BEIRUT1017 (last accessed 4 August 2014).

65 Nash, Matt, 'The Sheikh vs. the Prince', *Now Lebanon,* 16 March 2012, http://nowlebanon.com/NewsArchiveDetails.aspx?ID=376781#ixzz26ZXdzGhR, http://leaks.hohesc.us/?view=08BEIRUT1017 (last accessed 4 August 2014).

66 LBCI statement, 'LBCI sets the record straight on PAC feud', 25 April 2012, www.lbcgroup.tv/news/27811/lbci-sets-the-record-straight-on-pac-feud (last accessed 8 October 2013).

67 From Randa El Daher's Twitter account, 26 April 2010, @randa_eldaher https://twitter.com/randa_eldaher.

68 LBC was reportedly contracted to restructure Yemen TV. Said Nada Mufarrej, 'LBCI regains its vigour and light production' (LBCI Tasta'īdu ʿāfiyatahā wa tuntiju ʿāl-khafīf), *Al-Akhbar,* 27 June 2012, http://www.al-akhbar.com/node/96350 (last accessed 8 October 2013). In 2004 LBC partnered with Harris Corporation on a US\$96 million contract for training and content provision for Al-Iraqiya Radio and TV. Kraidy and Khalil, *Arab Television Industries*, pp. 25–30.

69 LBCI press release announcing the launch of LBCI-Drama (Ar.), 16 August 2012, http://www.lbcgroup.tv/news/45911/LBCI-DRAMA (last accessed 8 October 2013).

70 LBCI News, 'LDC, a new satellite channel', 25 November 2012, http://www.lbcgroup.tv/news/62058/ldc-a-new-satellite-channel (last accessed 8 October 2013).

71 Farran, Rabih, 'Pierre Daher, alone against everyone' (Pierre al-Daher wāḥīddan ḍudda-l-jamy'), *Al-Akhbar,* 24 March 2012, https://www.al-akhbar.com/node/58964 (last accessed 8 October 2013).

72 *Star Academy* has proven to be a goldmine, gaining 80 per cent of the audience ratings in some countries in 2004. Kraidy, Marwan. M., 'Reality TV and multiple Arab modernities: A theoretical exploration', *Middle East Journal of Culture and Communication,* 1(1) (2008), p. 51.

73 Hamoui, Faten, 'Star Academy 9's contract completed' (wa-iktamala 'aqed Star Academy 9), Al-Safir, 10 May 2013, http://www.assafir.com/Article.asp x?EditionId=2456&ChannelId=59140&ArticleId=585&Author=%D9%81% D8%A7%D8%AA%D9%86 (last accessed 8 October 2013).

74 Watson, James, Media Communication: An Introduction to Theory and Process (Palgrave Macmillan, Basingstoke, 1998), p. 86.

75 Tunstall, Jeremy, and Palmer, Michael, Media Moguls (Routledge, London/ New York, NY, 1991), p. 105.

76 Williams, Kevin, Read All About It!: A History of the British Newspaper (Routledge, London/New York, NY, 2010), p. 208.

77 Quoted by Nötzold, Defining the Nation?, p. 532.

78 Official website: www.vanillaproduction.tv.

79 Randa el Daher declared on Twitter, on 18 April 2012, 'I'm proud to be Pierre's wife socially but professionally I'm not'.

80 Haddad, Layal, 'Bin Talal coup: What remains of LBC?', Al-Akhbar English, 8 January 2012, https://english.al-akhbar.com/content/bin-talal-coup-what-remains-lbc (last accessed 8 October 2013).

81 Farran, Pierre Daher.

82 Unverified allegations made both by the former prime minister Saad Hariri's office and by MTV, a local competitor to LBC, claimed that, in July 2012, Daher had met with the head of Syrian Intelligence and with Jamil Sayyed, a former pro-Syrian General Security Chief. According to the report by MTV, the Syrians presented Daher with a list of potential Arab donors who could fill the gap left by bin Talal's withdrawal; 'Hariri slams LBC over report, accuses Daher of serving Assad', The Daily Star, 23 August 2012, http://www.dailystar. com.lb/News/Politics/2012/Aug-23/185464-hariri-slams-lbc-over-report-ac-cuses-daher-of-serving-assad.ashx#ixzz264f20QfV (last accessed 8 October 2013). Hariri's accusation came in response to a report on LBCI claiming that the former prime minister had received what they cynically called an Eid gift of US$4 billion from Saudi Arabia and Qatar to alleviate his financial woes.

83 In the author's interview with Daher in Adma, Lebanon, the latter referred to a 'crisis' in political television programmes. Trainers were brought in and the newscast was made more dynamic. Dolly Ghanem retained a position on the morning current affairs show.

84 Data collected by Stat-IPSOS and published by Al-Akhbar show that, between 20 July and 17 August 2012, Al-Jadeed's newscast attracted 4.99 per cent of viewers above the age of 15, whereas LBCI attracted 4.91 per cent. See http://al-akhbar.com/node/167310 (last accessed 8 October 2013). However, such statistics are disputed due to the limited number of Television Audience Measurement (TAM) people-meters and the fact that they have not been installed in areas like the densely populated Southern Beirut suburb, a

Hezbollah stronghold. Others allege a conflict of interest, pointing out that Stat-IPSOS receives its funding from the media themselves and mainly from LBC, because some channels have boycotted it. Future TV took Stat-IPSOS to court for reporting higher audiences for LBC's *Star Academy* than its *Super Star*. According to the author's interview with Al-Jadeed's deputy director of news and political programming (Beirut, 28 October 2010), Al-Jadeed has also sued Stat-IPSOS for what they regard as 'biased' ratings.

85 The changes, as well as the shift in focus towards socio-economic issues, culminated in the viral and well-received newscast introduction 'Republic of shame' broadcast on 31 July 2012, which caustically critiqued the government for a series of shortcomings including the 'homosexuality' tests it had used on arrested men.

86 A pun, which can either mean 'Showing off?' or 'Can you see yourself?', is a campaign by Impact BBDO and LBCI that aims at raising awareness on a variety of issues, including traffic laws, corruption and racism. See http://www.cheyef7alak.com/aboutus (last accessed 8 October 2013).

87 Author's interview with Pierre Daher in Adma, 14 September 2011.

88 Muslims include Malek Maktabi, whose show *The Bold Red Line* sensationally handles taboo topics such as homosexuality and gender-based violence, and news anchor Dima Sadek. Daher himself (interviewed by the author in Adma, 14 September 2011) says that 82 per cent of LBC staff are Christian because of the station's geographical location north of Beirut and its previous political affiliation.

89 Twitter comment published on 27 April 2012 on Randa El Daher's account: https://twitter.com/randa_eldaher.

90 Author's interview with Pierre Daher in Adma, 14 September 2011.

Chapter 5

1 Blanford, Nicholas, *Killing Mr. Lebanon. The Assassination of Rafik Hariri and its Impact on the Middle East* (I.B.Tauris, London, 2009), p. 14.

2 Jaber, Ali, 'Lebanon's prime minister buying media', *Green Left*, 9 December 1992, http://www.greenleft.org.au/node/2458 (last accessed 13 August 2012).

3 Tunstall, Jeremy, and Palmer, Michael, *Media Moguls* (Routledge, London/New York, NY, 1991), p. 105.

4 Ibid.

5 Blanford, *Mr. Lebanon*, pp. 17–18.

6 Smaller construction businesses in Saudi Arabia complain that most government contracts in construction are awarded to the Hariri-owned Saudi Oger Group and the Bin Laden Group. See Allam, Abeer, 'Saudi construction monopoly alleged', *Financial Times*, 1 August 2011.

7 Dib, Kamal, *Warlords and Merchants. The Lebanese Business and Political Establishment* (Ithaca Press, Reading, 2004), p. 295.

8 Baumann, Hannes, 'The ascent of Rafiq Hariri and Sunni philanthropy', in F. Mermier and S. Mervin (eds), *Leaders et Partisans au Liban* (Karthala, Paris, 2012), pp. 95–8.

9 Hourani, Najib, 'Transnational pathways and politico-economic power: Globalisation and the Lebanese civil war', *Geopolitics*, 15 (2010), p. 298; Dib, *Warlords*, p. 294.

10 Schellen, Thomas, 'Counting on insurers', *Executive Magazine* 60 (May 2004); http://www.executive-magazine.com/getarticle.php?article=6013 (last accessed 31 August 2012).

11 Dib, *Warlords*, p. 295.

12 Blanford, *Mr. Lebanon*, p. 31.

13 Blanford, *Mr. Lebanon*, pp. 30–3.

14 In Lebanon, power is shared among 18 recognised sects. Parliamentary seats and higher offices in public administration are allocated in the ratio 6:5 for Christians and Muslims, as laid out in the unwritten National Pact of 1943. The Taif Accord renewed this sectarian system but adjusted the ratio to 5:5. Institutional powers were transferred from the Lebanese President, who always has to be Maronite, towards the Sunni Prime Minister and the Shi'i Speaker of Parliament. For details of Lebanon's political system see e.g. Kamal, Salibi, *A House of Many Mansions* (University of California Press, Berkeley, CA, 1988); Hanf, Theodor, *Co-existence in War-Time Lebanon* (I.B.Tauris, London, 1993).

15 Hariri's relations with Syria turned more tense after Bashar al-Assad took over the Lebanese portfolio and replaced long-time allies of his father with men more loyal to himself, such as Ghazi Kenaan and Rustom Ghazaleh.

16 Blanford, *Mr. Lebanon*, p. 43.

17 Gambill, Gary C., 'Lebanon's cell phone scandals', *Middle East Intelligence Bulletin*, 5 (1) (January 2003); http://www.meforum.org/meib/articles/0301_l2.htm (last accessed 22 August 2012).

18 Hariri, Hayat, 'The Political Economy of Postwar Reconstruction in Lebanon', MA thesis (Beirut, 2011), p. 59.

19 Hariri, 'The Political Economy of Postwar Reconstruction in Lebanon', p. 59.

20 Blanford, *Mr. Lebanon*, p. 43; Hariri, 'The Political Economy of Postwar Reconstruction in Lebanon', p. 59.

21 Blanford, *Mr. Lebanon*, p. 31.

22 He died in the aftermath of the Hariri assassination from third degree burns caused because he was sitting close to Hariri in the car that was blown up on 14 February 2005.

23 Blanford, *Mr. Lebanon*, p. 61.

24 Nötzold, Katharina, *Defining the Nation? Lebanese Television and Political Elites 1990–2005* (Frank & Timme, Berlin, 2009), p. 124.

25 Jaber, 'Lebanon's prime minister'.

26 Sakr, Naomi, *Satellite Realms: Transnational Television, Globalization and the Middle East* (I.B.Tauris, London, 2001), p. 76.

27 Naba, René, *Rafic Hariri. Un homme d'affaires premier ministre* (L'Harmattan, Paris, 1999), p. 69.

28 Sakr, *Satellite Realms*, p. 76.

29 Kutschera, Chris, 'France: The rise and fall of the Arab press', April 1997; http://www.chris-kutschera.com/A/arab_press.htm (last accessed 31 December 2012).

30 Author's interview with Diana Moqalled in Beirut, 18 February 2003.

31 Author's interview with Ali Jaber in Beirut, 13 May 2003.

32 Nötzold, *Defining the Nation?* p. 170.

33 Author's interviews with Future TV journalists in Beirut, 18 February 2003, 19 March 2003, 5 May 2003, 13 May 2003 and 21 May 2003.

34 On 14 March 2005 around 1 million Lebanese gathered on Beirut's Martyr Square for the biggest demonstration ever. Most demonstrators were Sunnis of the Future Movement, Druze of the Progressive Socialist Party, various Christian anti-Syrian groups who were close to the Lebanese Forces with their imprisoned leader Samir Geagea, the Kata'eb Party of Amine Gemayel and the Free Patriotic Movement (FPM) of exiled former General Michel Aoun and Lebanese of secular parties. Demonstrators were united under the Lebanese national flag. They demanded the truth about the assassination of Hariri, but their slogans also called for freedom and independence from Syrian political and military interference. This demonstration was seen as a show of force after the 8 March 2005 demonstration in downtown Beirut, which saw mainly Shi'i supporters of Hezbollah and Amal and smaller pro-Syrian parties 'thank Syria' for their presence in Lebanon. After Aoun returned from exile, he allied the FPM with Hezbollah and Amal for parliamentary elections in May 2005. Since then, the political blocs in Lebanon are mostly referred to in an overly simplistic manner as 'pro-Syrian March 8' and 'pro-Western March 14' alliances.

35 Boyd, Douglas, *Broadcasting in the Arab World* (Iowa State University Press, Ames, IA, 1993), p. 80; Harb, Zahera, *Channels of Resistance in Lebanon* (I.B.Tauris, London, 2011), p. 97.

36 'Q & A: Gebran Tueini', *Executive Magazine*, 57 (February 2004); http://www.executive-magazine.com/getarticle.php?article=5720 (last accessed 13 August 2012).

37 'Q & A: Gebran Tueini', *Executive Magazine*.

38 Wikileaks cable; https://www.wikileaks.org/plusd/cables/06BEIRUT305_a.html (last accessed 11 September 2013).

39 'Q & A: Gebran Tueini', *Executive Magazine*.

40 List of Shareholders of Future TV (National Audiovisual Media Council, *c.* 2002).

41 Nötzold, *Defining the Nation?* p. 173.

42 Article 13 of Media Law (see Nötzold, *Defining the Nation*, p. 126). This means that the 'adult' children of some shareholders are legally allowed to own shares (10 per cent each) in one and the same station where one of their parents is a shareholder. See ACRLI 2007, *Country Report: Media in Lebanon* (Beirut, 2007); http://www.arabruleoflaw.org/Files/Outline/EN_MediaReport_Lebanon.pdf (last accessed 27 April 2013).

43 Dabbous-Sensenig, Dima, 'Ending the War? The Lebanese Broadcasting Act of 1994', PhD thesis (Sheffield Hallam University, 2003).

44 Dabbous-Sensenig, 'Ending the War?', p. 143.

45 New TV (now Al-Jadeed) is managed by Tahseen Khayyat, a Sunni businessman from Sidon. He had been a long-standing critic of Hariri, and his station was known for inviting political talk show guests who would criticise Hariri.

46 *The Daily Star*, 3 January 2003.

47 See http://www.ogertelecom.com/subsidiaries.html (last accessed 3 May 2012).

48 'IDM Cyberia merger awaits approval', *Business News*, 16 February 2012; http://www.businessnews.com.lb/cms/Story/StoryDetails.aspx?ItemID=1435 (last accessed 11 July 2012).

49 See http://www.ogertelecom.com/Cyberia.html (last accessed 3 May 2012).

50 Kraidy, Marwan M., and Khalil, Joe F., *Arab Television Industries* (Palgrave Macmillan, Basingstoke/British Film Institute, London, 2009), p. 118.

51 *The Daily Star*, 26 August 2003.

52 For more details see Nötzold, *Defining the Nation*, p. 185, footnote 732.

53 Fattah, Hassan M., 'Zen Television reaches out to Arab youth', *TBS Journal*, 9 (Fall/Winter 2002); http://www.tbsjournal.com/Archives/Fall02/Zen.html (last accessed 22 August 2012).

54 Dukcevich, Davide, 'Forbes faces: Rafik Hariri's Zen Television', *Forbes*, 26 January 2001; http://www.forbes.com/2001/01/26/0126faces.html (last accessed 22 August 2012).

55 Ibid.

56 The first chapter of Allegra Stratton's book, *Muhajababes* (Constable, London, 2006), is devoted to Zen TV.

57 *The Daily Star*, 28 October 1999.

58 *The Daily Star*, 13 April 1999.

59 Interview with Hani Hammoud in Beirut, 21 May 2003.

60 See Nötzold, *Defining the Nation?* p. 177.

61 See Nötzold, *Defining the Nation?* pp. 261–311.

62 Cochrane, Paul, 'Lebanon's Media Sectarianism', *Arab Media and Society*, May 2007; http://www.arabmediasociety.com/articles/downloads/20070520151707_AMS2_Paul_Cochrane.pdf (last accessed 26 November 2007).

63 'Future TV to get new look, add all-news channel', *MEB Journal*, January 2007.

64 *Ibid.*

65 Barotta, Rita, 'Future News: News channel or new oracle?', 20 November 2007; http://www.menassat.com/?q=en/news-articles/2217-future-news-news-channel-or-new-oracle (last accessed 22 August 2012).

66 Dockery, Stephen, 'Future TV aims to get back on top with revamp', *The Daily Star*, 25 August 2012.

67 Ibid.

68 Ibid.

69 Vloeberghs, Ward, 'The Hariri political dynasty, *Mediterranean Politics* 17(2) (2012), p. 242.

70 Vloeberghs, 'The Hariri political dynasty', p. 242.

71 Ibid., pp. 241–3.

72 Cochrane, Paul, 'Who owns the banks', *Executive* 132, July 2010; http://www.executive-magazine.com/getarticle.php?article=13209 (last accessed 4 May 2012).

73 Vloeberghs, 'The Hariri Political dynasty', pp. 242–3.

74 For a list of advisors see Vloeberghs, 'The Hariri political dynasty', p. 244.

75 'The Saudi royal bailout of Saad Hariri', *Al-Akhbar*, 14 February 2012.

76 Vloeberghs, 'The Hariri political dynasty', p. 245.

77 LBCI News,'Hariri sells Oger Telecom', 7 October 2011.

78 El-Amin, Muhammad, 'IFC announces $124 million Medgulf investment', *The Daily Star*, 6 February 2012.

79 'Saad Hariri: One Year Leading by Remote Control', *Al-Akhbar*, 19 May 2012.

80 Hariri tweeted a 'Good morning' to Avichay Adraee, an Arabic-speaking spokesperson for the Israeli ministry of defence. Israel and Lebanon are still in a state of war and for Lebanese it is a criminal offence to have contact with Israelis. Hariri later claimed that he unwittingly tweeted this message. However, political bloggers such as *Beirut Spring* criticized and mocked Hariri's ignorance. See http://beirutspring.com/blog/2012/01/13/hariris-serious-twitter-gaffe/ (last accessed 13 August 2013).

81 See Dabbous-Sensenig, *Lebanese Broadcasting Act*; Nötzold, *Defining the Nation?*; Cochrane, 'Lebanon's media sectarianism'.

82 Issa, Antoun, 'Lebanon: Is politics a social media taboo?', 18 March 2011; http://globalvoicesonline.org/2011/03/18/lebanon-is-politics-a-social-media-taboo/ (last accessed 13 August 2013).

83   Dennis, Everette E., Martin, Justin D., and Wood, Robb, 'How people in the Middle East actually use social media', *The Atlantic*, 24 April 2013; http://www.theatlantic.com/international/archive/2013/04/how-people-in-the-middle-east-actually-use-social-media/275246/ (last accessed 13 August 2013).

84   'Social media in the Arab world: Influencing societal and cultural change?', *Arab Social Media Report,* 2(1) (July 2012).

85   Vloeberghs, 'The Hariri political dynasty', p. 246.

Chapter 6

1   *Halabisa* is like a bouillon of boiled yellow peas with spices.

2   Interview with Saleh Kamel on the programme *Ana* at Dream TV, http://www.youtube.com/watch?v=7d8efy-IWiE&feature=related (last accessed 20 August 2012).

3   *Sheikh* is an honorary title indicating respect for someone in a position of leadership. Kamel is often referred to as 'Sheikh Saleh'.

4   'Saudi tycoon discusses region, challenges', cover interview, *Business Life*, http://businesslife.net/en/Cover-Interview/saudi-tycoon-discusses-region-challenges.html (last accessed 18 August 2012).

5   Roy, Olivier, *Globalised Islam* (Hurst, London, 2006, 2nd edn), pp. 97–9.

6   Bayat, Asef, 'What is Post-Islamism?', *Isim Review* 16, Autumn (2005), p. 5.

7   Ibid., p. 5.

8   Roy, *Globalised Islam*, p. 97.

9   Ibid., p. 97.

10   Ibid., p. 244.

11   Tunstall, Jeremy, and Palmer, Michael, *Media Moguls* (Routledge, London/New York, NY, 1991), p. 106.

12   *Ana* at Dream TV.

13   Ibid.

14   See Chapter 7 in this book, on Walid al-Ibrahim.

15   See Chapter 8 in this book, on Alwaleed bin Talal.

16   Sakr, Naomi, *Satellite Realms: Transnational Television, Globalization and the Middle East* (I.B.Tauris, London, 2001), p. 44.

17   Interview with the private secretary of Saleh Kamel in Egypt, 8 January 2012.

18   Kraidy, Marwan M., and Khalil, Joe F., *Arab Television Industries* (Palgrave Macmillan, Basingstoke/British Film Institute, London, 2009), p. 62.

19   Interview with the private secretary of Saleh Kamel.

20   Interview with Abdallah Schleifer in Egypt, 2 January 2012.

21   See http://www.youtube.com/watch?v=NgJQGbS3_j0 (uploaded by Al-Arabiya 23 January 2011).

22   Interview with the private secretary of Saleh Kamel.

23 Gher, Leo A., and Amin, Hussein Y., 'New and old media access and ownership in the Arab world', *International Communication Gazette* 61 (1999), pp. 59–88.

24 Ibid., pp. 59–88.

25 Kraidy and Khalil, *Arab Television Industries*, p. 21.

26 Galal, Ehab, 'Medier i den arabiske verden' (Media in the Arab world), in *Mellemøsthåndbogen: Fakta om landene i Mellemøsten og Nordafrika* (Syddansk Universitetsforlag, Odense, 2005), pp. 61–73; Sakr, *Satellite Realms: Transnational Television, Globalization and the Middle East*, p. 109.

27 Sakr, Naomi, *Arab Television Today* (I.B.Tauris, London, 2007), p. 190.

28 Ibid., p. 191.

29 Galal, Ehab, 'Modern Salafi broadcasting: Iqra channel', in K. Hroub (ed.), *Religious Broadcasting in the Middle East* (C. Hurst & Co., London, 2012), pp. 57–80.

30 Ibid., pp. 57–80.

31 Ibid., pp. 57–80.

32 Kraidy and Khalil, *Arab Television Industries*, p. 22. See also Chapter 4 in this book, on Pierre Daher.

33 Interview conducted by *Transnational Broadcasting Studies* 1, Fall (1998), http://www.tbsjournal.com/Archives/Fall98/Interviews1/Sheikh_Saleh/sheikh_saleh.html (last accessed 29 December 2012). See also Chapter 8 in this book, on Alwaleed bin Talal.

34 Ibid.

35 Sullivan, Sarah, 'ART relaunches as "total entertainment solution"', *TBS Archives* 6, Spring/Summer (2001), http://www.tbsjournal.com/Archives/Spring01/ART.html (last accessed 9 September 2013).

36 Arab News, 'Saleh Kamel accuses West of double standard', *Arab News*, 5 November 2002, http://www.arabnews.com/node/225706 (last accessed 19 August 2012). Fakkar, Galal, 'Saleh Kamel to launch major media projects', *Arab News*, 7 January 2003, http://www.arabnews.com/node/227314 (last accessed 18 August 2012).

37 Sakr, *Satellite Realms: Transnational Television, Globalization and the Middle East*, pp. 27–65.

38 Ibid., p. 47.

39 Ibid., pp. 43, 78.

40 Ibid., p. 47.

41 Interview with the private secretary of Saleh Kamel.

42 Ibid.

43 See http://www.youtube.com/watch?v=l9bF-8PlfLU&feature=related (uploaded by IqraaTube 3 January 2012; last accessed 5 January 2013).

44 Kraidy and Khalil, *Arab Television Industries*, p. 71.

45 Kraidy and Khalil also notice the similarity with *The Apprentice*. Ibid., p. 71.

46 See http://www.youtube.com/watch?v=l9bF-8PlfLU&feature=related (up-loaded by IqraaTube 3 January 2012; last accessed 6 January 2013).

47 'Kingdom has SR 1 trillion worth of Zakat: Saleh Kamel', *Arab News*, 10 August 2012, http://www.arabnews.com/economy/kingdom-has-sr-1-trillion-worth-zakat-saleh-kamel (last accessed 17 August 2012).

48 Ibid.

49 'Saudi tycoon discusses region, challenges', *Business Life*.

50 'Saleh Kamel accuses West of double standard', *Arab News*.

51 The quote is taken from the English version of the channel's website. The presentation in English is largely a translation from the presentation in Arabic, which also contains a sentence that the channel aims to reach Muslims worldwide. See http://www.Iqraa-tv.net/En/Channel.asp (last accessed 2 May 2008). This version of the website has been unavailable since at least August 2009.

52 See also Galal, 'Modern Salafi broadcasting: Iqra channel', pp. 57–80.

53 'Saudi tycoon discusses region, challenges', *Business Life*.

54 'Saleh Kamel: Ta'sis bank islami fimiliaar dolaar' [Saleh Kamel: Establishment of an Islamic bank worth a billion dollars], *Al-Yaum al-Sabe'a*, 21 March 2012.

55 The content is posted on YouTube under the title 'The Wife of Saleh Kamel'.

56 See http://www.youtube.com/watch?v=NgJQGbS3_j0 (uploaded by Al-Arabiya, 23 January 2011).

57 *Ana* at Dream TV.

58 'Saudi tycoon discusses region, challenges', *Business Life*.

59 Interview with the private secretary of Saleh Kamel.

60 See http://www.youtube.com/watch?v=NgJQGbS3_j0 (uploaded by Al-Arabiya, 23 January 2011).

61 Ibid.

62 Roy, *Globalised Islam*, pp. 232–33.

63 See, for example, his interview in 'Saudi tycoon discusses region, challenges', *Business Life*.

64 Roy, *Globalised Islam*, p. 244.

Chapter 7

1 'Rich List 2009 – Sheikh Walid al-Ibrahim: $2.9bn', ArabianBusiness.com, http://www.arabianbusiness.com/rich-list-2009/list?view=profile&item id=150329 (last accessed 4 August 2014).

2 Tunstall, Jeremy, and Palmer, Michael, *Media Moguls* (Routledge, London/New York, NY, 1991), pp. 105, 107, 108.

3 Al-Ghathami, Abdullah, *The Tale of Modernity in the Kingdom of Saudi Arabia* (Arab Cultural Centre, Beirut/Casablanca, 2005) pp. 169–73.

4 Ibid., p. 29.

5 Kraidy, Marwan M., 'The Saudi modernity wars according to 'Abdullah Al-Ghathami: A template for the study of Arab culture and media', in T. Sabry (ed.), *Arab Cultural Studies: Mapping the Field* (I.B.Tauris, London, 2012), p. 238.

6 As paraphrased and translated by Kraidy. Ibid., p. 249.

7 Lerner, Daniel, *The Passing of Traditional Society: Modernizing the Middle East* (Free Press of Glencoe, New York, NY, 1958), p. 46.

8 Ghathami, *The Tale of Modernity*, p. 39, quoted and translated by Kraidy, 'The Saudi modernity wars', p. 237.

9 Ghathami, *The Tale of Modernity*, p. 146, quoted and translated by Kraidy, 'The Saudi modernity wars', p. 248.

10 Ghathami, *The Tale of Modernity*, pp. 100, 207; Kraidy, 'The Saudi modernity wars', p. 247.

11 The website of Al Fdool Tribe (in Arabic): http://www.alfothool.com/web/al-braheem.htm (last accessed 17 September 2012).

12 Boyd, Douglas, 'Saudi Arabia's international media strategy: Influence through multinational ownership', paper presented in Maryland, August 1998, quoted by Sakr, Naomi, *Satellite Realms: Transnational Television, Globalization and the Middle East* (I.B.Tauris, London, 2001), p. 81.

13 Kamil, Yumnah, 'Saudi media moguls gobble up the Arabic market', August 1999, http://arabwestreport.info/j311/index.php/details/1/2520 (last accessed 4 October 2012).

14 See Chapter 6 in this book, on Saleh Kamel.

15 Sakr, *Satellite Realms*, p. 45.

16 Ibid., p. 42.

17 Sakr, Naomi, *Arab Television Today* (I.B.Tauris, London, 2007), p. 169.

18 Saeed, MuhammadAl-Sayyed, 'New trends and forces in the Arab media arena', in Emirates Center for Strategic Studies and Research (ed.), *Arab Media in the Information Age* (Emirates Center for Stragic Studies and Research, Abu Dhabi, 2006), p. 35.

19 Ibid., p. 35.

20 Amin, Hussein, and Boyd, Douglas, 'The development of direct broadcast television to and within the Middle East', *Journal of South Asian and Middle East Studies* 18 (2) Winter (1994), p. 46.

21 Sakr, *Arab Television Today*, p. 169.

22 Ryssdal, Kai, 'A talk with Middle East media mogul', Marketplace.org, 12 March 2008, http://www.marketplace.org/topics/world/middle-east-work/talk-middle-east-media-mogul (last accessed 20 October 2012).

23 Akeel, Maha, *Saudi Women in the Media* (Al Mar'a al-Saudiyya fi-l-'alam) (Arab Scientific Publishers, Beirut, 2010), p. 114.

24 Dossari, Salman, 'Q&A with MBC Chairman Al Waleed al Ibrahim', *Al-Sharq al-Awsat English*, 8 February 2008, http://www.asharq-e.com/print. asp?artid=id11713 (last accessed 15 November 2012).

25 Author's interview in Dubai, 22 March 2011.

26 al Rasheed, Madawi, 'An assessment of Saudi political, religious and media expansion', in M. al-Rasheed (ed.), *Kingdom Without Borders* (Hurst Publishers, London, 2008), pp. 13, 17, 18.

27 Author's interview in London, 29 October 2011.

28 Quoted in Sakr, *Arab Television Today*, p. 112.

29 Dossari, 'Q&A with Arab media mogul Waleed al-Ibrahim', *Al-Sharq al-Awsat English* website, 23 November 2006, www.asharqalawsat.com/english/news.asp?artid=id7129 (last accessed 15 November 2012).

30 Ryssdal, 'A talk with Middle East media mogul'.

31 Author's interview in Dubai, 22 March 2011.

32 Ibid.

33 Author's interview in Dubai, 13 March, 2011.

34 'Saudi fatwa row spoils Ramadan TV season', *Menassat*, 15 September 2008, http://www.menassat.com/?q=en/news-articles/4619-saudi-fatwa-row-spoils-ramadan-tv-season (last accessed 15 November 2012).

35 Chetwynd, Josh, 'At 20, MBC delivers Arab TV vision', *Variety*, 18 February 2012, http://www.variety.com/article/VR1118050467?refcatid=32 (last accessed 25 November 2012).

36 Salamandra, Christa, 'The Muhannad effect: Media panic, melodrama, and the Arab female gaze', *Anthropological Quarterly* 85(1) (2012), p. 62.

37 Ibid., p. 69.

38 Sands, Phil, 'Noor star defends racy soap', *The National*, 28 July 2008, http://www.thenational.ae/news/world/middle-east/noor-star-defends-racy-tv-soap#full (last accessed 16 September 2012).

39 MBC Club, 'Tash Ma Tash from Saudi Televsion to the MBC' (Tash Ma Tash min al-tilfisiun al-saudi ila MBC), 2005, http://www.startimes.com/f.aspx?t=647905 (last accessed 15 October 2012).

40 Saudi Forum website (Arabic), http://www.afif.ws/sahat/sitemap/t-21267. html (last accessed 6 November 2009).

41 Human Rights Watch, 'Saudi Arabia events of 2009', in Human Rights Watch, *World Report 2010*, http://www.hrw.org/world-report-2010/saudi-arabia (last accessed 12 September 2012).

42 Author's interview in Dubai, 22 March 2011.

43 Kraidy, Marwan M., *Reality Television and Arab Politics: Contention in Public Life* (Cambridge University Press, New York, NY, 2010), p. 61.

44 Quoted by Kraidy. Ibid., p. 62.

45 Dossari, 'Q&A with Arab media mogul'.

46 Al-Arabiya, 'MBC to produce series on Islam's second caliph', AlArabiya.net, 30 September 2010, http://www.alarabiya.net/articles/2010/09/30/120811. html (last accessed 8 October 2012).

47 Al-Arabiya, 'Behind the scenes of the biggest Arabic TV series', AlArabiya. net, 27 August 2012, http://english.alarabiya.net/articles/2012/08/27/234549. html (last accessed 17 October 2012).

48 Author's interview in Dubai, 13 March 2011.

49 The term is credited to Paul DiMaggio, a Princeton sociology professor, who first used it in 1998.

50 Author's interview in London, 29 October 2011.

51 MBC Group Profile, Audience Profile of Al-Arabiya – KSA IPSOS MBC Group Profile 2011, company document, p. 7.

52 Dossari, 'Q&A with MBC Chairman'.

53 Dossari, 'Q&A with Arab media mogul'.

54 Jaafar, Ali, 'Sheikh Waleed al-Ibrahim expands media empire', *Variety*, 21 November 2007, http://www.variety.com/article/VR1117976421?refCatId=13 (last accessed 11 October 2012).

55 Naidoo, Amelia, 'Internet's fine, but TV is most trusted', Gulfnews.com, 23 March 2011, http://gulfnews.com/news/region/internet-s-fine-but-tv-is-most-trusted-1.781068 (last accessed 20 October 2012).

56 Author's interview in Dubai, 22 March 2011.

57 Ryssdal, 'A talk with Middle East media mogul'.

Chapter 8

1 Curtin, Michael, *Playing to the World's Biggest Audience: The Globalization of Chinese Film and TV* (University of California Press, Berkeley, CA, 2007), p. 23.

2 Ibid., p. 10.

3 This is the title of Chapter 3 of Kraidy, Marwan, *Reality Television and Arab Politics: Contention in Public Life* (Cambridge University Press, Cambridge, 2010), pp. 66–90.

4 McGinley, Shane, 'Alwaleed fortune soars 32 per cent', *Arabian Business*, 4 November 2012, http://www.arabianbusiness.com/prince-alwaleed-s-fortune-soars-32--478413.html (last accessed 10 December 2012).

5 'Prince Alwaleed Bin Talal: Man of the year (1999)', *ArabAd* 9 (1) (1999).

6 Ibid.

7 Braude, Joseph, 'Rock the Casbah', *Radar Magazine*, 5 October 2006, http://www.radaronline.com/features/2006/10/the_prince_of_pop.php (last accessed 5 October 2006).

8 Agnew, Richard, 'The Arabian kings of cash', *Arabian Business*, 21 August 2005; Khan, Riz, *AlWaleed: Businessman, Billionaire, Prince* (Harper Collins, London, 2005).

9 Kraidy, Marwan M., and Khalil, Joe F., *Arab Television Industries* (Palgrave Macmillan, Basingstoke/British Film Institute, London, 2009).

10 'LBCSAT and Rotana television channels merge to form media powerhouse', company press release, 9 August 2007. On Pierre Daher, see Chapter 4 in this book.

11 'LBCSAT and Rotana channels merge in one entity', *Al-Riyadh*, 9 August 2007 [Arabic].

12 Akoum, Caroline, 'Has the era of Arab media alliances arrived?', *Al-Sharq al-Awsat*, 13 August 2007 [Arabic].

13 'LBC finally merged with Rotana!', *Al-Akhbar*, 9 August 2007 [Arabic].

14 'Competition between Rotana and Alam El Phan moves to the courts', *Al-Riyadh*, 12 May 2009 [Arabic].

15 Haddad, Viviane, 'Monopolistic production companies push stars towards self-productions', *Al-Sharq al-Awsat*, 7 August 2009 [Arabic].

16 Farran, Rabi, 'Concerts and releases rejuvenate art scenes', *Al-Akhbar*, 9 September 2010 [Arabic].

17 Wikileaks, 'Ideological and ownership trends in the Saudi medias', 09RIYADH651, US Embassy in Riyadh, 11 May 2009.

18 Knickmeyer, Ellen, and Efrati, Amir, 'Twitter's fit for a prince', *The Wall Street Journal*, 20 December 2011, http://online.wsj.com/article/SB1000142405297 02047911045771077338313439976.htm (last accessed 24 December 2012).

19 Kraidy and Khalil, *Arab Television Industries*, pp. 19–22; Sakr, Naomi, *Satellite Realms: Transnational Television, Globalization and the Middle East* (I.B.Tauris, London, 2001), pp. 45–9; Sakr, Naomi, *Arab Television Today* (I.B.Tauris, London, 2007), pp. 194–9.

20 Curtin, *Playing to the World's Biggest Audience: The Globalization of Chinese Film and TV*, p. 14.

21 Kraidy and Khalil, *Arab Television Industries*, p. 23.

22 Kraidy, Marwan M., and Khalil, Joe F., 'Youth, media, and culture in the Arab world', in S. Livingstone and K. Drotner (eds), *International Handbook of Children, Media and Culture* (Sage, London, 2008), pp. 330–44.

23 Dagher, Farah, 'Welcome to the empire of The Arabs' Murdoch', *Al-Akhbar*, 6 January 2012 [Arabic]; Toumi, Habib, 'Al Waleed chooses Bahrain as site for Al Arab news channel', Gulf News, 29 December 2011, http://www.gulfnews. com (last accessed 6 September 2012).

24 Curtin, *Playing to the World's Biggest Audience*, p. 19.

25 Ibid., p. 21.

26 Kraidy, *Reality Television and Arab Politics*; Sakr, Naomi, 'Placing political economy in relation to cultural studies: Reflections on the case of cinema

in Saudi Arabia', in T. Sabry (ed.), *Arab Cultural Studies: Mapping the Field* (I.B.Tauris, London, 2012).

27 Kraidy and Khalil, 'Youth, media, and culture in the Arab world', pp. 330–44.

28 Ibid., pp. 330–44; Sakr, *Arab Television Today* , pp. 154–5.

29 Sakr, *Arab Television Today*, p. 176.

30 Echchaibi, Nabil, 'From the pulpit to the studio: Islam's internal battle', *Media Development* 1 (2007).

31 'Sheikh Saleh Kamel. Featured interview', *Transnational Broadcasting Studies* 1(1) (1998), http://www.tbsjournal.com/Archives/Fall98/Interviews1/Sheikh_Saleh/sheikh_saleh.html (Link no longer working.) On Saleh Kamel, see Chapter 6 in this book.

32 'Prince Alwaleed Bin Talal: Man of the year (1999)', *ArabAd*.

33 Mansour, Muhammad, 'LBC's welcome to Saudi productions: Media charlatanism harmful to both sides!', *Al-Quds Al-Arabi*, 13 December 2007 [Arabic].

34 Ibid.

35 Kraidy, *Reality Television and Arab Politics*, p. 87.

36 Rabahi, Tawfiq, 'Saudi loyalty and dissent […] from abroad, and war of attrition in Qassem and Haddad's topics', *Al-Quds Al-Arabi*, 17 July 2007 [Arabic].

37 Ibid.

38 Ibid.

39 Abuzeid, Rania, 'Alwaleed expands media empire', *The National*, 6 July 2008.

40 Al-Rasheed, Madawi, 'The Saudi sect joins Lebanon's seventeen sects', *Al-Quds Al-Arabi*, 12 April 2008 [Arabic].

41 Ibid.

42 These debates make their way to English-language Saudi publications like *Saudi Gazette* and *Arab News*, but less so to Arabic language publications.

43 Al-Rasheed, 'The Saudi sect joins Lebanon's seventeen sects'.

44 Ayoub, S., '*Al-Nahar*, end of an era: More than 50 editors and employees laid off', *Al-Akhbar*, 28 September 2009 [Arabic].

45 Haddad, L., 'Al-Nahar's influenza infects media institutions', *Al-Akhbar*, 1 October 2009 [Arabic].

46 Curtin, *Playing to the World's Biggest Audience*, p. 11.

47 Alwaleed also encountered resistance in Egypt, where he purchased vast amounts of television archives under circumstances that observers found opaque, and where the cultural and media establishment feared the Saudiisation of culture and taste.

48 Al-Hakeem, Bassem, 'Pierre Daher tries to calm the game', *Al-Akhbar*, 6 January 2012 [Arabic].

49 Dagher, 'Welcome to the empire of The Arabs' Murdoch'.

50 Kingdom Holding Company, 'Prince Alwaleed strongly commends Saudi Ministry Council decision in regards to Saudization', official press release, 3 December 2012.

51 Curtin, *Playing to the World's Biggest Audience*, p. 109.

Chapter 9

1 Burt, Tim, 'From Tunisian desert to Hollywood dealmaking', *Financial Times*, 31 May 2005, http://www.tarakbenammar.com/uploads/assets//pdf/financialtimes310505.pdf (last accessed 15 June 2013).

2 Ibid.

3 In 2006, his companies were valued at around €450–550 million. Borzi, Nicola, 'Ben Ammar rilancia su tv digitale e cinema', *il Sole 24 ore*, 23 September 2006, http://www.tarakbenammar.com/uploads/assets//pdf/Il_sole_24_ore_sept06_TBA.pdf (last accessed 15 June 2013).

4 Halliday, Josh, 'Saudi prince launches libel action against *Forbes* magazine over Rich List', the *Guardian*, 6 June 2013, http://www.theguardian.com/media/2013/jun/06/saudi-prince-libel-action-forbes-rich-list (last accessed 15 June 2013).

5 Borzi, 'Ben Ammar rilancia su tv digitale e cinema'.

6 'Murdoch, Alwaleed, Berlusconi do deals with Tarak Ben Ammar', *Bloomberg*, 28 July 2011, http://www.bloomberg.com/apps/news?pid=newsarchive&sid=abIcvC6avpQ0&refer=germany (last accessed 15 June 2013).

7 Burt, 'From Tunisian desert to Hollywood dealmaking'.

8 Somebody 'who owns and operates major media companies, who takes entrepreneurial risks, and who conducts these media businesses in a personal or eccentric style'. Tunstall, Jeremy, and Palmer, Michael, *Media Moguls* (Routledge, London/New York, NY, 1991), p. 105.

9 'The mogul may be supported by several barons, who normally manage divisions or companies within the mogul's larger interests. The baron can be a chief executive, he may also take entrepreneurial risks, but he is not the ultimate owner or controller of the overall enterprises.' Ibid., p. 105.

10 Karl Marx has also made use of the figure of the Mogul dynasty of India to illustrate Oriental despotism and convey the image of absolute power.

11 Schumpeter, Joseph Alois, *The Theory of Economic Development* (Harvard University Press, Cambridge, MA, 1934).

12 Landstrom, Hans, *Pioneers in Entrepreneurship and Small Business Research* (Springer Science, Boston, MA, 2005), p. 34.

13 Schumpeter, *The Theory of Economic Development*, p. xix.

14 Ibid., p. 74.

15 Castells, Manuel, *The Rise of the Network Society: The Information Age: Economy, Society, and Culture,* Vol. I (Wiley-Blackwell, Malden and Oxford, 2010, 2nd edn with new preface).

16 The *Financial Times* also identifies this move to be at the core of his business strategy. See Burt, 'From Tunisian desert to Hollywood dealmaking'.

17 Croteau, David, and Hoynes, William, *The Business of Media: Corporate Media and the Public Interest* (Pine Forge Press, Sage, Thousand Oaks, CA, 2006, 2nd edn), p. 100.

18 'There are many who see this trend towards vertical disintegration and territorial localisation as heralding a benign post-Fordist era of flexible specialisation and cultural districts. It is important, however, to emphasise that vertical disintegration applies primarily to the production sector.'; Morley, David, and Robins, Kevin, *Spaces of Identity. Global Media, Electronic Landscapes and Cultural Boundaries* (Routledge, London, 1995), p. 33.

19 This phenomenon is well described by web-entrepreneur and director of MIT Media Lab Joichi Ito: 'We are now shifting from what I call the "delivery problem" to the "discovery problem". Whereas the difficulty use to lie in the mechanics of getting the product to the user, now the challenge is getting the attention of the customer.' Interview with *The Harper Studio,* 28 November 2008, http://theharperstudio.com/2008/11/creative-commons-ceo-joi-ito-explains-the-discovery-problem/ (last accessed 15 June 2013).

20 For an explanation of the reasons behind an increased interest in more vertical integration, see Croteau and Hoynes, *The Business of Media,* p. 100.

21 Aksoy and Robins, quoted by Morley and Robins, *Spaces of Identity. Global Media, Electronic Landscapes and Cultural Boundaries,* p. 33.

22 Noam, Eli M., *Media Ownership and Concentration in America* (Oxford University Press, New York, NY, 2009), p. 342.

23 Ibid., pp. 3–33, for a discussion of these dynamics.

24 Quoted by Croteau and Hoynes, *The Business of Media,* pp. 100–10.

25 Burt, 'From Tunisian desert to Hollywood dealmaking'.

26 'Murdoch, Alwaleed, Berlusconi do deals with Tarak Ben Ammar', *Bloomberg.*

27 Castells, *The Rise of the Network Society.*

28 'Murdoch, Alwaleed, Berlusconi do deals with Tarak Ben Ammar', *Bloomberg.*

29 'The jasmine media mogul', *Screen International,* April 2011.

30 Jafaar, Ali, 'Ammar moves between film, finance', *Variety,* 8 February 2008, http://www.variety.com/article/VR1117980584?refCatId=10 (last accessed 15 June 2013).

31 'Murdoch, Alwaleed, Berlusconi do deals with Tarak Ben Ammar', *Bloomberg.*

32 Ibid.

33 Scherer, Steve, and Totaro, Lorenzo, 'Berlusconi denies Qaddafi business tie that corporate documents confirm', *Bloomberg News,* 20 August 2010, http://

www.bloomberg.com/news/2010-08-20/berlusconi-denies-qaddafi-business-tie-that-corporate-documents-confirm.html (last accessed 15 June 2013).

34 'Murdoch, Alwaleed, Berlusconi do deals with Tarak Ben Ammar', *Bloomberg*.

35 Ibid.

36 Ibid.

37 Burt, 'From Tunisian desert to Hollywood dealmaking'.

38 Source, Telecom Italia official website: http://www.telecomitalia.com/tit/it/governance/board-of-directors/composition.html (last accessed 4 August 2014).

39 Prima TV is now controlled (with 95 per cent) by Ben Ammar's Holland Coordinator and Service Company Italia SPA and (with 5 per cent) by French group TF1. Source: Dfree official website, http://www.dfree.tv/societa.asp (last accessed 4 August 2014).

40 Goodfellow, Melanie, 'Tarak Ben Ammar buys private Egyptian TV channel ONTV', *Screen Daily*, 5 December 2012, http://www.screendaily.com/news/-tarak-ben-ammar-buys-private-egyptian-tv-channel-ontv/5049708.article (last accessed 15 June 2013).

41 Tunstall and Palmer, *Media Moguls*, pp. 107–8.

42 Tarek Ben Ammar's personal website: http://www.tarakbenammar.com/en/univers/professionnalisation. (Link no longer working.)

43 Personal interview with film maker Mourad Ben Cheikh in Tunis, October 2011.

44 Tarek Ben Ammar's personal website: http://www.tarakbenammar.com/en/univers/professionnalisation. (Link no longer working.)

45 Nessma TV, official presentation. Document provided by the channel, October 2011.

46 Nayeri, Farah, and Remondini, Chiara, 'Mediaset, Ben Ammar agree to buy 50 per cent in Nessma TV', *Bloomberg News,* 21 May 2008, http://www.bloomberg.com/apps/news?pid=newsarchive&sid=a66UkNQbtm14 (last accessed 15 June 2013).

47 Tarek Ben Ammar's personal website: http://www.tarakbenammar.com/en/actualites. (Link no longer working.)

48 Nayeri and Remondini, 'Mediaset, Ben Ammar agree to buy 50 per cent in Nessma TV'.

49 See http://www.tarakbenammar.com/en/actualites#3. (Link no longer working.)

50 Later, in 1994, when Bettino Craxi had to flee the country to avoid conviction on corruption charges, he found refuge in Hammamet, Tunisia, where he died and was buried.

51 Interview with Soufiane Ben Farhat, journalist at La Presse and former employee of Nessma, in Tunis, October 2011; interview with Elias Gharbi, former programmes host at Nessma, in Tunis, October 2011; interview with

Jamel Arfaoui, journalist and programme producer at Nessma, in Tunis, October 2011.

52 Interview with Nebil Keroui in Tunis, October 2011.

53 Interview with Jamel Arfaoui in Tunis, October 2011.

54 On the ownership structure of Lafitrade, see van Gelder, Jan Willem, and Spaargaren, Petra, 'Investments of Middle East and North African governments in the Netherlands', research paper by *Profundo Economic Research*, 9 March 2011, pp. 18–19, http://media.rtl.nl/media/actueel/rtlnieuws/2011/rapportprofundo.pdf (last accessed 15 June 2013).

55 Hooper, John, 'The Gaddafi–Berlusconi connection', the *Guardian*, 4 September 2009, http://www.guardian.co.uk/commentisfree/2009/sep/04/gaddafi-berlusconi-business (last accessed 15 June 2013).

56 il Sole 24 ore, 'Ben Ammar: il fondo sovrano libico è in affari con Fininvest, ma non in Italia. La mappa delle partecipazioni', 6 March 2011, http://www.ilsole24ore.com/art/notizie/2011-03-06/ammar-fondo-sovrano-libico-203523.shtml?uuid=Aazam0DD (last accessed 15 June 2013).

57 Scherer and Totaro, 'Berlusconi denies Qaddafi business tie that corporate documents confirm'.

58 Elia, Christian, 'Libia, il Colonnello e il Cavaliere', *PeaceReporter,* 27 August 2010, http://it.peacereporter.net/articolo/23812/Libia,+il+Colonnello+e+il+Cavaliere (last accessed 15 June 2013).

59 Ibid.

60 Latza Nadeau, Barbie, 'Gaddafi's Italian connection', *The Daily Beast,* 27 August 2011, http://www.thedailybeast.com/articles/2011/08/27/gaddafi-s-connections-to-italy-and-berlusconi.html (last accessed 15 June 2013).

61 In May 2012, Ponzellini resigned from his position at Impregilo, after being charged with financial fraud and corruption. Il Fatto Quotidiano, 'BPM, Ponzellini lascia Impregilo."Così la società opererà in trasparenza"', 31 May 2012, http://www.ilfattoquotidiano.it/2012/05/31/inchiesta-bpm-ponzellini-lascia-impregilo-cosi-societa-operera-in-trasparenza/248058/ (last accessed 15 June 2013).

62 Della Ratta, Donatella, 'Berlusconi's musalsal aired on Tunisian Nessma TV', Mediaoriente.com, 28 August 2009, http://mediaoriente.com/2009/08/28/berlusconis-musalsal-aired-on-tunisian-nessma-tv/ (last accessed 15 June 2013).

63 Ibid.

64 Weaver, Matthew, 'Muammar Gaddafi condemns Tunisia uprising', the *Guardian*, 16 January 2011, http://www.guardian.co.uk/world/2011/jan/16/muammar-gaddafi-condemns-tunisia-uprising (last accessed 15 June 2013).

65 Personal interview in Tunis, October 2011.

66 Ben Ali and Ben Ammar had officially met, in August 2010, to talk about Nessma TV and its role in supporting diversity and media pluralism. 'Pour

un paysage audiovisuel riche et diversifié', *La Presse*, 18 August 2010, http://www.lapresse.tn/18082010/11004/pour-un-paysage-audiovisuel-riche-et-diversifie.html (last accessed 15 June 2013).

67 Soufiane Ben Farhat, a journalist at Tunisian newspaper *La Presse*, who was working with Nessma TV at the time and who was present at the studio debate on the Sidi Bouzid issue, in a personal interview in Tunis, October 2011. This has been confirmed by Jamel Arfaoui, a journalist and political commentator, who also joined the Sidi Bouzid show on Nessma; personal interview in Tunis, October 2011. Nebil Keroui, the director general of the channel, has also confirmed that Ben Ammar was aware of the Sidi Bouzid show, although he was away in France at the time. Also, according to his version of the story, it is not Ben Ali who called Ben Ammar, but the Ministry of Communication, who called Keroui himself and asked Nessma to do a TV show 'to counter Al-Jazeera and France 24 propaganda'. Personal interview in Tunis, October 2011.

68 Moez Sinaoui, who was at the time Director of Communication at Nessma TV, also confirmed the anecdote during an informal chat in the framework of the Euro-Med media meeting held in Barcelona on 1–2 March 2013.

69 Personal interview in Tunis, October 2011.

70 Ben Farhat, Arfaoui and Keroui, personal interviews in Tunis, October 2011.

71 Personal interview in Tunis, October 2011.

72 Heydemann, Steven, *Upgrading Authoritarianism in the Arab World* (The Saban Center for Middle East Policy at the Brookings Institution, Washington, DC, October 2007), p. VII, http://www.brookings.edu/~/media/research/files/papers/2007/10/arabworld/10arabworld.pdf (last accessed 15 June 2013).

73 Ibid., p. VII.

74 Hostrup Haugbolle, Rikke, and Cavatorta, Francesco, '"Vive la grande famille des médias tunisiens". Media reform, authoritarian resilience and societal responses in Tunisia,' *The Journal of North African Studies* xxvii(1) (2012), p. 1, http://www.tandfonline.com/doi/abs/10.1080/13629387.2011.558308 (first version published 14 July 2011).

75 Ibid., p.3.

76 Personal interview in Tunis, October 2011.

77 Ibid.

78 Ibid.

79 'Protesters attack TV station over film *Persepolis*', BBC News, 9 October 2011, http://www.bbc.co.uk/news/world-africa-15233442 (last accessed 15 June 2013).

80 Lyman, Eric J., 'Tarak Ben Ammar acquires ONTV in the mogul's first foray into Egypt', *The Hollywood Reporter*, 5 December 2012, http://www.hollywoodreporter.com/news/tarak-ben-ammar-aquires-ontv-398163 (last accessed 15 June 2013).

81 Quoted by Jafaar, 'Ammar moves between film, finance'.

82 Quoted in Shams El-Din, Mai, 'Sawiris sells ONtv to Tunisian businessman', *Egypt Independent*, 16 December 2012, http://www.egyptindependent.com/news/sawiris-sells-ontv-tunisian-businessman (last accessed 15 June 2013).

Chapter 10

1 Sfakianakis, John, 'The whales of the Nile: Networks, businessmen, and bureaucrats during the era of privatization in Egypt', in S. Heydemann (ed.), *Networks of Privilege in the Middle East: The Politics of Economic Reform Revisited* (Palgrave Macmillan, Basingstoke/New York, NY, 2004). Sfakianakis based his title on the plural word *hitan*, as stated on p. 80.

2 Edition of 10 March 2005.

3 Tunstall, Jeremy, and Palmer, Michael, 'Introduction', in J. Tunstall (ed.), *Media Occupations and Professions: A Reader* (Oxford University Press, Oxford, 2001), pp. 4–5.

4 Knee, Jonathan, Greenwald, Bruce, and Seave, Ava, *The Curse of the Mogul: What's Wrong with the World's Leading Media Companies* (Portfolio/Penguin Group, New York, NY, 2009), p. 4.

5 Ibid., pp. 267–8.

6 Jarvis, Jeff, 'The last mogul moments', *BuzzMachine*, 26 July 2011, http://buzzmachine.com/2011/07/ (last accessed 12 October 2011).

7 Mitchell, Timothy, *Rule of Experts: Egypt, Techno-Politics, Modernity* (University of California Press, Berkeley, CA, 2002), p. 30.

8 Harvey, David, 'The enigma of capital and the crisis this time', Paper prepared for the American Sociological Association, Atlanta, 16 August 2010, http://davidharvey.org/2010/08/the-enigma-of-capital-and-the-crisis-this-time/ (last accessed 4 May 2013).

9 Sakr, Naomi, 'Where Arab media magnates stand *vis-à-vis* globalized media flows: Insights from Egypt and Saudi Arabia', *International Journal of Communication* 7 (2013), pp. 2297–8.

10 Mitchell, *Rule of Experts*, p. 31.

11 Ibid., p 33.

12 Ibid., pp. 30, 33.

13 Ibid., p. 53.

14 Darwish, Mustafa, *Dream Makers on the Nile: A Portrait of Egyptian Cinema* (American University in Cairo Press, Cairo, 1998), pp. 9–13.

15 Shafik, Viola, *Popular Egyptian Cinema: Gender, Class, and Nation* (American University in Cairo Press, Cairo, 2007), pp. 21–2.

16 Ghoneim, Ahmed Farouk, 'The audio-visual sector in Egypt', in P. Guerrieri, P. Lelio Iapadre and G. Koopmann (eds), *Cultural Diversity and International*

Economic Integration: The Global Governance of the Audio-Visual Sector (Edward Elgar, Cheltenham, 2005), pp. 203–4.

17 Ibid., p. 203.

18 El-Bishlawi, Khaireya, 'A capital production', *Al-Ahram Weekly*, no. 377, 14–20 May 1998.

19 Eberhard Kienle states that evidence for such pressure ultimately 'boils down to hearsay and rumors', although the regime had plenty of reasons to want to please the Sawiris family to 'convince them to further support the regime'. See Kienle, Eberhard, 'Reconciling privilege and reform: Fiscal policy in Egypt, 1991–2000', in S. Heydemann (ed.), *Networks of Privilege in the Middle East: The Politics of Economic Reform Revisited* (Palgrave Macmillan, Basingstoke, 2004), pp. 289–90.

20 Baker, Stephanie, and Kassem, Mahmoud, 'Billionaire facing death threats says Egypt risks becoming Iran', *Bloomberg News*, 26 October 2011, http://mobile.bloomberg.com/news/2011-10-26/billionaire-facing-death-threats-says-egypt-risks-becoming-iran?category=%2Fmarkets-magazine%2F (last accessed 31 October 2011).

21 Mitchell, *Rule of Experts*, p. 284.

22 'The new Pharaohs', *The Economist*, 10 March 2005.

23 Kamel, Sherif, 'Evolution of mobile technology in Egypt', in M. Khosrowpour (ed.), *Innovations through Information Technology* (Information Resources Management Association, New Orleans, LA, 2004), p. 726.

24 El-Bishlawi, 'A capital production'.

25 UNESCO data quoted by Ghoneim, 'The audio-visual sector in Egypt', p. 206.

26 According to Columbia and TriStar agent Tarek Sabri, quoted by El-Bishlawi, 'A capital production'.

27 Author's interview with Magda Maurice, editor of *Shashati* (*My Screen*), in Cairo, 24 February 1999.

28 According to EFG-Hermes board member Ahmed Heikal, quoted by *Middle East Economic Digest*, 5 March 1999, p. 18.

29 El-Bishlawi, 'A capital production'.

30 Howeidy, Amira, 'Private initiatives', *Al-Ahram Weekly*, 481, 11–17 May 2000.

31 Ibid.

32 Myers, Lisa, and Roston, Aram, 'Iraqi contract may benefit controversial businessman', *NBC News*, 13 November 2003, http://www.nbcnews.com/id/3476025/ns/nbcnightlynews/t/iraqi-contract-may-benefit-controversial-businessman/ (last accessed 20 May 2013).

33 Fahim, Joseph, 'Sawiris attacked at Heaven press conference; pandemonium ensues', *Daily News Egypt*, 29 November 2007.

34 Sakr, Naomi, 'Egyptian TV in the grip of government: Politics before profit in a fluid pan-Arab market', in D. Ward (ed.), *Television and Public Policy* (Lawrence Erlbaum Associations, New York, NY, 2008), p. 272.

35 Howeidy, 'Private initiatives'.

36 For more detailed analysis see Sakr, Naomi, 'Social media, television talk shows and political change in Egypt', *Television & New Media* 14(4) (2013), p. 326.

37 Sakr, Naomi, *Arab Television Today* (I.B.Tauris, London, 2007), p. 29.

38 Ibid., p. 114.

39 The Coalition Provisional Authority was dissolved in June 2004, when it handed power to the Interim Iraqi Government, which it had created.

40 Clark, Nicola, 'A calmer voice comes to nascent Iraqi television scene', *New York Times*, 16 August 2004.

41 Khalaf, Roula, and Wallis, William, 'Egyptian billionaire aims to build satellite TV empire', *Financial Times,* 21 May 2006.

42 Eutelsat, *Cable and Satellite TV Market, 2002*; Eutelsat, *Cable and Satellite TV Market, 2006*. Eutelsat's figure for Egypt in 2006 was equivalent to 50.3 per cent.

43 Fahim, Joseph, 'OTV hits the airwaves', *Daily News Egypt*, 30 January 2007.

44 Ibid.

45 Tryhorn, Chris, 'The Sawiris family: From entrepreneurs to media owners', the *Guardian*, 2 February 2010, http://www.guardian.co.uk/media/2010/feb/02/sawiris-independent (last accessed 8 April 2012).

46 See quotations in Fahim, 'OTV hits the airwaves'; Tryhorn, The Sawiris family: (last accessed 8 April 2012).

47 Buccianti, Alexandra, 'Les talk shows d'Egypte parlent aux Egyptiens', MA dissertation (Institut d'études politiques de Paris, Paris, 2010), p. 89.

48 Sawiris was assigned to speak on this topic at The Economist Conferences' Emerging Markets Summit on 16 September 2010. His talk can be watched at http://www.economistconferences.co.uk/video/emerging-markets-summit-2010/4397 (last accessed 20 May 2013).

49 Gara, Tom, and George-Cosh, David, 'Orascom founder says company has to evolve to survive', *The National*, 6 March 2010.

50 Gara and George-Cosh, 'Orascom founder says company has to evolve to survive'.

51 For example, the interview with Charlie Rose on PBS, 14 February 2011, http://www.charlierose.com/view/interview/11472 (last accessed 12 July 2012).

52 Ibid.

53 For more on the debate see Sakr, Naomi, *Transformations in Egyptian Journalism* (I.B.Tauris, London, 2013), pp. 13–14.

54 Baker and Kassem, 'Billionaire facing death threats says Egypt risks becoming Iran'.

55 Gray, Jessica, '2013: The year of MobiNil', *Business Today Egypt*, 11 December 2012, http://www.businesstodayegypt.com/article/artId:530/2013-The-Year-of-Mobinil/secId:3 (last accessed 21 May 2013).

56 For more on Tarek Ben Ammar see Chapter 9 in this book.

57 A video of the interview, on 5 March 2013, was posted at http://nilesports.com/news/2013/03/06/interview-with-egyptian-businessman-naguib-sawiris-march-5th-2013/ (last accessed 17 March 2013).

58 As translated by *AhramOnline*, 6 March 2013, http://english.ahram.org.eg/NewsContent/3/12/66259/Business/Economy/My-family-is-targeted-by-Brotherhood-Egypt-busines.aspx (last accessed 14 March 2013).

59 Interview conducted by Steve Chiotakis on 31 January 2011, http://www.marketplace.org/topics/world/new-egypt/naguib-sawiris-importance-de-mocracy-business-egypt (last accessed 1 October 2012).

60 Interviewed by Zeinab Badawi on 21 December 2012, http://www.bbc.co.uk/iplayer/episode/b01pd29d/HARDtalk_Naguib_Sawiris_Businessman_and_founder_Free_Egyptians_Party/ (last accessed 21 May 2013).

61 For more on Diab and Bahgat see Chapter 11 in this book.

62 Allam, Hannah, 'Egypt's press has become surprisingly free – and lively', *Knight Ridder Newspapers*, 23 February 2006, http://www.mcclatchydc.com/2006/02/23/v-print/13545/egypts-press-has-become-surprisingly.html (last accessed 22 May 2013).

63 Cooper, Kenneth J., 'Politics and priorities: Inside the Egyptian press', *Arab Media and Society* 6, Fall (2008).

64 Beach, Alistair, 'Newspaper article which criticised military ruler is banned', *The Independent*, 5 December 2011.

65 According to Sherif Wadood, a former CEO of *Al-Masry al-Youm*, quoted in the valedictory online article explaining the closure of *Egypt Independent*, 25 April 2013. See http://www.egyptindependent.com/news/final-issue-how-poor-management-destroyed-leading-voice (last accessed 21 May 2013).

66 Carr, Sarah, 'Goodbye, Al-Masry al-Youm', *Egypt Independent*, 26 April 2013, http://www.egyptindependent.com/opinion/goodbye-al-masry-al-youm (last accessed 21 May 2013).

67 Mitchell, *Rule of Experts*, p. 53.

68 Ibid., pp. 30–3.

Chapter 11

1 Bourdieu, Pierre, and Passeron, Jean-Claude, *Les héritiers. Les étudiants et la culture* (Editions de Minuit, Paris, 1964); *La reproduction, éléments pour une théorie du système d'enseignement* (Editions de Minuit, Paris, 1970).

2 I used the term 'confluence' to describe this interrelation. Tourya Guaaybess, *Les médias arabes* (CNRS, Paris, 2012 edn).

3 See http://www.goodnewsgroup.com.

4 Orbit TV is a satellite channel and part of the Saudi network Orbit.

5 See   http://www.cihrs.org/wp-content/uploads/2012/02/Elections-Report. pdf; Levinson, Charles, 'Plus ça change: The role of the media in Egypt's first contested presidential elections', *Transnational Broadcasting Studies* 15, January–June (2006).

6 *Al-Masry al-Youm*, 13 February 2011.

7 *Al-Masry al-Youm*, 26 December 2009, http://www.almasryalyoum.com/ node/7906 [in Arabic] (last accessed 4 August 2014).

8 Quoted among others by Abdoun, Safaa, 'Crackdown on the media takes new dimension in 2010', *Daily News Egypt*, 23 December 2010.

9 William Rugh qualifies media as loyalist if they support the regime: Rugh, William, *Arab Mass Media: Newspapers, Radio, and Television in Arab Politics* (Praeger, Westport, CT, 2004).

10 Al Tamimi, Jumana, 'Undiluted news revives Egypt papers', *Gulf News*, 10 February 2011.

11 Interview with the author in Cairo, January 2011.

12 Kassem, Hisham, 'How the *Cairo Times* came to be published out of Cyprus', in Islam, Roumeen (ed.), *The Right to Tell: The Role of Mass Media in Economic Development* (World Bank Institute, Washington, DC, 2002), pp. 275–80.

13 Interview with the author in Cairo, January 2011.

14 For more on Kassem see Sakr, Naomi, *Transformations in Egyptian Journalism* (I.B.Tauris, London, 2013), pp. 33–5.

15 Interview with the author in Cairo, January 2011.

16 Black, Jeffrey, 'Egypt's press: More free, still fettered', *Arab Media & Society* January (2008).

17 Knickmeyer, Ellen, 'In Egypt, a son is readied for succession', *Washington Post*, 11 October 2007.

18 Loza, Pierre, 'Egypt: Brotherhood coverage is pure journalism, not a political deal with *Al-Dostour*', *The Daily Star*, 19 September 2007.

19 Nasrawy, Saif, 'El-Baradei article central to sacking of Al-Dostour's chief editor', *Al-Masry al-Youm*, 5 October 2010.

20 Abdel-Rahman, Muhammad, 'Will Tahrir channel leave the square?', *Al-Akhbar*, 21 October 2011.

21 See *Al-Masry al-Youm*, Tahrir separates from *Al-Shabab* after Tawfiq sells share to *Amer*', 14 December2011.

22 The Supreme Council of Armed Forces.

23 See Chapter 10 in this book, on Sawiris.

24 Quoted in Sakr, Naomi, *Arab Television Today* (I.B.Tauris, London, 2007), p. 123.

25 *The report: Emerging Egypt 2008* (Oxford Business Group, 2009), p. 186.

26 Quoted by Michael, Maggie, 'Egypt's emboldened press now feeling the backlash', *Associated Press*, 22 October 2010.

27 This interview was recorded on 14 February 2011. See http://www.charlierose.com/view/interview/11472. (Link no longer working.)

28 Afify, Heba, 'Naguib Sawiris launches liberal "Free Egyptians Party2"', *Al-Masry al-Youm*, 4 April 2011.

29 See http://www.bahgat.com/dpages.aspx?id=122 (last accessed 4 August 2014).

30 Solovieva, Daria, 'Amid media wars, a need for evolution', *Business Today Egypt*, 13 January 2012.

31 Osman, Ahmed, 'Rude awakening: Dream drops top talkers', *TBS* 12, Spring–Summer (2004).

32 See http://swegypt.net/news/ANTI-BIN%20LADEN%20MEDIA%20KIT. FINAL.pdf. (Link no longer working.)

33 Hamdy, Naila, 'El Mehwar the mercurial, *TBS* 9, Winter (2002), http://www. tbsjournal.com/Archives/Fall02/Mehwar.html. (Link no longer working.)

34 Hamdy, 'El Mehwar the mercurial'.

35 See http://25online.tv/index.php?lang=en (Link no longer working.)

36 'Ethical' is used here to refer to the difficulty for individual businessmen of doing business in a way acceptable to both the population and the government.

37 Guaaybess, Tourya, 'Reforming Egypt's broadcasting in the post-25 January era: The challenges of path dependence', in T. Guaaybess (ed.), *National Broadcasting and State Policy in Arab Countries* (Palgrave Macmillan, Basingstoke, 2013), pp. 49–68.

Bibliography

Akeel, Maha, *Saudi Women in the Media* [in Arabic] (Arab Scientific Publishers, Beirut, 2010).

Al-Ghathami, Abdullah, *The Story of Modernity in Saudi Arabia* [in Arabic] (The Arab Cultural Centre, Beirut, 2005).

Al-Rasheed, Madawi, 'An assessment of Saudi political, religious and media expansion', in M. Al-Rasheed (ed.), *Kingdom without Borders* (Hurst Publishers, London, 2008), pp. 1–38.

Al-Zubaidi, Layla, *Walking a Tightrope: News Media and Freedom of Expression in the Arab Middle East* (Heinrich Böll Foundation Middle East Office, Beirut, 2004).

Ayish, Muhammad I., *Arab World Television in the Age of Globalization: An Analysis of Emerging Political, Economic, Cultural and Technological Patterns* (Deutsches Orient-Institut, Hamburg, 2003).

Baumann, Hannes, 'The ascent of Rafiq Hariri and Sunni philanthropy', in F. Mermier and S. Mervin (eds), *Leaders et Partisans au Liban* (Khartala, Paris, 2012), pp. 81–106.

Black, Jeffrey, 'Egypt's press: More free, still fettered', *Arab Media & Society*, January 2008.

Blanford, Nicholas, *Killing Mr. Lebanon. The Assassination of Rafik Hariri and its Impact on the Middle East* (I.B.Tauris, London, 2009).

Bourdieu, Pierre, and Passeron, Jean-Claude, *Les Héritiers. Les Etudiants et la culture* (Editions de Minuit, Paris, 1964).

——— *La Reproduction, Eléments pour une théorie du système d'enseignement* (Editions de Minuit, Paris, 1970).

Boyd, Douglas, *Broadcasting in the Arab World* (Iowa State University Press, Ames, IA, 1993).

Buccianti, Alexandra, 'Les Talk Shows d'Egypte Parlent aux Egyptiens', MA dissertation (Institut d'études politiques de Paris, Paris, 2010).

Castells, Manuel, *The Rise of the Network Society: The Information Age: Economy, Society, and Culture*, Vol I, 2nd edn (Wiley-Blackwell, Cambridge, MA, 2010).

Cochrane, Paul, 'Lebanon's media sectarianism', *Arab Media and Society*, May (2007).

Croteau, David, and Hoynes, William, *The Business of Media: Corporate Media and the Public Interest*, 2nd edn (Pine Forge Press, Sage, Thousand Oaks, CA, 2006).

Curtin, Michael, *Playing to the World's Biggest Audience: The Globalization of Chinese Film and TV* (University of California Press, Berkeley, CA, 2007).

Dabbous-Sensenig, Dima, *Ending the War? The Lebanese Broadcasting Act of 1994*, PhD thesis (Sheffield Hallam University, Sheffield, 2003).

Darwish, Mustafa, *Dream Makers on the Nile: A Portrait of Egyptian Cinema* (American University in Cairo Press, Cairo, 1998).

Della Ratta, Donatella, *Dramas of the Authoritarian State: The Politics of Syrian TV Serials in the Pan Arab Market* (Department of Cross-Cultural and Regional Studies, Copenhagen University, Copenhagen, 2013).

Dib, Kamal, *Warlords and Merchants: The Lebanese Business and Political Establishment* (Ithaca Press, Reading, 2004).

Dodge, Toby, 'Bringing the bourgeoisie back in: Globalization and the birth of liberal authoritarianism in the Middle East', in T. Dodge and R. Higgott (eds), *Globalization and the Middle East: Islam, Economy, Society and Politics* (Royal Institute of International Affairs, London, 2002), pp. 169–87.

Doyle, Gillian, *Understanding Media Economics* (Sage, London, 2002).

El-Richani, Sarah, 'The Lebanese broadcasting system: A battle between political parallelism, commercialization and de-facto liberalism', in T. Guaaybess (ed.), *National Broadcasting and State Policy in Arab Countries* (Palgrave Macmillan, Basingstoke, 2013), pp. 68–82.

Fandy, Mamoun, *(Un)Civil War of Words: Media and Politics in the Arab World* (Praeger Security International, London/Westport, CT, 2008).

Fattah, Hassan M., 'Zen television reaches out to Arab youth', *Transnational Broadcasting Studies* 9, Fall/Winter (2002).

Freedman, Des, *The Politics of Media Policy* (Polity, Cambridge, 2008).

Galal, Ehab, 'Medier i den arabiske verden', in L. Erslev Andersen, S. Hove and M. Vingum Jensen (eds), *Mellemøsthåndbogen: Fakta om landene i Mellemøsten og Nordafrika* (Syddansk Universitetsforlag, Odense, 2005), pp. 61–73.

—— '"Modern" Salafi broadcasting: Iqra' channel', in K. Hroub (ed.), *Religious Broadcasting in the Middle East* (C Hurst & Co, London, 2012), pp. 57–80.

Ghoneim, Ahmed Farouk, 'The audio-visual sector in Egypt', in P. Guerrieri, P. Lelio Iapadre and G. Koopmann (eds), *Cultural Diversity and International*

Economic Integration: The Global Governance of the Audio-Visual Sector (Edward Elgar, Cheltenham, 2005), pp. 192–217.

Giddens, Anthony, 'The globalizing of modernity', in A. Sreberny (ed.), *Media in Global Context: A Reader* (Arnold, London, 1997), pp. 19–26.

Guaaybess, Tourya, *Les médias arabes, confluences médiatiques et dynamique sociale* (CNRS éditions, Paris, 2012).

—— 'Reforming Egypt's broadcasting in the post-25 January era: The challenges of path dependence', in T. Guaaybess (ed.) *National Broadcasting and State Policy in Arab Countries* (Palgrave Macmillan, Basingstoke, 2013), pp. 49–68.

Hallin, Daniel C., and Mancini, Paolo, *Comparing Media Systems: Three Models of Media and Politics* (Cambridge University Press, Cambridge, 2004).

Hamdy, Naila, 'El Mehwar the mercurial', *Transnational Broadcasting Studies* 9, Winter (2002).

Hamelink, Cees J., and Nordenstreng, Kaarle, 'Towards democratic media governance', in E. de Bens and C. J. Hamelink (eds), *Media between Culture and Commerce* (Intellect Books, Bristol, 2007), pp. 225–40.

Hanf, Theodor, *Co-existence in War-time Lebanon* (I.B.Tauris, London, 1993).

Harb, Zahera, *Channels of Resistance in Lebanon* (I.B.Tauris, London, 2011).

Hariri, Hayat, *The Political Economy of Postwar Reconstruction in Lebanon*, MA thesis (Lebanese American University, Beirut, 2011).

Heidenreich, Martin, Cooke, Philip, and Braczyk, Hans-Joachim, *Regional Innovation Systems: The Role of Governances in a Globalized World* (Routledge, London, 1998).

Heydemann, Steven, *Upgrading Authoritarianism in the Arab World* (The Saban Center for Middle East Policy at the Brookings Institution, Washington, DC, October 2007), http://www.brookings.edu/~/media/research/files/papers/2007/10/arabworld/10arabworld.pdf.

Hostrup Haugbolle, Rikke, and Cavatorta, Francesco, '"Vive la grande famille des médias tunisiens": Media reform, authoritarian resilience and societal responses in Tunisia', *The Journal of North African Studies* 17(1) January (2012), pp. 97–112.

Hottinger, Arnold, 'Zu'ama and parties in the Lebanese crisis of 1958', *The Middle East Journal*, 15(2) (1961), pp. 127–40.

Hourani, Najib, 'Transnational pathways and politico-economic power: globalisation and the Lebanese civil war', *Geopolitics*, 15(2) May (2010), pp. 290–311.

Karlsson, Charlie, and Picard, Robert G., *Media Clusters: Spatial Agglomeration and Content Capabilities* (Edward Elgar, Cheltenham, 2011).

Kassem, Hisham, 'How the *Cairo Times* came to be published out of Cyprus', in R. Islam (ed.) *The Right to Tell: The Role of Mass Media in Economic Development* (World Bank Institute, Washington, DC, 2002), pp. 275–80.

Khan, Riz, *AlWaleed: Businessman, Billionaire, Prince* (Harper Collins, London, 2005).

Kienle, Eberhard, 'Reconciling privilege and reform: fiscal policy in Egypt, 1991–2000', in S. Heydemann (ed.), *Networks of Privilege in the Middle East: The Politics of Economic Reform Revisited* (Palgrave Macmillan, Basingstoke, 2004), pp. 281–96.

Knee, Jonathan, Greenwald, Bruce, and Seave, Ava, *The Curse of the Mogul: What's Wrong with the World's Leading Media Companies* (Portfolio/Penguin Group, New York, NY, 2009).

Kraidy, Marwan M., 'Reality TV and multiple Arab modernities: A theoretical exploration', *Middle East Journal of Culture and Communication* 1(1) (2008), pp. 49–59.

—— *Reality Television and Arab Politics: Contention in Public Life* (Cambridge University Press, New York, NY, 2010).

—— 'The Saudi modernity wars according to Abdullah Al-Ghathami: A template for the study of Arab culture and media', in T. Sabry (ed.), *Arab Cultural Studies: Mapping the Field* (I.B.Tauris, London, 2012), pp. 234–54.

Kraidy, Marwan M., and Khalil, Joe F., 'Youth, media, and culture in the Arab world', in S. Livingstone and K. Drotner (eds), *International Handbook of Children, Media and Culture* (Sage, London, 2008), pp. 330–44.

—— *Arab Television Industries* (Palgrave Macmillan, Basingstoke/British Film Institute, London, 2009).

Landstrom, Hans, *Pioneers in Entrepreneurship and Small Business Research* (Springer Science, Boston, MA, 2005).

Lerner, Daniel, *The Passing of Traditional Society: Modernizing the Middle East* (Free Press of Glencoe, New York, NY, 1958).

Levinson, Charles, Plus ça change: The role of the media in Egypt's first contested presidential elections, *Transnational Broadcasting Studies* 15, January–June (2006).

Mancini, Paolo, 'Political complexity and alternative models of journalism: The Italian case', in M. Park and J. Curran, *De-Westernizing Media Studies* (Routledge, London, 2000), pp. 265–78.

McQuail, Dennis, 'Introduction: The current state of media governance in Europe', in G. Terzis (ed.), *European Media Governance: National and Regional Dimensions* (Intellect, Bristol, 2007), pp. 17–26.

Mellor, Noha, Rinnawi, Khalil, Dajani, Nabil, and Ayish, Muhammad I., *Arab Media: Globalization and Emerging Media Industries* (Polity Press, Cambridge, 2011).

Mitchell, Timothy, *Rule of Experts: Egypt, Techno-Politics, Modernity* (University of California Press, Berkeley, CA, 2002).

Morley, David, and Robins, Kevin, *Spaces of Identity. Global Media, Electronic Landscapes and Cultural Boundaries* (Routledge, London, 1995).

Naba, René, *Rafic Hariri. Un homme d'affaires premier ministre* (Harmattan, Paris, 1999).

Noam, Eli M., *Media Ownership and Concentration in America* (Oxford University Press, New York, NY, 2009).

Nötzold, Katharina, *Defining the Nation? Lebanese TV Stations: The Political Elites' Dominance over the Visual Space: Lebanese Television and Political Elites, 1990–2005* (Frank & Timme, Berlin, 2009).

Osman, Ahmed, 'Rude awakening: Dream drops top talkers', *Transnational Broadcasting Studies* 12, Spring–Summer (2004).

Roy, Olivier, *Globalised Islam* 2nd edn (Hurst, London, 2006).

Rugh, William A., *Arab Mass Media: Newspapers, Radio, and Television in Arab Politics* (Praeger Publishers, Westport, CT, 2004).

Saeed, MuhammadAl-Sayyed, 'New trends and forces in the Arab media arena', in *Arab Media in the Information Age* (The Emirates Center for Strategic Studies and Research, Abu Dhabi, 2006), pp. 27–59.

Sakr, Naomi, *Walls of Silence: Media and Censorship in Syria* (ARTICLE 19, London, 1998).

—— *Satellite Realms: Transnational Television, Globalization and the Middle East* (I.B.Tauris, London, 2001).

—— *Arab Television Today* (I.B.Tauris, London, 2007).

—— 'Egyptian TV in the grip of government: Politics before profit in a fluid pan-Arab market', in D. Ward (ed.), *Television and Public Policy* (Lawrence Erlbaum Associates, New York, NY, 2008), pp. 265–81.

—— 'Placing political economy in relation to cultural studies: Reflections on the case of cinema in Saudi Arabia', in T. Sabry (ed.), *Arab Cultural Studies: Mapping the Field* (I.B.Tauris, London, 2012), pp. 214–33.

—— *Transformations in Egyptian Journalism* (I.B.Tauris, London, 2013).

——— 'Where Arab media magnates stand *vis-à-vis* globalized media flows: Insights from Egypt and Saudi Arabia', *International Journal of Communication* 7 (2013), pp. 2285–302.

Salamandra, Christa, 'The Muhannad effect: Media panic, melodrama, and the Arab female gaze', *Anthropological Quarterly*, 85(1) (2012), pp. 45–78.

Salibi, Kamal, *A House of Many Mansions* (University of California Press, Berkeley, CA, 1988).

Schumpeter, Joseph Alois, *The Theory of Economic Development* (Harvard University Press, Cambridge, MA, 1934).

Seib, Philip M., *The Al Jazeera Effect: How the New Global Media Are Reshaping World Politics* (Potomac Books, Washington, DC, 2008).

Sfakianakis, John, 'The whales of the Nile: Networks, businessmen, and bureaucrats during the era of privatization in Egypt', in S. Heydemann (ed.), *Networks of Privilege in the Middle East: The Politics of Economic Reform Revisited* (Palgrave Macmillan, New York, NY/Basingstoke, 2004), pp. 77–100.

Shafik, Viola, *Popular Egyptian Cinema: Gender, Class, and Nation* (American University in Cairo Press, Cairo, 2007).

Siebert, Fred S., Peterson, Theodore, and Schramm, Wilbur, *Four Theories of the Press: The Authoritarian, Libertarian, Social Responsibility, and Soviet Communist Concepts of What the Press Should Be and Do* (University of Illinois Press, Urbana, IL, 1956).

Statham, Paul, and Trenz, Hans-Jörg, *The Politicization of Europe: Contesting the Constitution in the Mass Media* (Routledge, New York, NY, 2012).

Stratton, Allegra, *Muhajababes* (Constable, London, 2006).

Tunstall, Jeremy, and Palmer, Michael, *Media Moguls* (Routledge, London/New York, NY, 1991).

Tunstall, Jeremy, and Palmer, Michael, 'Introduction', in J. Tunstall (ed.) *Media Occupations and Professions: A Reader* (Oxford University Press, Oxford, 2001).

Vloeberghs, Ward, 'The Hariri political dynasty after the Arab Spring', *Mediterranean Politics* 17(2) July (2012), pp. 241–8.

Watson, James, *Media Communication: An Introduction to Theory and Process* (Macmillan, Basingstoke, 1998).

Williams, Kevin, *Read All About It! A History of the British Newspaper* (Routledge, London/New York, NY, 2010).

Zayani, Muhammad, *The Al-Jazeera Phenomenon: Critical Perspectives on New Arab Media* (Paradigm Publishers, Boulder, CO, 2005).

Index